HashiCorp Terraform Associate (003) Exam Guide

Exam Guide

Prepare to pass the Terraform Associate exam on your first attempt

Chandra Mohan Dhanasekaran

Manjunath H. Gowda

HashiCorp Terraform Associate (003) Exam Guide

Authors: Chandra Mohan Dhanasekaran and Manjunath H. Gowda

Reviewers: Salim Tekin and Mehdi Laruelle

Publishing Product Manager: Anindya Sil

Senior-Development Editor: Ketan Giri

Development Editor: Kalyani S.

Presentation Designer: Salma Patel

Editorial Board: Vijin Boricha, Megan Carlisle, Simon Cox, Ketan Giri, Saurabh Kadave, Alex Mazonowicz, Gandhali Raut, and Ankita Thakur

First Published: May 2024

Production Reference: 1310524

Published by Packt Publishing Ltd.
Grosvenor House
11 St Paul's Square
Birmingham
B3 1RB

ISBN: 978-1-80461-884-4

www.packtpub.com

Contributors

About the Authors

Chandra Mohan Dhanasekaran, a.k.a. Chandru D, is an AWS Certified Solutions Architect at Philips, focused on designing world-class resilient and cost-efficient solutions for customers in the public cloud. His previous experience includes stints at banking giants including JP Morgan Chase & Co. and Danske Bank, the largest bank in Denmark and very popular in the Nordic countries. He has close to 15 years of professional IT experience in different domains and various technology stacks ranging from mainframes to frontend, distributed, and container technologies. He has always had a profound love for mainframe systems and is fascinated by the advantages of using IaC tools and cloud services. You can find him at almost all AWS events and meetups around Bengaluru, and he loves to connect with people.

He always looks to explore new and blossoming open source technologies and is a fan of serverless technologies and Kubernetes. You can connect with him on LinkedIn: `https://www.linkedin.com/in/chandrud`

Outside of work, he loves cooking for the kids at the weekend and enjoys jogging whenever he finds time. He's also a die-hard Manchester United fan and watching "Rafa" (Rafael Nadal) around the tennis court is something he can't afford to miss!

Manjunath H. Gowda is a VP of cloud engineering at Lentra.ai. Previously, he worked at AWS as a solutions architect, helping customers migrate to AWS and build cloud-native solutions in the AWS cloud. While working as a freelance consultant, he helped several startups with their AWS architecture, cost optimization, infrastructure security assessment, and automation using IaC tools. He has a special interest in cloud security and infra-automation using IaC tools such as CloudFormation and Terraform.

When not in front of a laptop, he plays cricket and loves long-distance cycling. He is a loyal RCB fan who genuinely believes in the RCB slogan, "Ee sala cup namde".

You can connect with him at `https://www.linkedin.com/in/manju712/`.

About the Reviewers

Salim Tekin is a seasoned Senior DevOps Engineer, currently spearheading the optimization of the Data Science Platform at Generali Germany. Prior to this role, he served as a Cloud Engineer Consultant at Deloitte, where he specialized in crafting tailored cloud solutions. Before his tenure at Deloitte, Salim showcased his versatility as an ADAS Engineer at Bertrandt, simultaneously holding the role of Product Owner for Connectivity Backend on the 'Harry' project. With a rich skill set including Certified Kubernetes Administration and Development, AWS & GCP Architecture, and proficiency in tools like Terraform and Prometheus, Salim excels in driving efficiency and scalability in complex technological landscapes. Holding a Diploma in Industrial Engineering with a focus on Electronics & Informatics, Salim combines academic prowess with practical expertise to deliver impactful solutions. Outside of work, Salim enjoys staying abreast of the latest technological advancements and spending time with family and friends.

Mehdi Laruelle is a seasoned professional with a diverse background in the industry. With extensive experience working for major players and startups, he's honed his skills as a consultant, particularly in the realm of cloud, DevOps culture and tools. His proficiency extends to HashiCorp software like Terraform and Vault, among others. Passionate about sharing knowledge, Mehdi actively engages in training, writing articles, and organizing meetups. As the co-organizer of the HashiCorp User Group France meetup, he fosters a community of learning and collaboration. His expertise is widely recognized, earning him distinctions as a HashiCorp Ambassador, AWS Community Builder, and AWS Authorized Instructor (AAI). You can find him on GitHub under the username "mehdilaruelle".

Table of Contents

2

3

4

Terraform Commands and State Management   79

7

Debugging and Troubleshooting Terraform   161

8

Terraform Functions   181

9

Understanding HCP Terraform's Capabilities   225

10

11

Preface

With the cloud being the new normal for the deployment of applications, **Infrastructure as Code (IaC)** becomes very important in managing the infrastructure used to host these applications. HashiCorp's Terraform is leading this space, with many startups and enterprises choosing it over the cloud-native IaC services for infrastructure management.

The knowledge, working experience, and certification of Terraform will definitely give engineers an edge over their peers.

This book will help you get a good understanding of Terraform concepts and prepare for the certification. The chapters in the book follow the certification content and cover all the key concepts that you're expected to understand to pass the certification.

By the end of the book, you will be confident in managing a Terraform-based setup and deciding which Terraform edition to use for your use case, and will be ready to take the certification.

Who This Book Is For

Administrators, CloudOps engineers, DevOps engineers, developers, architects, any other roles related to infrastructure management, and anyone who wants to keep up with the latest in infrastructure management will all benefit from learning Terraform.

Having some programming background will help you quickly learn Terraform, but this is not mandatory.

Having a working knowledge of any of the cloud platforms will also help when it comes to trying out the Terraform code.

What This Book Covers

Chapter 1, Introduction to Infrastructure as Code (IaC) and Concepts, will help you get a clear understanding of IaC concepts and build your knowledge of the Terraform tool.

Chapter 2, Why Do We Need Terraform?, will give you an idea about the advantages of IaC when compared to the manual provisioning of infrastructure. The chapter will also discuss the Terraform tool and its benefits over other tools/services used for IaC.

Chapter 3, Basics of Terraform and Core Workflow, will introduce you to the building blocks that make Terraform an efficient tool to use. It will help you get a basic idea of what constitutes Terraform.

Chapter 4, Terraform Commands and State Management, is about the various commands you will use while working with Terraform CLI. While some commands are part of almost every infrastructure workflow, some may not be regularly used. But every command has its own significance.

Chapter 5, Terraform Modules, will introduce you to modules, one of the core concepts of Terraform because of their extensive use in the production environment.

Chapter 6, Terraform Backends and Resource Management, will cover remote backend configurations with supported backends and the ways to configure them. You will also take a look at some use cases.

Chapter 7, Debugging and Troubleshooting Terraform, talks about the issues you generally face while managing Terraform and how to either avoid, debug, or fix them.

Chapter 8, Terraform Functions, will cover the different built-in functions and their syntax with examples for better understanding.

Chapter 9, Understanding HCP Terraform's Capabilities, will introduce you to HCP Terraform and Terraform Enterprise, the managed Terraform offerings by HashiCorp.

Chapter 10, Miscellaneous Topics, will cover topics relevant to the certification exam that could not be covered in the other chapters. These could add value when you encounter special use cases.

Online Practice Resources

With this book, you will unlock unlimited access to our online exam-prep platform (*Figure 0.1*). This is your place to practice everything you learn in the book. How to access the resources. To learn how to access the online resources, refer to *Chapter 11,* Accessing the Online Practice Resources at the end of this book.

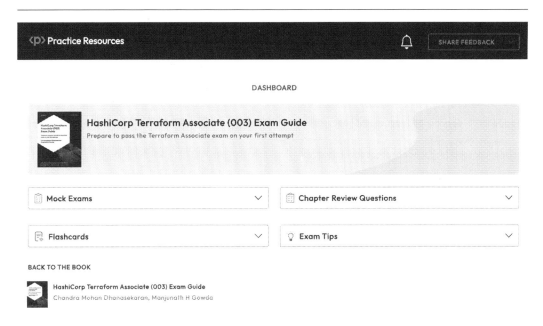

Figure 0.1 – Online exam-prep platform on a desktop device

Sharpen your knowledge of Terraform concepts with multiple sets of mock exams, interactive flashcards, and exam tips accessible from all modern web browsers.

> **Note**
>
> If you are using the digital version of this book, we advise you to type the code and command lines yourself or access the code from the book's GitHub repository (a link is available in the next section). Doing so will help you avoid any potential errors related to the copying and pasting of code.

Download the Example Code Files

You can download the example code files for this book from GitHub at `https://github.com/` `PacktPublishing/Hashicorp-Certified-Terraform-Associate-003-Exam-` `guide-Second-Edition`. If there are any updates to the code, the GitHub repository will be updated.

We also have other code bundles from our rich catalog of books and videos available at `https://` `github.com/PacktPublishing/`. Check them out.

Download the Color Images

We also provide a PDF file that has color images of the screenshots/diagrams used in this book. You can download it here: `https://packt.link/6ryKi`.

Conventions Used

`Code in text`: Indicates code words in text, database table names, folder names, filenames, file extensions, pathnames, dummy URLs, user input, and Twitter handles. Here is an example: In the following command, the file is downloaded under `~/Downloads` and hence the command is being run from the `Downloads` folder.

A block of code is set as follows:

```
terraform {
  required_providers {
    aws = {
      source = "hashicorp/aws"
      version = "~> 5.0"
    }
  }
}
provider "aws" {
  region = "ap-south-1"
}
```

Add the code highlight example before the command line sentence:

When we wish to draw your attention to a particular part of a code block, the relevant lines or items are set in bold:

```
terraform {
  required_providers {
    local name = {
      source = «source location
      »version = «version constraint
```

```
    »}
  }
}
```

Any command line or output is written as follows:

```
brew tap hashicorp/tap
```

Bold: Indicates a new term, an important word, or words that you see onscreen. Here is an example: This is exactly where **Infrastructure as Code (IaC)** adds value.

> **Tips or important notes**
> Appear like this.

Get in Touch

Feedback from our readers is always welcome.

General feedback: If you have questions about any aspect of this book, email us at customercare@packtpub.com and mention the book title in the subject of your message.

Errata: Although we have taken every care to ensure the accuracy of our content, mistakes do happen. If you have found a mistake in this book, we would be grateful if you would report this to us. Please visit www.packtpub.com/support/errata and fill in the form. We ensure that all valid errata are promptly updated in the GitHub repository, with the relevant information available in the Readme.md file. You can access the GitHub repository at https://packt.link/ykI4S.

Piracy: If you come across any illegal copies of our works in any form on the internet, we would be grateful if you would provide us with the location address or website name. Please contact us at copyright@packt.com with a link to the material.

If you are interested in becoming an author: If there is a topic that you have expertise in and you are interested in either writing or contributing to a book, please visit authors.packtpub.com.

Setting up the Environment

Before exploring the book, you need to set up Terraform CLI and configure one of the cloud platforms for Terraform usage. We use the AWS cloud platform in this book.

Terraform works seamlessly across multiple operating systems. It offers multiple installation options. The following sections will help you understand the Terraform components and the installation and configuration of Terraform for AWS:

- Components of Terraform
- Terraform installation:
  - macOS
  - Linux
  - Windows
- Configuring Terraform with AWS

By the end of this section, you will understand the different components of Terraform and the different ways of installing Terraform across Linux, Windows, and macOS.

Components of Terraform

When Terraform was launched in 2014, it was a single component that included the provider plugins as part of the binary. In 2017, HashiCorp made the decision to separate the providers to allow the provider's code to be managed independently from the Terraform binary (from Terraform version 0.10).

Currently, Terraform has a plugin-based architecture in which the Terraform core makes a **remote procedure call** (**RPC**) to the Terraform plugins to provision and manage the infrastructure.

Terraform is composed of two components:

- **Terraform core**: This is a statically compiled binary written in the Go programming language. Once it has been compiled, you get a binary file that is used as the command-line tool. This binary is downloaded by users and acts as an entry point. The core communicates with the plugins, reads the configuration files, creates a plan, and manages the resources.
- **Terraform plugins**: Terraform plugins are the binaries that expose an implementation for a specific service/provider, such as AWS, GCP, or Salesforce. These plugins get invoked by the Terraform core over RPC. The providers are a type of plugin that needs to be installed separately. These provider plugins are responsible for authenticating and initializing the libraries to make the API calls to the infrastructure provider.

At the time of this book, Terraform supports the Windows, macOS, FreeBSD, OpenBSD, Solaris, and Linux (Ubuntu/Debian, CentOS/RHEL, Fedora, and Amazon Linux) operating systems. *Figure 0.2* summarizes the details of the Terraform installation.

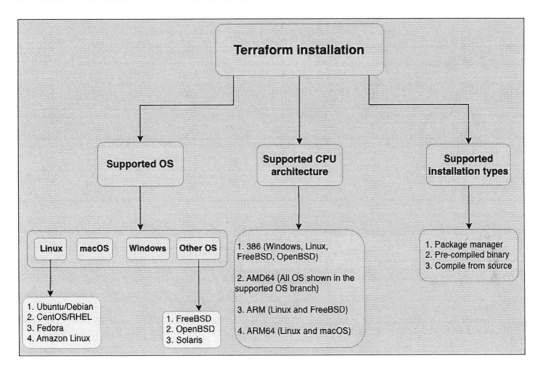

Figure 0.2: Terraform installation

In the following section, you will learn how to install Terraform on macOS, Linux, and Windows.

Terraform Installation

The Terraform installation process varies depending on the operating system and the CPU architecture.

macOS

You can install Terraform on macOS using a package manager (Homebrew), by downloading the pre-compiled binary, or by compiling it from the source. In this section, you will learn how to install via the package manager and pre-compiled binary.

Package Manager – Homebrew

Homebrew is a free, open source package management system for macOS. The following steps will help you install Terraform using the Homebrew package manager:

1. Install the HashiCorp tap containing the Terraform binary by running the following command:

    ```
    brew tap hashicorp/tap
    ```

2. Install Terraform by running the following command:

    ```
    brew install hashicorp/tap/terraform
    ```

3. After installation, you should see some output similar to that shown in *Figure 0.3*. There may be some variation in the messages received depending on the presence of a previous installation of Terraform.

```
~$brew install hashicorp/tap/terraform
==> Fetching hashicorp/tap/terraform
==> Downloading https://releases.hashicorp.com/terraform/1.7.3/terraform_1.7.3_darwin_arm64.zip
Already downloaded: /Users/manjunath/Library/Caches/Homebrew/downloads/a0ca203fddc90ae140c9d76ebdf8991f960ab
3c01a8baf1df7626550e389b7d6—terraform_1.7.3_darwin_arm64.zip
==> Installing terraform from hashicorp/tap
==> Downloading https://formulae.brew.sh/api/formula.jws.json
################################################################################### 100.0%
==> Downloading https://formulae.brew.sh/api/cask.jws.json
################################################################################### 100.0%
Warning: Cask homebrew/cask/terraform was renamed to homebrew/core/terraform.
🍺  /opt/homebrew/Cellar/terraform/1.7.3: 3 files, 88.6MB, built in 4 seconds
==> Running `brew cleanup terraform`...
Disable this behaviour by setting HOMEBREW_NO_INSTALL_CLEANUP.
Hide these hints with HOMEBREW_NO_ENV_HINTS (see `man brew`).
~$
```

Figure 0.3: Terraform installation using Homebrew

4. Test the installation of Terraform by running the following command, which shows the version:

    ```
    terraform -v
    ```

5. You should see some output like that shown in *Figure 0.04*. The version shown on your terminal may be a different one.

```
~$terraform -v
Terraform v1.7.3
on darwin_arm64
+ provider registry.terraform.io/hashicorp/aws v4.64.0
~$
```

Figure 0.4: Terraform installation validation

Pre-Compiled Binary Download

If you are looking for a specific version of Terraform, it is recommended to go with the **pre-compiled binary** option. Another reason to go with this installation option is that the package managers may not always have the latest version of the software.

Pre-compiled binaries are available in both AMD64 and ARM64. Make sure to choose the right binary depending on your CPU architecture. The following steps will help you install Terraform using a pre-compiled binary:

1. Navigate to the following URL that has the latest version of pre-compiled binary:

    `https://developer.hashicorp.com/terraform/install`

2. You should see the binaries, as shown in *Figure 0.5*.

Binary download

AMD64		ARM64	
Version: 1.7.3	Download ⬇	Version: 1.7.3	Download ⬇

Figure 0.5: Pre-compiled binary for macOS

3. Depending on the CPU architecture of your laptop or server, you can choose AMD64 or ARM64.

4. The binary is downloaded in ZIP format. Navigate to the path where the file was downloaded and unzip it. In the following command, the file is downloaded under ~/Downloads and hence the command is being run from the Downloads folder:

    ```
    ~/Downloads $ unzip terraform_1.7.3_darwin_arm64.zip
    ```

5. You should see the Terraform binary file, as shown in *Figure 0.6*.

```
~/Downloads $ls
terraform_1.7.3_darwin_arm64.zip
~/Downloads $
~/Downloads $unzip terraform_1.7.3_darwin_arm64.zip
Archive:  terraform_1.7.3_darwin_arm64.zip
  inflating: terraform
~/Downloads $
~/Downloads $ls --color=auto
terraform                        terraform_1.7.3_darwin_arm64.zip
~/Downloads $
```

Figure 0.6: Unzipping the Terraform ZIP file

6. Now, move the Terraform binary to the appropriate directory on the filesystem. Typically, it is moved to /usr/local/bin:

```
mv ~/Downloads/terraform /usr/local/bin/
```

7. Now you can test the Terraform installation by running the following command:

```
terraform -v
```

You should see the output detailing the Terraform version as shown in *Figure 0.7*.

```
~/Downloads $terraform -v
Terraform v1.7.3
on darwin_arm64
```

Figure 0.7: Pre-compiled binary installation validation

> **Note**
>
> If you get an error when you run terraform -v, make sure your PATH variable has the location where the Terraform binary is moved to. Here, the binary is moved to /usr/local/bin, and this should be present in your PATH environment variable on your operating system.

Linux

Terraform is available for Ubuntu/Debian-based OS, CentOS/RHEL-based OS, Fedora, and Amazon Linux operating systems. All operating systems support installation via the package manager, pre-compiled binary, and compilation from the source.

In the following sections, you will learn how to install Terraform in Ubuntu and Amazon Linux.

Package Manager

Use the package manager specific to your Linux OS distribution to install Terraform. Here, you will be using Ubuntu and Amazon Linux as examples. For other OS, refer to https://developer.hashicorp.com/terraform/install.

Ubuntu

The following steps will help you install Terraform via the package manager in Ubuntu:

1. Download HashiCorp's GPG key onto your OS:

```
wget -O- https://apt.releases.hashicorp.com/gpg | sudo gpg --dearmor
-o /usr/share/keyrings/hashicorp-archive-keyring.gpg
```

2. Add HashiCorp's `apt` repository that contains Terraform:

```
echo "deb [signed-by=/usr/share/keyrings/hashicorp-archive-keyring.
gpg] https://apt.releases.hashicorp.com $(lsb_release
-cs) main" | sudo tee /etc/apt/sources.list.d/hashicorp.list
```

3. Update the repo and install Terraform:

```
sudo apt update && sudo apt install terraform
```

4. Test the installation:

```
terraform version
```

If you get the version details as output, then Terraform has been installed successfully.

Amazon Linux

The following steps will help you install Terraform via the package manager in Amazon Linux:

1. Install `yum-config-manager` to manage the repositories:

```
sudo yum install -y yum-utils shadow-utils
```

2. Add the HashiCorp Linux repository:

```
sudo yum-config-manager --add-repo https://rpm.releases.hashicorp.
com/AmazonLinux/hashicorp.repo
```

3. Install Terraform:

```
sudo yum -y install terraform
```

4. Test the installation:

```
terraform version
```

- If you get the version details as output, then Terraform has been installed successfully.

Pre-Compiled Binary Download

Copy the appropriate binary's link for your OS and CPU architecture from the following URL:

```
https://developer.hashicorp.com/terraform/install
```

All the operating systems have similar steps: install the `unzip` application, download the Terraform binary, unzip the archive, move the binary to the right location, and test it. To avoid repetition, this section will cover Ubuntu only. For other OS, please make the required changes in the commands (mostly in the `unzip` installation) before proceeding with this method.

Ubuntu

The following steps will help you install Terraform using a pre-compiled binary in Ubuntu:

1. Install the unzip package, which is required to unzip the Terraform file:

   ```
   sudo apt-get install unzip
   ```

2. Download the Terraform binary that needs to be installed (you need to copy this link from the HashiCorp downloads URL):

   ```
   wget https://releases.hashicorp.com/terraform/1.7.3/
   terraform_1.7.3_linux_amd64.zip
   ```

3. Extract the downloaded file archive:

   ```
   unzip terraform_1.7.3_linux_amd64.zip
   ```

4. Move the extracted file into a directory as defined in the PATH variable:

   ```
   mv terraform /usr/local/bin/
   ```

5. Test the installation:

   ```
   terraform version
   ```

   - If you get the version details, Terraform is installed successfully.

Compile from Source

The **compile from source** option is typically used for operating systems that are not directly supported by Terraform, but where you still want to install it.

The steps to compile the Terraform from source remain the same across the Linux OS. You will have to make sure you use an appropriate package manager to install go. The following steps are done on Ubuntu:

1. To compile the Terraform binary from source, clone the HashiCorp Terraform repository:

   ```
   git clone https://github.com/hashicorp/terraform.git
   ```

2. Navigate to the new directory:

   ```
   cd terraform
   ```

3. Install go, which is required to compile the binary:

   ```
   sudo snap install go
   ```

4. Now compile the binary by running the following command. The compiled binary is stored in `$GOPATH/bin/terraform`:

    ```
    go install
    ```

5. Move the compiled Terraform binary file into a directory searched for executables. You will first have to navigate to the `bin` folder of the `go` installation and run the following command:

    ```
    mv terraform /usr/local/bin/
    ```

6. Test the installation:

    ```
    terraform version
    ```

   - If you get the version details, Terraform has been installed successfully.

Windows

You can install Terraform on Windows using the **Chocolatey** package manager. You do not have to add the location of the Terraform binary in the PATH variable when installed through Chocolatey. The following steps will help you install Terraform in Windows using Chocolatey:

1. Open the PowerShell CLI as an administrator.

2. Enter the following command, which will install the Chocolatey package manager. This has been tested on Windows Server 2022 for the installation of Chocolatey. Please make use of the command appropriate for your version of Windows to install Chocolatey:

    ```
    Set-ExecutionPolicy Bypass -Scope Process -Force; [System.
    Net.ServicePointManager]::SecurityProtocol = [System.
    Net.ServicePointManager]::SecurityProtocol -bor 3072; iex
    ((New-Object System.Net.WebClient).DownloadString('https://
    chocolatey.org/install.ps1'))
    ```

3. Once the installation succeeds, test it by running the following command:

    ```
    choco version
    ```

4. Output like that in *Figure 0.8* confirms the successful installation of Chocolatey:

    ```
    PS C:\Users\Administrator> choco version
    Chocolatey v2.2.2
    ```

    Figure 0.8: Chocolatey installation validation

5. Use Chocolatey to install Terraform by running the following command:

```
choco install -y terraform
```

The output will look like *Figure 0.9* when Terraform is successfully installed:

```
PS C:\Users\Administrator> choco install terraform
Chocolatey v2.2.2
Installing the following packages:
terraform
By installing, you accept licenses for the packages.
Progress: Downloading terraform 1.7.3... 100%

terraform v1.7.3 [Approved]
terraform package files install completed. Performing other installation steps.
The package terraform wants to run 'chocolateyInstall.ps1'.
Note: If you don't run this script, the installation will fail.
Note: To confirm automatically next time, use '-y' or consider:
choco feature enable -n allowGlobalConfirmation
Do you want to run the script?([Y]es/[A]ll - yes to all/[N]o/[P]rint): Y

Removing old terraform plugins
Downloading terraform 64 bit
  from 'https://releases.hashicorp.com/terraform/1.7.3/terraform_1.7.3_windows_amd64.zip'
Progress: 100% - Completed download of C:\Users\Administrator\AppData\Local\Temp\chocolatey\terraform\1.7.3\terraform_1.
7.3_windows_amd64.zip (25.05 MB).
Download of terraform_1.7.3_windows_amd64.zip (25.05 MB) completed.
Hashes match.
Extracting C:\Users\Administrator\AppData\Local\Temp\chocolatey\terraform\1.7.3\terraform_1.7.3_windows_amd64.zip to C:\
ProgramData\chocolatey\lib\terraform\tools...
C:\ProgramData\chocolatey\lib\terraform\tools
 ShimGen has successfully created a shim for terraform.exe
```

Figure 0.9: Terraform installation via Chocolatey

6. Test the installation:

```
terraform version
```

7. If you get the version details as output, then Terraform has been installed successfully.

Pre-Compiled Binary Download

The following steps will help you install Terraform on Windows using a pre-compiled binary:

1. Depending on your operating system's CPU architecture, download either the 386 or AMD64 binary from the following HashiCorp URL:

    https://developer.hashicorp.com/terraform/install

2. The file you download will be in ZIP format. Extract the contents of the archive to get the terraform.exe file.

3. Create a new folder named terraform under C:\Program Files (x86) and move this terraform.exe file into that folder (i.e., to C:\Program Files (x86)\terraform).

4. You will have to add the Terraform binary file's location in the PATH environment variable to make it available for the command line.

5. Open the command line and execute SystemPropertiesAdvanced. This should open the **System Properties** window on the **Advanced** tab, as shown in *Figure 0.10*. (Alternatively, you can search for advanced system settings in the search bar.)

Figure 0.10: System properties

6.   Click on **Environment Variables**. This should open a new window.

7.   Select **Path** under **System variables** and click **Edit** as shown in *Figure 0.11*. This should open another screen.

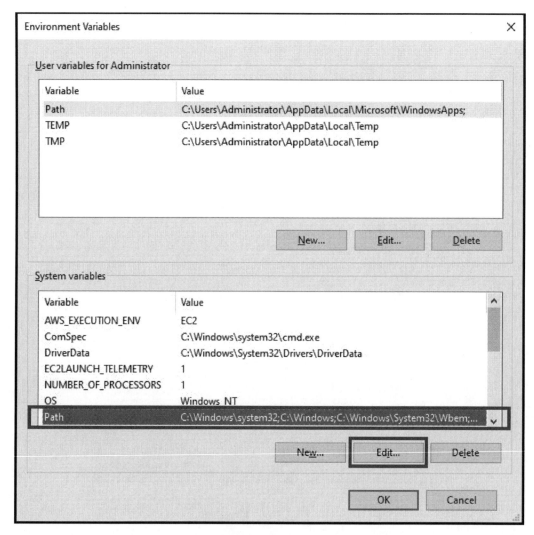

Figure 0.11: Modifying the PATH environment variable

8. On the new screen, either add the `terraform.exe` file's location manually as shown in *Figure 0.12*, or browse to the location of the `terraform.exe` file to select it. Once the new location appears on the screen, click **OK** to save it.

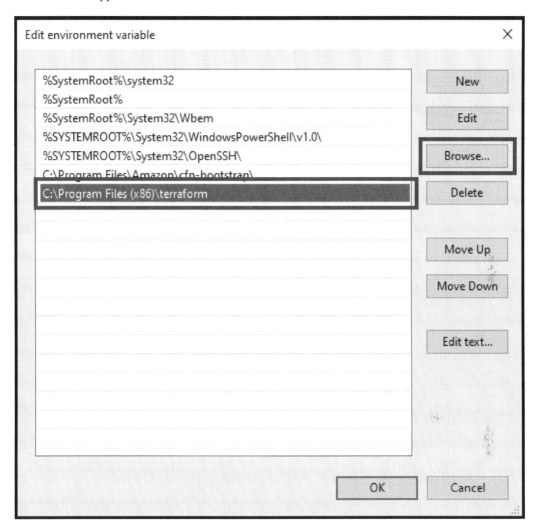

Figure 0.12: Adding the Terraform location to the PATH environment variable

9. In the command line, run the following command, which should show the Terraform version if the configuration was successful:

```
terraform version
```

Configure Terraform for AWS

For Terraform to manage the resources in any platform, it must first authenticate against the platform. The following steps will help you in configuring Terraform to interact with AWS to manage the resources:

- Make sure you have installed Terraform and the AWS CLI. You can follow the steps given at the following URL to install the AWS CLI:

  `https://docs.aws.amazon.com/cli/latest/userguide/getting-started-install.html`

- Terraform can authenticate against AWS using the following methods:

  - Parameters in the provider configuration (access key and secret access key in given in the provider config)

  - Environment variables (access key and secret access key passed through environment variables)

  - Shared credentials files (credentials are taken from `$HOME/.aws/credentials`)

  - Shared configuration files (credentials are taken from `$HOME/.aws/config`)

  - Container credentials (credentials are taken from the container's `task` role)

  - Instance profile credentials (only if you are running Terraform on EC2 with an IAM role associated)

  - Assuming an IAM role (very useful for AWS multi-account login)

In the following steps, you will learn how to configure the Terraform to authenticate to AWS via **Shared credentials files**:

1. Log in to the AWS Management Console and create an IAM user with enough permissions to manage the required resources. Detailed instructions to create an IAM user are provided at `https://packt.link/7afrg`.

2. Generate the access key and secret access key for this IAM user from the IAM dashboard. Copy the access key and secret access key, as they will be required in later steps.

3. Configure the AWS CLI to use the credentials that were copied in the previous step by running the following command:

```
aws configure
```

4. You will be prompted for the access key, secret key, Region, and output format. Paste these details according to the prompt as shown in *Figure 0.13*.

```
~ $aws configure
AWS Access Key ID [None]: AKIAYC3
AWS Secret Access Key [None]: EdMKRvx40S5                    4VJo5NzU05gA
Default region name [None]: ap-south-1
Default output format [None]: json
~ $
```

Figure 0.13: Configuring the AWS CLI

5. Once you enter the details, the credentials get stored in the ~/.aws/credentials file in Linux and macOS.

6. You can use the following block to finish the final configuration required for Terraform to talk to AWS. Create a file named provider.tf containing the following code:

```
terraform {
  required_providers {
    aws = {
      source  = "hashicorp/aws"
      version = "~> 5.0"
    }
  }
}
provider "aws" {
  region = "ap-south-1"
}
```

> **Note**
>
> Note that we have not made any reference to the file where the credentials are stored or the profile used by the AWS CLI. If we are using the default options, we do not have to explicitly specify this as Terraform will automatically detect and use them.

When you run `terraform init` and `terraform plan` with the provider code, it should go through without any issues as shown in *Figure 0.14*:

```
terraform init
terraform plan
```

```
● /Users/packt/Desktop $terraform init

Initializing the backend...

Initializing provider plugins...
- Finding hashicorp/aws versions matching "~> 5.0"...
- Installing hashicorp/aws v5.37.0...
- Installed hashicorp/aws v5.37.0 (signed by HashiCorp)

Terraform has created a lock file .terraform.lock.hcl to record the provider
selections it made above. Include this file in your version control repository
so that Terraform can guarantee to make the same selections by default when
you run "terraform init" in the future.

Terraform has been successfully initialized!

You may now begin working with Terraform. Try running "terraform plan" to see
any changes that are required for your infrastructure. All Terraform commands
should now work.

If you ever set or change modules or backend configuration for Terraform,
rerun this command to reinitialize your working directory. If you forget, other
commands will detect it and remind you to do so if necessary.
● /Users/packt/Desktop $terraform plan

No changes. Your infrastructure matches the configuration.
```

Figure 0.14: Configuring AWS provider

You can test the connectivity to AWS by adding a simple VPC creation code from the public module either in the same `provider.tf` file or by creating a new file named `vpc.tf` (make sure both files are in the same folder) and then running `terraform plan`:

```
module "vpc" {
  source  = "terraform-aws-modules/vpc/aws"
  version = "5.5.2"
}
```

You will see `terraform plan` trying to create four resources (NACL, security group, route table, and VPC). Only the VPC plan is shown in *Figure 0.15* for brevity, but note that the plan shows the overall addition of four resources.

```
# module.vpc.aws_vpc.this[0] will be created
+ resource "aws_vpc" "this" {
    + arn                                  = (known after apply)
    + cidr_block                           = "10.0.0.0/16"
    + default_network_acl_id               = (known after apply)
    + default_route_table_id               = (known after apply)
    + default_security_group_id            = (known after apply)
    + dhcp_options_id                      = (known after apply)
    + enable_dns_hostnames                 = true
    + enable_dns_support                   = true
    + enable_network_address_usage_metrics = (known after apply)
    + id                                   = (known after apply)
    + instance_tenancy                     = "default"
    + ipv6_association_id                  = (known after apply)
    + ipv6_cidr_block                      = (known after apply)
    + ipv6_cidr_block_network_border_group = (known after apply)
    + main_route_table_id                  = (known after apply)
    + owner_id                             = (known after apply)
    + tags                                 = {
        + "Name" = ""
      }
    + tags_all                             = (known after apply)
  }

Plan: 4 to add, 0 to change, 0 to destroy.
```

Figure 0.15: Terraform plan for VPC creation in AWS

The `terraform plan` output confirms that we have successfully configured Terraform to communicate with AWS to manage the resources.

> **Note**
>
> There are multiple editors that can be used for writing Terraform code. The choice of editor is very subjective. However, the most common ones are **Visual Studio Code** (**VSCode**), Atom, and PyCharm. Irrespective of the editor you choose, make sure you install the Terraform plugin/extension, which helps a lot when writing Terraform code.

Share Your Thoughts

Once you've read *HashiCorp Terraform Associate (003) Exam Guide*, we'd love to hear your thoughts! Scan the QR code below to go straight to the Amazon review page for this book and share your feedback.

https://packt.link/r/1804618845

Your review is important to us and the tech community and will help us make sure we're delivering excellent quality content.

Download a Free PDF Copy of This Book

Thanks for purchasing this book!

Do you like to read on the go but are unable to carry your print books everywhere?

Is your eBook purchase not compatible with the device of your choice?

Don't worry, now with every Packt book you get a DRM-free PDF version of that book at no cost.

Read anywhere, any place, on any device. Search, copy, and paste code from your favorite technical books directly into your application.

The perks don't stop there, you can get exclusive access to discounts, newsletters, and great free content in your inbox daily.

Follow these simple steps to get the benefits:

1. Scan the QR code or visit the link below:

https://packt.link/free-ebook/9781804618844

2. Submit your proof of purchase.
3. That's it! We'll send your free PDF and other benefits to your email directly.

1

Introduction to Infrastructure as Code (IaC) and Concepts

In the ever-evolving era of technology, the software applications being built are expected to be scalable in nature at the very minimum. The term **scalability** means the ability of an application or system to always match the growing needs of its user base and handle the increase in the number of users without any problems. This is applicable to all types of applications, including web applications, backend microservices, and internal apps. Such scalable apps are well suited for deployment in the cloud rather than on-premises because of the dynamic resource needs and because automating the scaling process (both scaling up and scaling down) will reap greater benefits. This is exactly where **Infrastructure as Code** (**IaC**) adds value.

In this chapter, you will explore IaC in detail and the various aspects of this framework through the following topics:

- What is IaC?
- Basic concepts of IaC
- IaC tools on the market
- IaC use cases
- Benefits of IaC

By the end of this chapter, you will have a firm understanding of IaC concepts, which will help you build your knowledge of the Terraform tool and focus on getting the HashiCorp Terraform Associate 003 certification in the subsequent chapters.

Making the Most Out of This Book – Your Certification and Beyond

This book and its accompanying online resources are designed to be a complete preparation tool for your **AZ-204 Exam**.

The book is written in a way that you can apply everything you've learned here even after your certification. The online practice resources that come with this book (*Figure 1.1*) are designed to improve your test-taking skills. They are loaded with timed mock exams, interactive flashcards, and exam tips to help you work on your exam readiness from now till your test day.

> **Before You Proceed**
>
> To learn how to access these resources, head over to *Chapter 11, Accessing the Online Practice Resources*, at the end of the book.

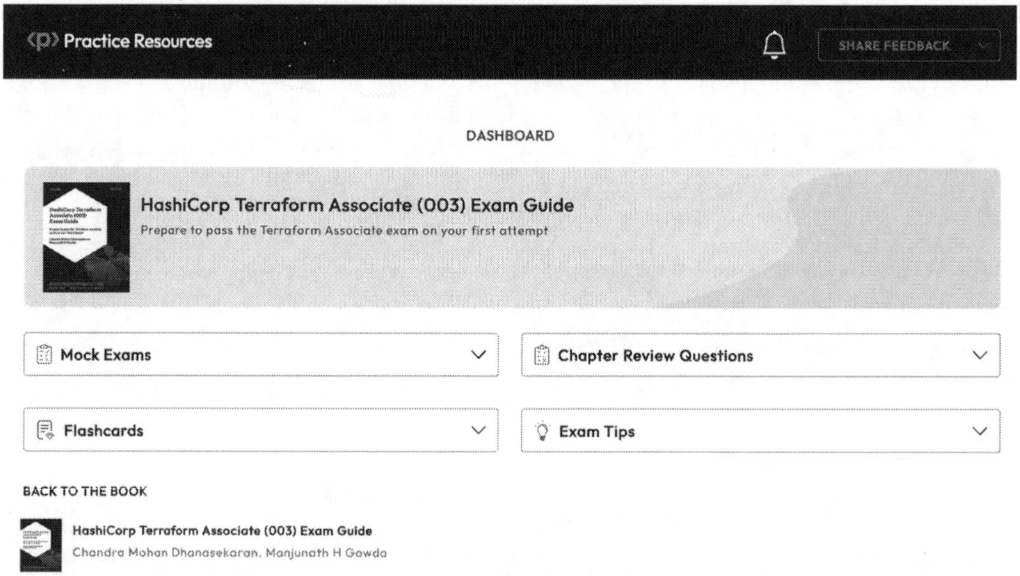

Figure 1.1 – Dashboard interface of the online practice resources

Here are some tips on how to make the most out of this book so that you can clear your certification and retain your knowledge beyond your exam:

1. Read each section thoroughly.

2. **Make ample notes**: You can use your favorite online note-taking tool or use a physical notebook. The free online resources also give you access to an online version of this book. Click the BACK TO THE BOOK link from the Dashboard to access the book in **Packt Reader**. You can highlight specific sections of the book there.

3. **Chapter Review Questions**: At the end of this chapter, you'll find a link to review questions for this chapter. These are designed to test your knowledge of the chapter. Aim to score at least **75%** before moving on to the next chapter. You'll find detailed instructions on how to make the most of these questions at the end of this chapter in the *Exam Readiness Drill - Chapter Review Questions* section. That way, you're improving your exam-taking skills after each chapter, rather than at the end.

4. **Flashcards**: After you've gone through the book and scored **75%** more in each of the chapter review questions, start reviewing the online flashcards. They will help you memorize key concepts.

5. **Mock Exams**: Solve the mock exams that come with the book till your exam day. If you get some answers wrong, go back to the book and revisit the concepts you're weak in.

6. **Exam Tips**: Review these from time to time to improve your exam readiness even further.

This chapter covers the following main topics:

- The benefits of cloud computing
- Cloud deployment models
- Cloud service models
- The core concepts of Azure

Technical Requirements

This is an introductory chapter on IaC that covers aspects such as use cases, different tools, and benefits that require no prior experience. However, basic knowledge of code development practices, public and private clouds, automation, DevOps, containers, and virtualization will help you understand the chapter better.

There are a couple of exercises at the end of this chapter to help you get a feel for using IaC tools. To complete them, you need the following:

- **Amazon Web Services (AWS)** account ID with administrator access
- AWS CLI version 2.x.x
- Terraform CLI version 1.5.x or later
- Visual Studio Code or any text editor

The GitHub repository for the chapter contains the graphics and sample scripts used in the chapter and can be found here:

```
https://github.com/PacktPublishing/Hashicorp-Certified-Terraform-
Associate-003-Exam-guide-Second-Edition/tree/main/ch1
```

What Is IaC?

In simple terms, **IaC** is the process of managing and provisioning an infrastructure through code instead of manual processes. In software engineering, you usually come across code development in programming languages such as Java, Python, and so many others that follow the **Software Development Life Cycle (SDLC)** process and then store them in a version-controlled source management tool such as GitHub or Bitbucket when they're ready. They are then deployed in the appropriate infrastructure where needed, either manually or with the help of an automated CI/CD pipeline.

The concept of IaC revolves around similar practices, such as creating a set of configuration scripts that will exactly provide the same infrastructure every time when executed and are also version controlled and properly tested.

IaC tools help us define the infrastructure in human-readable configuration files that can be applied multiple times, and they provide the same infrastructure every time without any changes from the desired state.

Figure 1.1 shows the IaC workflow and how it can transform the configuration scripts or files into real-world infrastructure components.

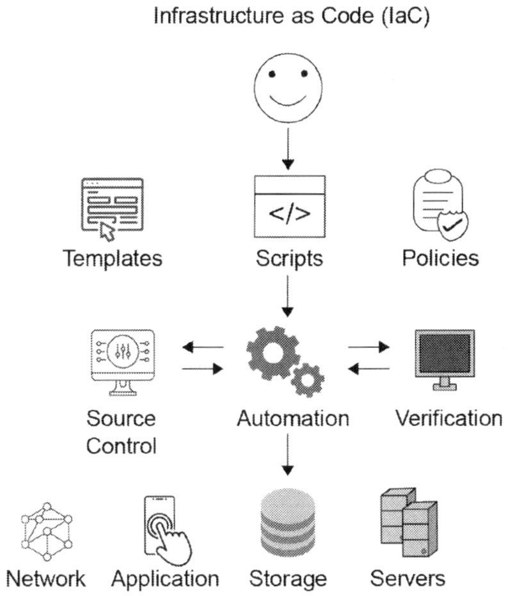

Figure 1.2 – IaC workflow

Scenario

"Company X wants to build a next-generation e-commerce web application that will be used by millions of its customers. The solution will have multiple microservices working with different architectures and will be deployed in a cloud that needs to run 24x7 for 365 days a year."

There are two ways to provide the infrastructure needed to run this application:

- Traditional approach
- IaC-based approach

In the traditional approach, there are clear segregations of responsibilities among the different teams involved, such as application development teams for app development, infrastructure teams for provisioning the resources to deploy the application, and operations teams to support the solution in production.

Once the entire solution has been developed and is ready for production, the development team will get in touch with the infrastructure team and share the requirements to run the application, usually with the ticketing mechanism. Then the infrastructure team will have a dedicated person/team to work on the task and make necessary planning for the deployment.

The planning process will involve procuring the dependent software and the required licenses and installing them on the server where the app will be running. The team will also spend time creating the scripts that need to be run manually before the deployment to get the environment ready.

The operations team will work on the monitoring part of the web application and come up with approaches such as health checks and mail notifications when there are any issues to support the deployment. There will be situations where the incoming traffic will increase rapidly, which requires scaling, and they might need to contact the infrastructure team to deploy multiple instances to serve the traffic, and the manual process will repeat once again. If there are any manual errors in this approach, that will delay the deployment of additional instances, which will affect the business.

As you can see, there are different bottlenecks in the overall execution and the temporary delays will have a bigger impact, and that is where the IaC approach will add real value.

In the IaC approach, based on DevOps principles, the application development team will also be responsible for the infrastructure provisioning, and they might support the application in production.

Once the application is ready to be deployed, the team focuses on creating the configuration scripts that will provision the required infrastructure on the cloud or on-premises setup. The team would be comfortable with going with the cloud-based deployment to make use of fully managed services and the pay-as-you-go model to avoid upfront costs.

The configuration scripts will focus on getting the initial setup ready, and they can be modified according to the varying needs of the application traffic. As the requirements state, the solution is expected to be available 24x7 for 365 days a year, but the volume of traffic will not always stay the same. The application does not need to run with the full set of resources during the night or early in the morning because the traffic will be lower. At the same time, the traffic will be enormous on offer days or during holidays, and this can be managed with very few changes to the configuration scripts and with no manual or operational overhead.

The entire provisioning process can also be automated to scale up/down the resources based on the incoming traffic so that the configuration can be auto applied to eliminate manual intervention. This allows the application developers not to worry about the infrastructure part at all; it is taken care of so that they can purely focus on implementing the business logic in the applications they design.

The IaC approach comes with the following benefits:

- Easy maintenance

- Less turnaround time

- Automated deployment and scaling

- Less/no manual intervention

Now you can proceed with the basic concepts and characteristics of IaC tools to further deepen your understanding of the topic.

Basic Concepts of IaC

IaC tools and practices are built based on the concepts described here. It helps to have a solid understanding of these concepts before exploring the advanced topics.

Declarative Approach versus Imperative Approach

Most IaC tools use the declarative approach of defining the required infrastructure, in contrast with the traditional imperative programming style. Before you get to know the declarative approach, you can take a look at what the imperative programming approach achieves.

The imperative programming approach primarily deals with detailed instructions about how exactly the infrastructure provisioning has to be achieved. This could be similar to the execution of setup scripts in the right sequence to set up a virtual machine or laptop, or similar.

In contrast, the declarative programming approach details the "what," and describes the desired state of the infrastructure provisioning. This approach does not get into the implementation details, unlike the previous approach. But it tries to keep the configuration in the desired state as much as possible.

IaC tools such as Terraform support the declarative approach, and Chef supports both the declarative and the imperative approach.

Version Control

In software development, it is very common to keep the generated source code in version-controlled repositories such as GitHub and Bitbucket. This will keep the snapshots of the software from each development iteration and help us with reverting the changes and proper tracking.

In IaC too, version control is required to keep track of infrastructure changes, and this may not be needed if you just work with the scripts that are always run for every new request. Version control also helps us go back to a particular version if there are problems with the latest upgrades or the software versions used.

Idempotency

The idempotency behaviour of IaC tools comes along with the declarative approach, and it basically means that the scripts will produce the same output irrespective of the number of times they are executed. This is vitally important because the intention is not to duplicate/overprovision the required infrastructure if the scripts need to be executed more than once.

This is again different from the traditional programming languages, which might produce new output every time scripts are executed. For example, if a Java program is created to add a SQL database entry every time it is executed, the row will be inserted in every execution, and you can even say that the program will create a new output every time.

But with IaC provisioning, you can say that you want the code to add an EC2 instance to an AWS account and that is the desired state. In this case, even if the configuration scripts run multiple times, you always need only one EC2 instance, and this is supported by retaining the current state in state files in Terraform and always comparing it with the desired state. If there is no difference between the current state and the desired state, the code will not perform any action and will return an output message such as "The infrastructure matches the configuration, and no changes are required."

Infrastructure Provisioning and Configuration Management

With the IaC tools firmly taking their place in the IT landscape, you also need to understand the difference between infrastructure provisioning and configuration management. This will help you pick the right toolset.

Infrastructure provisioning deals with the creation of resources such as EC2 instances, virtual machines, and database tables, and setting up container orchestration tools such as Kubernetes before you start running your application workloads on them. Container orchestration tools manage and automate the life cycle of containers at scale and provide out-of-the-box features such as scaling, networking, and load balancing. Basically, you need infrastructure provisioning to be working perfectly from day one of the setup.

Configuration management is something usually referred to as a "day-two process" where you have to manage the infrastructure with the security updates, install the latest dependencies, configure the application setup, and so on. There are tools such as Ansible and Chef that support both infrastructure provisioning and configuration management, which you will explore in the next section.

IaC Tools in the Market

Traditionally, infrastructure provisioning has been taken care of as part of the software configuration management process by the concerned teams. Now, the scope of infrastructure provisioning has broadened more than ever, and each application team is expected to take care of the infrastructure they need. With this, the importance of selecting the right IaC tool becomes vitally important.

You are now familiar with IaC concepts and the way they help teams bootstrap their deployment infrastructure process. You will now learn about different IaC tools in the market and how you can choose the right one based on your requirements and the capabilities of the selected tool.

How to Choose the Right IaC Tool

Before you decide on the most suitable IaC tool, there are some basic questions that need to be answered to help you make the right decision:

- What are the different skillsets within the team (i.e., C#, Python, Golang, TypeScript, or none of them)?

- What cloud platform are you planning to deploy resources into?

- Are you comfortable with the declarative approach or the imperative approach of infrastructure provisioning, and which method are you most familiar with (push versus pull)?

- Are you concerned only about infrastructure provisioning or configuration management as well?

The following are the most widely used IaC tools:

- HashiCorp Terraform
- Progress Chef (formerly known as Chef)
- Puppet
- Pulumi
- AWS CloudFormation

HashiCorp Terraform

Terraform is the IaC tool developed by HashiCorp. It is user-friendly and easy to use for new developers. The tool was initially released in July 2014, and it is written in the Golang language.

Terraform supports multi-cloud platforms such as AWS, Microsoft Azure, **Google Cloud Platform (GCP)**, and several others. Terraform has an extensive list of providers that can be categorized as **Official**, **Community**, **Partner**, and **Archived**. The providers provide the logical abstraction for the API interactions and are responsible for exposing the resources.

Users of Terraform define the required infrastructure resources in a set of configuration files written in a declarative configuration language known as **HashiCorp Configuration Language (HCL)**. The configuration files are saved with the `.tf` extension, and JSON is also supported as an alternative to HCL to define resource configuration.

A sample Terraform configuration file called `main.tf` is provided for reference. It creates an EC2 instance of type `t3.large` with the specified **Amazon Machine Image (AMI)** ID.

The script contains different blocks, such as `terraform`, `provider`, `variable`, `resource`, and `output`, and each has its own purpose. The `terraform` block indicates the Terraform provider to use, and the `provider` block configures this Terraform provider with the specified parameters. The `variable` block will take the user input, or it can have default values that will be used in the `resource` block. It will show the output in the terminal when the script is executed:

```
terraform {
  required_providers {
    aws = {
      source  = "hashicorp/aws"
      version = "~> 5.0"
    }
  }
}

provider "aws" {
  region = "us-east-1"
}

variable "ami" {
  default = "ami-00e93213821bcacf8"
  description = "Amazon Machine Image ID for Bottlerocket"
}

resource "aws_instance" "demo" {
  ami = var.ami
  instance_type = "t3.large"
  tags = {
    name = "Demo System"
  }
}

output "instance_id" {
  instance = aws_instance.demo.id
}
```

Progress Chef

Progress Chef (formerly known as Chef) is an IaC and configuration management tool initially released in January 2009. It is written in Ruby and Erlang.

The tool uses pure Ruby, a **Domain-Specific Language** (**DSL**) for writing system configurations popularly known as **recipes**. The recipes describe the servers and utilities to be managed and how they need to be configured. When grouped together, the recipes form "cookbooks" with the main intention of making management easier. The cookbooks can also contain other components, such as attributes, templates, and files. Progress Chef is also integrated with multiple cloud platforms, such as AWS, Azure, and GCP, and always ensures that the provisioned servers are available in the desired state.

Similar to the concept of community providers in Terraform, Progress Chef has **Chef Marketplace**, which has community workbooks that you can use as dependencies in custom workbooks.

Creating Your First Recipe

Say you want to install **OpenJDK 1.8** using **Chef**. You need to create a cookbook and then add a recipe. Here are the steps you can follow:

1. First, generate the cookbook using the `chef generate` command once the Chef Development Kit is installed on your workstation/laptop:

   ```
   $ chef generate cookbook cookbooks/java
   ```

2. Once the cookbook has been created, create a default recipe to install `epel-release` and `java-1.8.0-openjdk` with the following content:

   ```
   package 'epel-release' do
     action :install
   end

   package 'java-1.7.0-openjdk' do
     action :install
   end
   ```

With these steps, you should be able to install OpenJDK 1.8 on your workstation.

Puppet

Puppet is another IaC tool that's used for infrastructure provisioning and configuration management that uses its own declarative language to describe the configuration. The tool was initially released in 2005 and has both an open source version, Puppet Software, and a closed source version, Puppet Enterprise.

Puppet software also supports the use of Ruby DSL to define the configuration. It also supports the resource configuration of Unix and Windows systems.

With this tool, the configuration information is stored in Puppet manifests, which are compiled into a system-specific catalogue with the details on resources and resource dependencies with the help of a utility called **Facter**.

The tool uses a client-server architecture. The client is usually called a Puppet agent, and it interacts with the Puppet server installed on one or more servers. The Puppet agent runs in machines to be managed by Puppet, and it fetches the configuration information from the server and applies the changes. The final status report is sent back to the server on the execution results.

For example, a Unix user can be defined as a resource using Puppet's declarative language, as shown here:

```
user { 'alan':
  ensure => present,
  uid     => '1000',
  shell   => '/bin/bash',
  home    => '/var/tmp'
}
```

Pulumi

Pulumi is different from the tools you have read about so far because it takes the conventional approach of using traditional programming languages to set up infrastructure. It therefore becomes really easy for software programmers to onboard themselves onto the IaC bandwagon with their current expertise.

Pulumi supports programming languages such as TypeScript, JavaScript, Python, Go, .NET, and Java, and markup languages such as YAML to interact with cloud resources with the use of Pulumi SDK.

This tool was initially released in June 2018, and it comes with the Pulumi CLI, runtime, libraries, and a hosted service. These work together to deliver a robust and efficient way of provisioning, updating, and managing cloud infrastructure.

To declare new infrastructure resources in your program, you allocate resource objects whose properties correspond to the desired state of your infrastructure. These properties are also used between resources to handle any necessary dependencies and can be exported outside of the stack, if needed.

Programs usually reside in a project's working directory that contains the source code for the program and metadata on how to run the program. After writing your program, you can run the `pulumi up` **Pulumi CLI command** from within your project directory. This command creates an isolated and configurable instance of your program, known as a stack. Stacks are similar to different deployment environments that you use when testing and rolling out application updates. This can allow you to have different configuration values for each environment where the resources are going to be deployed.

The following Java program shows how to create an EC2 instance of type `t2.micro` with the `test-sg` security group, which allows port `80` access:

```
package testproject;

import com.pulumi.Context;
import com.pulumi.Exports;
import com.pulumi.Pulumi;
```

```
import com.pulumi.aws.ec2.Instance;
import com.pulumi.aws.ec2.InstanceArgs;
import com.pulumi.aws.ec2.SecurityGroup;
import com.pulumi.aws.ec2.SecurityGroupArgs;
import com.pulumi.aws.ec2.inputs.SecurityGroupIngressArgs;
import java.util.List;

public class App {
    public static void main(String[] args) {
        Pulumi.run(App::stack);
    }

    public static void stack(Context ctx) {
        final var group = new SecurityGroup("test-sg",
            SecurityGroupArgs.builder()
            .description("Enable HTTP access")
            .ingress(SecurityGroupIngressArgs.builder()
                .protocol("tcp")
                .fromPort(80)
                .toPort(80)
                .cidrBlocks("0.0.0.0/0")
                .build())
            .build());
        final var server = new Instance("web-server",
            InstanceArgs.builder()
                .ami("ami-032930428bf1abbff")
                .instanceType("t2.micro")
                .vpcSecurityGroupIds(group.name().
applyValue(List::of))
                .build());
        ctx.export("publicIp", server.publicIp());
        ctx.export("publicDns", server.publicDns());
    }
}
```

AWS CloudFormation

AWS CloudFormation is a service provided by AWS that helps users create AWS resources in an automated and secure manner. It allows users to spend less time managing their infrastructure resources so they can focus more on applications that will be running on AWS.

With AWS CloudFormation, the user can create template files that describe all the resources needed (for example, EC2 instances, RDS instances, or any S3 buckets) and the tool will take care of provisioning them. CloudFormation takes care of handling the resource dependencies automatically.

A CloudFormation template consists of several sections, including resources, parameters, mappings, conditions, outputs, and metadata. The most important section is the `resources` section, which defines the AWS resources to be created or modified:

- **Resources**: Details the AWS components that are created, updated, or deleted when the CloudFormation stack is created, updated, or modified

- **Parameters**: Used to pass custom input to the template

- **Mappings**: Set of key-value pairs that can be used to map the user input to the corresponding output values

- **Conditions**: Defines conditional statements within the CloudFormation template

- **Outputs**: Exports the information about the resources created by the template

- **Metadata**: Additional information about the template or resources within the template

An example CloudFormation template that creates an EC2 instance and associates it with the Elastic IP address is given here for reference:

```
{
    "AWSTemplateFormatVersion": "2010-09-09",
    "Description": "AWS CloudFormation Sample Template to associate an
Elastic IP address with an Amazon EC2 instance",
    "Parameters": {
        "InstanceType": {
            "Description": "EC2 instance type",
            "Type": "String",
            "Default": "t1.micro",
            "AllowedValues": [
                "t1.micro"
            ],
            "ConstraintDescription": "Must be a valid EC2 instance
type."
        },
        "KeyName": {
            "Description": "Existing EC2 KeyPair name to enable SSH
access to the instances",
            "Type": "AWS::EC2::KeyPair::KeyName",
            "ConstraintDescription": "Name of an existing EC2
KeyPair."
        }
    },
    "Mappings": {
        "AWSInstanceType2Arch": {
            "t1.micro": {
```

```
                    "Arch": "HVM64"
                }
            },
            "AWSInstanceType2NATArch": {
                "t1.micro": {
                    "Arch": "NATHVM64"
                }
            },
            "AWSRegionArch2AMI": {
                "us-east-1": {
                    "HVM64": "ami-032930428bf1abbff",
                    "HVMG2": "ami-0aeb704d503081ea6"
                }
            }
        },
        "Resources": {
            "EC2Instance": {
                "Type": "AWS::EC2::Instance",
                "Properties": {
                    "UserData": {
                        "Fn::Base64": {
                            "Fn::Join": [
                                "",
                                [
                                    "IPAddress=",
                                    {
                                        "Ref": "IPAddress"
                                    }
                                ]
                            ]
                        }
                    },
                    "InstanceType": {
                        "Ref": "InstanceType"
                    },
                    "KeyName": {
                        "Ref": "KeyName"
                    },
                    "ImageId": {
                        "Fn::FindInMap": [
                            "AWSRegionArch2AMI",
                            {
                                "Ref": "AWS::Region"
```

```json
                    },
                    {
                        "Fn::FindInMap": [
                            "AWSInstanceType2Arch",
                            {
                                "Ref": "InstanceType"
                            },
                            "Arch"
                        ]
                    }
                ]
            }
        }
    },
    "IPAddress": {
        "Type": "AWS::EC2::EIP"
    },
    "IPAssoc": {
        "Type": "AWS::EC2::EIPAssociation",
        "Properties": {
            "InstanceId": {
                "Ref": "EC2Instance"
            },
            "EIP": {
                "Ref": "IPAddress"
            }
        }
    }
},
"Outputs": {
    "InstanceId": {
        "Description": "InstanceId of the newly created EC2
instance",
        "Value": {
            "Ref": "EC2Instance"
        }
    },
    "InstanceIPAddress": {
        "Description": "IP address of the newly created EC2
instance",
        "Value": {
            "Ref": "IPAddress"
        }
    }
```

```
        }
    }
```

IaC Use Cases

This section will cover the most important use cases where IaC adds value and increases the developer's or team's productivity.

Multi-Cloud Deployments

For mission-critical applications, provisioning infrastructure in multi-cloud deployments will increase fault tolerance and reduce their dependency on one particular cloud provider so that they can be highly available if there are any issues. But multi-cloud deployments come with the increased complexity of handling each provider with their own setup, different tools/services, and different configuration procedures. IaC tools such as Terraform allow us to have the same workflow to deploy applications in multi-cloud environments and handle cross-cloud dependencies.

Application Deployments, Scaling, and Monitoring Tools

IaC tools can be used to efficiently deploy, release, scale, and monitor infrastructure for multi-tier applications. The multi-tier application architecture usually consists of a web layer that's accessible from the internet for customers to interact with, a backend layer that exposes the data to the web layer, and a database layer that actually stores the data. This style allows you to individually scale the components and provides the separation of concerns. Using IaC will help you deploy the components together and handle dependencies. For example, the database layer should be provisioned before the web layer or the backend layer.

Policy Compliance and Management

There could be situations where we can enforce policies on the types of resources the internal team uses for development for compliance reasons, and IaC helps here as well. There are policy-as-code frameworks such as Sentinel that can be used to implement policies before the resources are provisioned.

Testing Environments and Software Demos

The applications are usually developed and tested in different environments, such as development, QA, and pre-prod, before the code is deployed in production. The different environments mostly have different scaling requirements, but with the same set of tools and dependencies, and IaC tools can help provide the infrastructure based on the environment with the same set of scripts.

IaC tools will also help set the space/environment for software demos that might be needed temporarily and that do not have to go through the ticketing process or reviews, mainly for bootstrapping the testing environments in no time, when compared to the traditional way of installing software and setting up project-related things.

Benefits of IaC

IaC comes with a lot of benefits in every phase of software development and also after the product is implemented in production. This removes a lot of bottlenecks in real-world problems around the installation and management of software products and other open-source tools used in the background.

Some of the key benefits are listed here.

Rapid Deployments and Tool Integration

As discussed earlier in the chapter, IaC practices, along with the cloud migration strategy, help organizations reduce their initial capital expenses and focus more on the applications that will be deployed in the cloud.

In this way, organizations can get started with application development with very minimal costs and take full advantage of the pay-as-you-go model with the cloud. Cloud service providers always strive to provide the best customer experience and at the same time enhance their products with value-added services.

For example, AWS provides managed services such as **Amazon Managed Streaming for Apache Kakfa (Amazon MSK)** and Managed Service for Prometheus. These help customers easily integrate popular tools such as Apache Kafka and Prometheus with their applications in the cloud with AWS doing all the heavy lifting.

With the use of IaC tools such as Terraform and Crossplane, supporting services and actual services needed for compute and storage can be integrated easily and deployed with clear dependencies with very little manual effort.

Lower Costs and Error Reduction

Going with the IaC approach of infrastructure provisioning and configuration management will help organizations and individual teams reduce their management costs to surprising levels.

Here is another example: an organization, BLUE, uses the IaC approach, and another organization, RED, sticks with the manual approach of providing infrastructure for internal application teams.

Application teams at BLUE initially have to spend their time setting up their IaC scripts based on the application requirements, and these scripts can be reused in every deployment in all possible environments. They need very little to no help from the infrastructure team because of the stability IaC provides.

But the same scenario will not work with RED. They have to assign and allocate individuals every time a service request is raised, and they have to figure out deployment scripts and need constant communication with the application teams. If there are any problems, they need to do more work, and they need more capacity to support the same set of applications.

This clearly shows the advantages BLUE has over RED with regard to capacity costs and lower chances of error with infrastructure provisioning.

Configuration Drift Elimination

IaC automatically takes care of the configuration drift problem with its architecture. To understand this better, learn what exactly configuration drift is. This particularly arises when the actual state of the deployment **Configuration Items (CIs)** is different from the original intended state of the deployment.

For example, person A and person B from the same team with the same level of access are working on setting up an EC2 instance to run the application. Person A has created a **Secure Shell (SSH)** configuration script to allow SSH access, and at the same time, person B has created scripts that did not work as expected.

This creates a scenario where the original intended state might be affected by the problematic scripts created by the other individual and, eventually, the instance might become unusable. This scenario can easily be eliminated with the IaC approach, where the original desired state is always remembered and constantly checked against the current configuration.

If any differences are found, the scripts can be executed once again so the problematic resources can be removed and recreated with the desired status.

Improved Infrastructure Consistency

The IaC methodology also ensures that the provisioned infrastructure is always consistent with the desired configuration and that there are no deviations. Once the configuration scripts are in place after careful design, the scripts will always perform the same actions that result in the same infrastructure with the exact setup, irrespective of the number of executions or the execution environment in the current context.

This helps teams focus more on the application logic and the improvements in the design rather than worrying about the underlying infrastructure.

DevOps and CI/CD

DevOps and CI/CD have taken the world by storm, and one of the core principles of these advanced techniques is automation. Since automation is one of the core benefits you get from using IaC, it works well in this landscape.

DevOps and CI/CD tools such as Jenkins and GitLab work closely with open-source tools and third-party vendor products in the form of plugins, the build or test pipelines integrate them, and the triggers can be automated as well. The alignment of development and operations teams with the CI/CD processes using IaC through a DevOps approach leads to fewer errors and allows for automated deployments.

When integrated with IaC, DevOps best practices also help the infrastructure provisioning process where the same code is used for deployment in every environment and the code is going through the same testing pipeline, and version control helps maintain the different versions of infrastructure code.

Don't Repeat Yourself (DRY)

With the benefits being discussed so far, it is evident that IaC helps with the deployment process in different environments with the same code base. This completely removes the redundant steps that have to be performed manually every time for each deployment in the traditional approach.

Hence, this approach supports the DRY principle to reduce manual effort and increase overall efficiency.

> **Note**
>
> As indicated earlier in the chapter, you need the AWS CLI set up with credentials for your AWS account and the Terraform CLI to complete the exercises.
>
> It is assumed that the setup is ready by this point; you will find every step on the internet if you face any issues at all.

Creating a Simple AWS DynamoDB Table Using a CloudFormation Template

You are now going to create a new CloudFormation template that will provision a DynamoDB table based on user input when executed, and you will output the details of the table created at the end of the exercise. This will help you get a firm understanding of the IaC tool's ability to provision the required infrastructure in a declarative fashion. Here are the steps:

1. Create the template with the template version field and a short description of the template in JSON format:

```
{
    "AWSTemplateFormatVersion": "2010-09-09",
    "Description": "AWS CloudFormation Template to create a
simple DynamoDB_Table"
}
```

2. Next, you will define the `Parameters` block to get the user inputs and configure the default, minimum, and maximum values:

```
    "Parameters": {
        "ElementName": {
            "Description": "Primary Key Name",
            "Type": "String",
            "AllowedPattern": "[a-zA-Z0-9]*",
            "MinLength": "1",
            "MaxLength": "2048",
            "ConstraintDescription": "Only alphanumeric
characters are allowed"
        },
        "ElementType": {
            "Description": "Primary Key Type",
            "Type": "String",
            "Default": "S",
            "AllowedPattern": "[S|N]",
            "MinLength": "1",
            "MaxLength": "1",
            "ConstraintDescription": "Pattern values must be
either S or N"
        },
        "ReadCapacityUnits": {
            "Description": "Provisioned read throughput",
            "Type": "Number",
            "Default": "5",
            "MinValue": "5",
            "MaxValue": "1000",
            "ConstraintDescription": "RCU must be between 5 and
1000"
        },
        "WriteCapacityUnits": {
            "Description": "Provisioned write throughput",
            "Type": "Number",
            "Default": "10",
```

```
            "MinValue": "5",
            "MaxValue": "1000",
            "ConstraintDescription": "WCU must be between 5 and
    1000"
        }
    },
```

3. You can now create the `Resources` block, which is responsible for provisioning the DynamoDB resource:

```
"Resources": {
    "myDynamoDBTable": {
        "Type": "AWS::DynamoDB::Table",
        "Properties": {
            "AttributeDefinitions": [
                {
                    "AttributeName": {
                        "Ref": "ElementName"
                    },
                    "AttributeType": {
                        "Ref": "ElementType"
                    }
                }
            ],
            "KeySchema": [
                {
                    "AttributeName": {
                        "Ref": "ElementName"
                    },
                    "KeyType": "HASH"
                }
            ],
            "ProvisionedThroughput": {
                "ReadCapacityUnits": {
                    "Ref": "ReadCapacityUnits"
                },
                "WriteCapacityUnits": {
                    "Ref": "WriteCapacityUnits"
                }
            }
        }
    },
```

4. The final step is to create the `Outputs` block, which will output the name of the table you have just created:

```
"Outputs": {
    "TableName": {
        "Value": {
            "Ref": "myDynamoDBTable"
        },
        "Description": "DynamoDB table name"
    }
}
```

5. Run the template in the AWS CLI with the following command:

```
aws cloudformation create-stack --stack-name DynamoDB-
Test --template-body file://./aws-dynamodb-template-cfn.json
--parameters ParameterKey=ElementName,ParameterValue=CustomerID
ParameterKey=ElementType,ParameterValue=S --region us-east-1
```

6. Upon successful execution, you will get the `StackId` value for the template in the CLI output and you will be able to see the table in the console, as shown in *Figure 1.2*:

```
{
    "StackId": "arn:aws:cloudformation:us-east-
1:xxxxxxxxxxxx:stack/DynamoDB-Test/23b50a90-56cb-11ee-b665-
0a54a53b11f8"
}
```

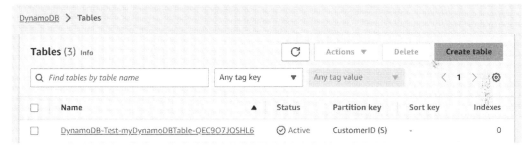

Figure 1.3 – Table in the console

You have successfully created a DynamoDB table using a CloudFormation template in this exercise, and this can be done with a template in YAML format as well.

Creating an AWS S3 Bucket Using Terraform

This exercise will explore the use of another popular IaC tool, Terraform, which we will focus on throughout the book. This will help you get a feel for its usage and learn how its simplified workflow can create real-world resources without any hassle:

1. Create a working directory, for example, `create-s3-bucket-terraform`, on a local machine where you will add your Terraform scripts for this exercise:

   ```
   $ mkdir create-s3-bucket-terraform
   ```

2. You can now create the first configuration file inside the directory called `provider.tf` to configure the AWS Terraform provider, which will be used in the background:

   ```
   terraform {
     required_providers {
       aws = {
         source  = "hashicorp/aws"
         version = "~> 5.14"
       }
     }

     required_version = ">= 1.4"
   }

   provider "aws" {
     profile = "default"
     region  = "ap-south-1"
   }
   ```

   Here, the first `terraform` configuration block is used to enforce the version constraints and to apply the configuration. The execution will be successful only if the specified criteria match.

   The `required_providers` sub-block is used to specify the provider requirements, such as the source and the version that will be downloaded in the next step. The `provider` block will specify some default settings for the resources that will be provisioned.

3. It is now time to define the actual S3 bucket resource in the new file, `main.tf`, with the `aws_s3_bucket` AWS resource with some default tags. Please note that the bucket name we specify must be unique across all the AWS Regions; otherwise, the resource creation might fail. That's the reason we add a random prefix:

   ```
   resource "aws_s3_bucket" "test-bucket" {
     bucket = "test-s3-bucket-kquiyrt"

     tags = {
       Name        = "S3Bucket"
   ```

```
        CreatedBy = "TestUser"
    }
}
```

4. The S3 bucket will be created with the default settings with the resource definition in the previous step, but we will additionally try to enable versioning for the bucket with the `aws_s3_bucket_versioning` resource:

```
resource "aws_s3_bucket_versioning" "enable_version" {
  bucket = aws_s3_bucket.test-bucket.bucket
  versioning_configuration {
    status = "Enabled"
  }
}
```

5. You are ready now to test our script with the Terraform CLI. Running the `terraform init` command will download all the provider plugins referenced in the code:

```
$ terraform init
```

You should be seeing a similar output to the one shown here:

```
Initializing the backend...

Initializing provider plugins...
- Finding hashicorp/aws versions matching "~> 5.14"...
- Installing hashicorp/aws v5.15.0...
- Installed hashicorp/aws v5.15.0 (signed by HashiCorp)

Terraform has created a lock file .terraform.lock.hcl to record the provider
selections it made above. Include this file in your version control repository
so that Terraform can guarantee to make the same selections by default when
you run "terraform init" in the future.

Terraform has been successfully initialized!

You may now begin working with Terraform. Try running "terraform plan" to see
any changes that are required for your infrastructure. All Terraform commands
should now work.

If you ever set or change modules or backend configuration for Terraform,
rerun this command to reinitialize your working directory. If you forget, other
commands will detect it and remind you to do so if necessary.
```

Figure 1.4: The output will look like this

6. You can then run the `terraform plan` command to see a preview of the resources that will be provisioned with the `apply` command. You can see that there are two resources that will be provisioned, one each for the S3 bucket and the versioning:

```
$ terraform plan
. . .
. . .
Plan: 2 to add, 0 to change, 0 to destroy.
```

7. You can run the `terraform apply` command to provision the resources and then view it from the AWS Management Console. When prompted for yes/no, please proceed with yes, or we can also use the `-auto-approve` option with the original command:

```
$ terraform apply
. . .
aws_s3_bucket.test-bucket: Creating...
aws_s3_bucket.test-bucket: Creation complete after 7s [id=test-s3-bucket-kquiyrt]
aws_s3_bucket_versioning.versioning_demo: Creating...
aws_s3_bucket_versioning.versioning_demo: Creation complete after 3s [id=test-s3-bucket-kquiyrt]

Apply complete! Resources: 2 added, 0 changed, 0 destroyed.
```

8. In the AWS Management Console, you should be able to see the S3 bucket with the versioning option enabled, as shown in *Figures 1.5* and *1.6*.

Figure 1.5 – Bucket in the console

Figure 1.6 – S3 bucket with versioning option enabled

You will now be able to successfully create an S3 bucket in the AWS account using Terraform with the required configuration settings.

Summary

In this chapter, the IaC concept was discussed in detail, and some popular IaC tools were covered to help you understand the differences between them. You then read through various use cases demonstrating the implementation of the IaC approach, and these were followed up with the benefits of using them.

After having done the practical exercises using CloudFormation and Terraform tools, you now also have a better idea about the actual working of these tools and how they differ from each other.

Exam Readiness Drill – Chapter Review Questions

Apart from a solid understanding of key concepts, being able to think quickly under time pressure is a skill that will help you ace your certification exam. That is why working on these skills early on in your learning journey is key.

Chapter review questions are designed to improve your test-taking skills progressively with each chapter you learn and review your understanding of key concepts in the chapter at the same time. You'll find these at the end of each chapter.

> **How to Access these Resources**
>
> To learn how to access these resources, head over to the chapter titled *Chapter 11, Accessing the Online Practice Resources.*

To open the Chapter Review Questions for this chapter, perform the following steps:

1. Click the link – `https://packt.link/HCorp003Ch1.`

    Alternatively, you can scan the following **QR code** (*Figure 1.7*):

Figure 1.7 – QR code that opens Chapter Review Questions for logged-in users

2. Once you log in, you'll see a page similar to the one shown in *Figure 1.8*:

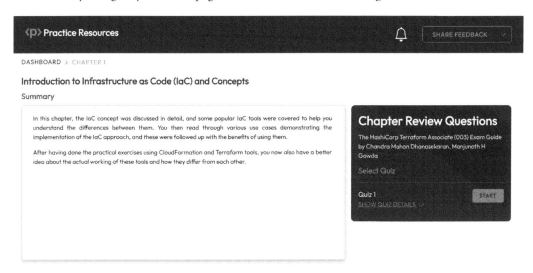

Figure 1.8 – Chapter Review Questions for Chapter 1

3. Once ready, start the following practice drills, re-attempting the quiz multiple times.

Exam Readiness Drill

For the first three attempts, don't worry about the time limit.

ATTEMPT 1

The first time, aim for at least **40%**. Look at the answers you got wrong and read the relevant sections in the chapter again to fix your learning gaps.

ATTEMPT 2

The second time, aim for at least **60%**. Look at the answers you got wrong and read the relevant sections in the chapter again to fix any remaining learning gaps.

ATTEMPT 3

The third time, aim for at least **75%**. Once you score 75% or more, you start working on your timing.

> Tip
>
> You may take more than **three** attempts to reach 75%. That's okay. Just review the relevant sections in the chapter till you get there.

Working On Timing

Target: Your aim is to keep the score the same while trying to answer these questions as quickly as possible. Here's an example of how your next attempts should look like:

Attempt	Score	Time Taken
Attempt 5	77%	21 mins 30 seconds
Attempt 6	78%	18 mins 34 seconds
Attempt 7	76%	14 mins 44 seconds

Table 1.1 – Sample timing practice drills on the online platform

> Note
>
> The time limits shown in the above table are just examples. Set your own time limits with each attempt based on the time limit of the quiz on the website.

With each new attempt, your score should stay above **75%** while your "time taken" to complete should "decrease". Repeat as many attempts as you want till you feel confident dealing with the time pressure.

2
Why Do We Need Terraform?

This chapter will help you understand how infrastructure provisioning was done in different periods of IT history, the challenges associated with it, and how infrastructure automation tools solved those problems.

You will learn what **Infrastructure as Code (IaC)** is and its advantages when compared to the manual provisioning of infrastructure. Then, this chapter will discuss the various tools/services available on the market for Infrastructure as Code, and their pros and cons with respect to Terraform.

Further, the chapter will discuss the Terraform tool and its advantages over other tools/services used for Infrastructure as Code. Finally, the chapter will conclude by providing an overview of the licensing change made by HashiCorp.

History of Infrastructure Provisioning

Historically, infrastructure deployment has undergone three key technological changes:

- The datacenter period
- The virtualization period
- The cloud period

In the datacenter period, infrastructure deployment and configuration were fully manual. Right from putting up the racks; stacking the servers, routers, and switches; installing operating systems and cabling them; and ensuring offsite backup for disaster recovery. There was very little scope for automation in infrastructure tasks. Automation tasks were limited to installing the OS via the **Unattended Install** option, configuring the software, and so on.

In the virtualization period, infrastructure deployment got better. VMware was the pioneer in creating production-grade virtualization offerings. Some of the time-consuming tasks, such as operating system installation and application configuration, could then be deployed in a matter of minutes. Further, centralized backup and patching helped reduce the duration and complexity of tasks. Although virtual machines could be provisioned instantly, this was limited by the hardware you had already purchased for your VMware-based setup in your datacenter.

Some automation started taking place at this stage with HashiCorp's Vagrant tool.

Vagrant helped quickly provision the development environment by adding the required resources and their dependencies in the Vagrant configuration files. These files were then used by the Vagrant tool to create the virtual machine in the VMware Workstation. This helped with quickly creating test environments and pre-production environments to test certain features before moving them to production. Since the provisioning and de-provisioning of the servers was done using the configuration files, the process could be automated easily, making it quicker and less error-prone.

Though the amount of infrastructure automation increased at this stage, it was limited to vendor-specific tools. Professionals were still using VMware-specific tools and technologies to automate production-grade setups. The same tools could not be carried to other vendors' solutions.

To summarize the discussion so far, the following were the challenges of infrastructure automation in the datacenter and virtualization periods:

- Manual processes were error-prone

- High expenses

- A long time was needed to set up the infrastructure required for application deployment

- A lack of tight integrations between various products

- Dependence on vendor-specific automation tools in the virtualization world

- Deploying applications in a different geographical region was a herculean task

It was the cloud era that paved the way for infrastructure automation in a significant manner by solving some of the above key challenges.

Why Is the Cloud Model a Good Fit for Infrastructure Automation?

The cloud model is considered suitable for infrastructure automation for the following reasons:

- Any creation/deletion/modification of a resource in the cloud can be done by calling an API

- There is seamless integration between the various resources of the cloud that can be stitched together for a production-grade solution

- You can access the same set of resources in different geographical regions to deploy the same solution

- The compute, network, security, and SaaS tools are software-defined and can be created, modified, and integrated into the virtual environment

Now that you have reviewed the history of infrastructure provisioning and the challenges associated with each period, you are ready to explore the automation of infrastructure provisioning using **IaC**.

Infrastructure Automation Using IaC

As the name implies, IaC refers to managing infrastructure resources in the form of code instead of manual provisioning. This involves the creation, modification, and deletion of all the infrastructure resources via code.

One of the key principles of DevOps is automation. IaC precisely fits into this principle. Apart from automation, IaC also provides the advantage of using the same best practices that are used for application code in the **Software Development Life Cycle (SDLC)**. This implies that, now, even infrastructure could be versioned and pipelines can be created for continuous deployment since it is all in code.

The following section presents the key advantages that IaC provides over manual deployments.

Advantages of IaC

While looking at the advantages of IaC, it will be compared against manual deployment. Some of the key advantages are listed below:

- **Quicker deployment timelines**: When the whole solution is in code that has been vetted, tested, and approved, it is easy to deploy everything in one go. This takes less time than the same deployment being done manually.

- **Consistently repeatable deployments**: As the resources are provisioned with the same set of APIs, you can expect the same behavior every single time it gets deployed. The uniformity of the deployment behavior provides assurance about the stability of the solution.

- **Version controlled via a source code management tool such as Git**: The configurations and integrations of all the resources can be carried out in code, which is stored in a tool such as Git. This helps you with versioning, merge requests, approvals, and so on. If there is an issue with the latest deployment, it is easy to roll back to the previous version.

- **Better operational efficiency**: Automating the process of launching and managing resources allows quicker deployment, which frees up the operations team to work on other important items rather than spending time just setting up the environments.

- **Self-service**: If you want to empower the development team to deploy the infrastructure, you can set certain guidelines for the modules/templates. They can use these guidelines for self-service and don't have to depend on other teams.

- **Accountability**: All code written, every modification made, and every line deleted is tracked in the version control system. It is easy to assign accountability to the person responsible for any tasks performed.

- **Increased security**: IaC embeds security from the base level and in each layer, such as the network, app, and database layers. Once these are validated by the infosec team, they can be used by all teams. This improves the overall security posture of the organization.

In the next section, you will review the various techniques used in the industry for provisioning infrastructure automatically and how they compare against Terraform.

Various Options for Implementing IaC

There are many ways of implementing IaC. Which option you choose depends on various factors, such as the level of automation required, the skills available in the team, the cloud platform chosen for application deployment, the plan for a multi-cloud presence, and so on. In the following sections, you will go through the options that are regularly used in the industry. Though there are options, Terraform has emerged as a go-to tool for IaC.

Ad Hoc Scripts

Ad hoc scripts are typically written in Shell script, Perl, or Python to automate some of the infrastructure provisioning by directly calling the API and writing the required logic to integrate the resource into the solution. The disadvantage of this is that there is no standardization, and hence each person may solve a problem using different logic and resources in the scripting languages. Scripts written today may not make sense to the same person after three months.

Configuration Management Tools

Configuration management tools such as Chef, Puppet, and Ansible are meant to be used for managing the configuration of software within the operating system. These tools also support infrastructure provisioning. All three of these tools were launched before Terraform and were used by engineers for infrastructure automation. However, this is not their primary functionality. It is important to use the right tool for the right job. Using the wrong tool could give sub-optimal results or could require more effort from you to achieve the same result that could have been achieved using the right tool with minimal effort.

If you want to create the infrastructure for a three-tier architecture-based solution, you may end up spending a similar amount of time on all three tools to create the initial infrastructure. However, the complexity starts when you start modifying the infrastructure.

Consider an example where you want to increase the number of servers from three to six:

- Write commands that will give the number of servers running in the account

- Write logic to calculate the new instances to be launched

- Finally, write code to launch these additional instances

In the case of Terraform, it is as simple as changing the number of servers from three to six. Terraform takes care of figuring out what needs to be done to get the servers to six.

Cloud-Based IaC Services

Each of the major cloud vendors has its own service for IaC functionality:

- AWS has CloudFormation and **Cloud Development Kit (CDK)**

- Microsoft Azure has Azure Resource Manager

- GCP has Cloud Deployment Manager

Each of these services has very tight integration with the services of the particular cloud, and their support for new services in that cloud will be significantly quicker than any third-party tool, such as Terraform or Pulumi. However, if you need to be present in multiple clouds, are unsure about sticking with a single cloud provider, or just want the team to learn how to use one tool that can be used across the infrastructure, platform, and SaaS tools provisioning automation, then it is better to choose a tool like Terraform that is not dependent on any single vendor but works across them all.

Cloud-Agnostic IaC Tools

Terraform by HashiCorp is a pioneer in cloud-agnostic IaC tools (i.e., able to run on any cloud without getting tied to a single cloud). In recent years, a new tool called Pulumi has also been slowly adopted. Pulumi lets users write code to deploy applications in the language of their choice. Currently, it supports Node.js, Python, Go, .NET, Java, and YAML format.

> **Note**
>
> The **AWS Cloud Development Kit (AWS CDK)** lets you define the AWS cloud infrastructure in a general-purpose programming language such as TypeScript, JavaScript, Python, Java, C#/.NET, or Go. Both Pulumi and AWS CDK expect you to have some programming language knowledge to make the best use of the tool.

What Is Terraform?

Terraform is an IaC tool that lets you create and manage your infrastructure by writing code in a simple language called **HashiCorp Configuration Language (HCL)**.

The following section describes the features of Terraform and explains how the problems of manual provisioning and other IaC options are solved by Terraform.

Features of Terraform

We will explore the primary features of Terraform in this section.

Cloud/Vendor Agnostic

A tool that is very specifically oriented toward a particular platform becomes highly dependent on the features of the platform and hinders customers' ability to switch to another platform when they want to. It is very important for an IaC tool to be cloud-/vendor-agnostic (i.e., able to run on any cloud without getting tied to a single cloud/vendor) for such customers. Unlike many IaC tools provided by cloud vendors, Terraform is fully cloud-/vendor-agnostic and works with all the major cloud providers and also the majority of other vendors.

A Pioneer in IaC

Terraform was launched by HashiCorp in 2014 when the IT industry used either scripts, cloud-specific tools, or configuration management tools for infrastructure automation. It pioneered a new way of solving the infra-automation problem and brought in multi-cloud support. This was done by using a declarative approach to provisioning infrastructure, along with having "current state and desired state" as the central idea, where Terraform assesses the current infrastructure state with the desired state of infrastructure as defined by the user and then makes relevant changes to change the current state to the desired state. Trust in the HashiCorp brand prompted customers to use Terraform in production even before the general availability of version 1.0, which was announced in 2021. The tool has only improved with newer releases, by adding more features, such as HCP Terraform integration, moved blocks for code refactoring, support for **Open Policy Agent (OPA)**, the ability to import manually created resources, testing frameworks, and so on, and integration with new partners.

Wide Partner Integration

Terraform can be used to provision and manage resources on any of the cloud platforms and SaaS offerings. Terraform already has thousands of partners integrated with it. Partners typically integrate with Terraform by creating a plugin that is downloaded by the customer along with the Terraform binary. There is a new set of partners who have products for code scanning, observability, cost management, security, and so on. If you want to support the automation of your product via Terraform, you can write your own custom provider plugin.

Declarative

Procedural and declarative ways of coding are an important consideration in understanding IaC.

In the procedural style, the focus is on clearly defining the steps to achieve the desired end state. Ad hoc scripts and tools such as Ansible and Chef are all procedural language-based. In contrast, declarative style only requires you to outline the end state and the tool takes care of driving the workflow to this end. Terraform uses a declarative approach for infrastructure automation. Hence, the code is easier to write for a newbie.

Idempotent

When you run the same command/instruction multiple times and achieve the same result as you got the first time, the command/instruction is called **idempotent**. Terraform is idempotent. For example, if you have a Terraform file that creates an EC2 instance (a virtual machine in AWS) and you run it for the first time, it will create an EC2 instance. Running it a second or third time will not create additional instances as the desired state has already been achieved.

Easy Learning Curve

Terraform supports two formats to write and manage configuration files: JSON and **HashiCorp Configuration Language (HCL)**.

JSON is typically used by systems for parsing but is tough for humans. In contrast, HCL is very easy to learn and implement even for someone with no programming background.

Version Controlled

The Terraform code written for infrastructure management is managed using a source code management tool such as Git. This code is pushed to platforms such as GitHub, GitLab, and so on to keep it in a central location. Storing it centrally helps with team collaborations, rolling back to previous versions in case of issues with the latest version, and creating a pipeline for automated infrastructure deployment.

Automation

Manual provisioning of infrastructure is manageable for a simple use case. When you are dealing with the creation of thousands of resources, the manual method will cause delays and errors, and will also be expensive. Automation solves all these problems.

You may be tempted to do things manually, but anything that needs to be done more than once should be considered for automation. There is a one-time investment of time while you write the code that will then bring you the benefits of automation when you have to provision the same or similar resource multiple times.

Documentation

Documentation is crucial to explain the current state of your architecture and resources, but it gets out of date quickly in the cloud world. When Terraform is used for full management of the infrastructure, the Terraform code itself can give you the latest state of the resource or the solution that is deployed. Please note that using Terraform does not take away the need for documentation but can help to reduce exhaustive documentation.

Community Support

Terraform is widely used and supported by the community. Whenever cloud vendors add new features to existing products or launch new services, the community quickly adds them to Terraform and creates a merge request with the owners of the repo. Any bugs are also quickly detected and raised with the owners of the plugin for a fix.

Licensing Change from Version 1.5.5 (Aug 2023)

Terraform was an open source tool until August 10, 2023, and it changed to the **community edition** when HashiCorp changed the licensing of their products from **Mozilla Public License v2.0 (MPL 2.0)** to **Business Source License (BSL or BUSL) v1.1**.

Though the BSL license is open, free, and makes the source code available, it does not meet the "open source" criteria defined by **The Open Source Initiative (OSI)**, because of which the Terraform tool cannot be called "open source" anymore. This license is applicable from Terraform version 1.5.5.

As per the new license, "Organizations providing competitive offerings to HashiCorp will no longer be permitted to use the community edition products free of charge under our BSL license."

For more details on new licensing and how it impacts your environment, visit the following links:

- `https://www.hashicorp.com/blog/hashicorp-adopts-business-source-license`
- `https://www.hashicorp.com/license-faq`

Summary

In this chapter, you learned about the challenges of the manual provisioning of infrastructure, what IaC is, and what its advantages are. You also reviewed the importance of Terraform in the IaC landscape and examined what differentiates it from other tools on the market. This information will help you understand the big picture of infrastructure automation and the tools available on the market to solve the problems associated with it. This understanding will help you have a meaningful technical conversation with others about infrastructure automation.

There was a short discussion about the change of license that has stripped the term "open source" from the Terraform feature list.

Now that you understand why Terraform is required, you are ready to explore the basics of Terraform and its workflow in *Chapter 3, Basics of Terraform and Core Workflow.*

Exam Readiness Drill – Chapter Review Questions

Apart from a solid understanding of key concepts, being able to think quickly under time pressure is a skill that will help you ace your certification exam. That is why working on these skills early on in your learning journey is key.

Chapter review questions are designed to improve your test-taking skills progressively with each chapter you learn and review your understanding of key concepts in the chapter at the same time. You'll find these at the end of each chapter.

> **How to Access these Resources**
>
> To learn how to access these resources, head over to the chapter titled *Chapter 11, Accessing the Online Practice Resources*.

To open the Chapter Review Questions for this chapter, perform the following steps:

1. Click the link – `https://packt.link/HCorp003Ch2`.

    Alternatively, you can scan the following **QR code** (*Figure 2.1*):

Figure 2.1 – QR code that opens Chapter Review Questions for logged-in users

2.   Once you log in, you'll see a page similar to the one shown in *Figure 2.2*:

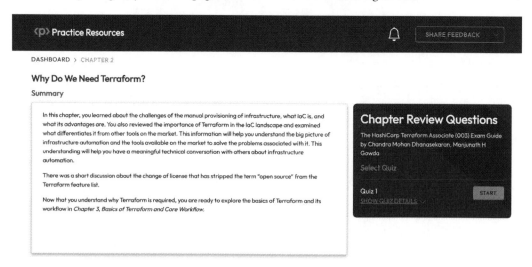

Figure 2.2 – Chapter Review Questions for Chapter 2

3.   Once ready, start the following practice drills, re-attempting the quiz multiple times.

Exam Readiness Drill

For the first three attempts, don't worry about the time limit.

ATTEMPT 1

The first time, aim for at least **40%**. Look at the answers you got wrong and read the relevant sections in the chapter again to fix your learning gaps.

ATTEMPT 2

The second time, aim for at least **60%**. Look at the answers you got wrong and read the relevant sections in the chapter again to fix any remaining learning gaps.

ATTEMPT 3

The third time, aim for at least **75%**. Once you score 75% or more, you start working on your timing.

> **Tip**
>
> You may take more than **three** attempts to reach 75%. That's okay. Just review the relevant sections in the chapter till you get there.

Working On Timing

Target: Your aim is to keep the score the same while trying to answer these questions as quickly as possible. Here's an example of how your next attempts should look like:

Attempt	Score	Time Taken
Attempt 5	77%	21 mins 30 seconds
Attempt 6	78%	18 mins 34 seconds
Attempt 7	76%	14 mins 44 seconds

Table 2.1 – Sample timing practice drills on the online platform

> **Note**
>
> The time limits shown in the above table are just examples. Set your own time limits with each attempt based on the time limit of the quiz on the website.

With each new attempt, your score should stay above **75%** while your "time taken" to complete should "decrease". Repeat as many attempts as you want till you feel confident dealing with the time pressure.

3

Basics of Terraform and Core Workflow

In the previous chapter, you saw various use cases and scenarios for adopting Terraform into infrastructure-provisioning workflows to reap real benefits. It is now time to cover the basic building blocks that make Terraform an efficient tool to use, whether you have ample experience in IT or you are just starting in your career.

This chapter will cover the following topics:

- How does Terraform work?
- Getting started with Terraform
- Terraform settings
- Terraform providers
- Dependency lock file
- Resources and data sources
- Variables and outputs
- Core workflow

Technical Requirements

In this chapter, you will deep dive into Terraform concepts and try out multiple programs or scripts that need the right setup. Please ensure that you have the following tools installed and ready to use:

- AWS account ID with administrator access credentials
- AWS CLI version 2.x.x

- Terraform CLI version 1.5.x or later
- Visual Studio Code or any text editor

The GitHub repository for the chapter contains the graphics and scripts used in the chapter and can be found using the following link:

```
https://github.com/PacktPublishing/Hashicorp-Certified-Terraform-
Associate-003-Exam-guide-Second-Edition/tree/main/ch3/getting-
started-in-terraform
```

How Terraform Works

The HashiCorp Terraform tool is an **Infrastructure as Code** (**IaC**) tool that can be used to create both cloud and on-premises resources with the help of human-readable configuration scripts. This set of scripts can be used numerous times to provision the exact same infrastructure with consistent workflows. Scripts can be shared and reused within the team if multiple developers are working on the same set of resources.

With the proper backend configuration to store the Terraform state file in a remote location/repository, resources created in different workstations can point to the same configuration, avoiding duplication and reducing costs.

You can now take a look at the basic workflow of Terraform and how it helps manage and track infrastructure in a more efficient way.

Terraform creates and manages resources in different cloud environments and other services with the help of **application programming interfaces** (**APIs**). Suppose you want to create an S3 bucket (a storage service that stores data as objects) in the AWS cloud and you have the necessary permissions to accomplish the task.

There are multiple ways to do that:

- Use the AWS Management Console and select the S3 service to create the bucket with basic permissions.
- Use the AWS CLI to create the bucket with the `aws s3 create-bucket` command.
- Use the AWS CloudFormation template.
- Use programs written in Java/Python/C# that use the AWS SDK to interact with the AWS cloud.

In all the preceding options, the final interaction with the AWS cloud happens with the help of the same APIs, but the way you access it slightly differs depending on the selected approach. Similarly, Terraform has also created an abstraction popularly known as **providers** and has hidden the internal details of how it interacts with APIs of different cloud providers and other services.

The official Terraform Registry page (`https://registry.terraform.io/`) lists thousands of providers, such as AWS, GCP, Azure, Docker, and Kubernetes, among several others.

Figure 3.1 – A high-level overview of Terraform providers

Getting Started with Terraform

As mentioned previously, it is assumed that the prerequisite tools are ready in your local workstation. To verify that everything is working without any issues, please try out the following commands and ensure that you get a similar output.

If you encounter any issues, please resolve them before proceeding with the topics for better understanding.

Terraform CLI Installation Check

The below command can be used to check the Terraform CLI version installed on your workstation:

```
$ terraform -version
```

The command output is as follows

```
C:\Users>terraform -version
Terraform v1.5.7
on windows_amd64
```

Figure 3.2 – Terraform version command output

AWS CLI Installation Check

The below command can be used to check the AWS CLI version installed on your workstation:

```
$ aws --version
```

The command output is as follows:

```
C:\Users>aws --version
aws-cli/2.15.16 Python/3.11.6 Windows/10 exe/AMD64 prompt/off
```

Figure 3.3 – AWS CLI version command output

If you see similar outputs, you are good to go and can try out the following exercise to get the feel of using Terraform to create a basic AWS IAM user resource and a pair of access keys for the IAM user to use programmatically.

Creating Your First Terraform Resource – AWS IAM User

In this subtopic, you will be creating an AWS IAM user resource and attaching a pair of access keys for it. Access keys are long-term credentials that you can attach to AWS IAM users or the root user account. They are used to sign your programmatic requests to the AWS CLI or the API directly (via the AWS SDK).

The resources you will be creating as part of this topic will end up in the AWS account that will be configured as follows. Please ensure that you have the right set of credentials before this step and that you have complete control of the AWS account. This will be very helpful when you want to visualize and track the changes being performed by Terraform in the background.

Setting up AWS Credentials

Here are the steps to set up AWS credentials:

1. The first step is to configure the environment variables in your workstation with the admin access credentials so the AWS Terraform provider will pick it for resource creation. If you do not have the credentials and possess only the root admin user and password, please log in to the console and create the access keys for the root user in the IAM menu.

2. Once you have the credentials, please execute the following commands before you create the Terraform configuration. The following commands will work for Linux. Please use the setx <ENV_VARIABLE_KEY> <ENV VARIABLE VALUE> command for Windows to set the environment variables.

Use the AWS access key ID instead of xxxx in the following command:

```
$ export AWS_ACCESS_KEY_ID=xxxx
```

Use the AWS secret access key instead of yyyy in the following command:

```
export AWS_SECRET_ACCESS_KEY=yyyy
```

Terraform Configuration

Now, you can create your own set of files inside the working directory to create the IAM user using Terraform. The files where you describe the infrastructure in Terraform are called the Terraform configuration.

Create a file named main.tf and paste the following configuration. Save it using any text editor:

```
terraform {
  required_providers {
    aws = {
      source  = "hashicorp/aws"
      version = "~> 5.0"
    }
  }

  required_version = ">= 1.5.0"
}

provider "aws" {
  region  = "us-east-1"
}

resource "aws_iam_user" "test_user" {
  name = "test-aws-user"
  path = "/test/"

  tags = {
    "createdby" = "terraform"
  }
}

resource "aws_iam_access_key" "user_access_keys" {
  user = aws_iam_user.test_user.name
}
```

This single file contains the entire configuration that can be deployed using Terraform CLI. Basically, the code has three different block types: a `terraform` block, a `provider` block, and a couple of `resource` blocks. The following are explanations of each of these blocks:

- **The terraform { } block**: The `terraform { }` block contains the Terraform settings along with the different providers that will be used for the configuration. In this case, you are using only one provider, `aws`, and the `required_providers` block is used to specify the source and the version attributes. The source attribute will optionally include a hostname, namespace, and provider type. If the hostname is not mentioned, the Terraform Registry, `registry.terraform.io`, is assumed.

  The `version` attribute will include the version, which is optional but still recommended. This is because specifying the version will ensure the configuration scripts work for the version specified and Terraform will not install something that is incompatible.

- **The provider { } block**: The `provider { }` block configures the provider you will use. The provider is nothing but a plugin that Terraform uses to create and manage resources by interacting with the cloud provider APIs.

  Since the credentials are already configured to use the AWS cloud provider, the `provider { }` block just contains the region, which is set to `us-east-1` (North Virginia). You want to create an IAM user that has a global scope and region is not applicable. But if you want to create an EC2 instance, the `region` parameter becomes important because the resource will be created in the region accordingly.

  You can also use multiple `provider { }` blocks if the configuration involves creating multiple resources from different providers. The `provider { }` blocks can also be dependent on values from other providers. For example, the secrets retrieved using the vault provider can be used to configure the AWS credentials, which is also possible when the credentials are secured in a vault.

- **The resource { } block**: The `resource { }` block is used to define the actual infrastructure resources and these are implementation-specific for each Terraform provider. In this example, you are using the `aws_iam_user` resource type, which will create an IAM user in the AWS public cloud. The resource name is `test_user` in the first `resource { }` block.

  Inside the `resource { }` block, the `path` and `name` parameters are additionally set to pass the required values. The defined resources can contain one or more parameters in addition to the mandatory ones and the provider documentation in the Terraform Registry will have additional details, such as usage and example resource blocks.

  There is also an additional parameter, `tags`, that can be used to tag the IAM user resource to set additional metadata for the created resource. In AWS, the resource tags have different purposes, such as resource segregation and billing usage, among others.

The second `resource {}` block will create AWS IAM access keys for the user just created in the previous block. The IAM access keys are used to set programmatic access with user permissions and have different use cases. If the IAM user permissions have to be used to configure the AWS CLI, then you need to create an AWS CLI profile with user access keys, and you need to use access keys similar to the one you are creating here.

IAM access keys are confidential information. If an intruder gets access to the access key, the AWS account can be compromised. So, you must secure the created credentials.

Creating the AWS IAM User

Now you have a basic understanding of the Terraform configuration script and can move on to creating the resources:

1. The first step is to initialize the working directory with the `terraform init` command. This command will download and install the providers defined in the script, in this case, the `aws` provider.

    When the `aws` provider is successfully downloaded and installed, you can see that Terraform keeps the content in the hidden `.terraform` directory inside your working directory. The `init` command will also indicate which provider version was installed in the terminal, and the same operation also creates the `.terraform.lock.hcl` file, which specifies the exact provider version used.

    This will help retain control of the provider versions installed in the future when the provider version changes with the latest upgrades. *Figure 3.4* shows the output of the `init` command for reference.

```
Initializing the backend...

Initializing provider plugins...
- Reusing previous version of hashicorp/aws from the dependency lock file
- Using previously-installed hashicorp/aws v5.19.0

Terraform has been successfully initialized!

You may now begin working with Terraform. Try running "terraform plan" to see
any changes that are required for your infrastructure. All Terraform commands
should now work.

If you ever set or change modules or backend configuration for Terraform,
rerun this command to reinitialize your working directory. If you forget, other
commands will detect it and remind you to do so if necessary.
```

Figure 3.4 – terraform init command output

2. The `terraform validate` command can be used after the `init` operation is successful to validate the Terraform configuration to identify any possible errors. If there are no errors, the message `Success! The configuration is valid` will be given as output.

3. In the Terraform documentation, it is also suggested that the `terraform fmt` command can be used for consistent formatting of the Terraform configuration scripts. If the command is executed without the `-recursive` option, only the scripts in the main directory will be formatted, and using it will format the scripts in the subdirectories as well.

4. The final step is to apply the configuration with the `terraform apply` command. The Terraform output in the terminal will be like in *Figure 3.5*.

```
Terraform used the selected providers to generate the following execution plan. Resource actions are indicated with the
following symbols:
  + create

Terraform will perform the following actions:

  # aws_iam_access_key.user_access_keys will be created
  + resource "aws_iam_access_key" "user_access_keys" {
      + create_date                   = (known after apply)
      + encrypted_secret              = (known after apply)
      + encrypted_ses_smtp_password_v4 = (known after apply)
      + id                            = (known after apply)
      + key_fingerprint               = (known after apply)
      + secret                        = (sensitive value)
      + ses_smtp_password_v4          = (sensitive value)
      + status                        = "Active"
      + user                          = "test-aws-user"
    }
```

```
  # aws_iam_user.test_user will be created
  + resource "aws_iam_user" "test_user" {
      + arn           = (known after apply)
      + force_destroy = false
      + id            = (known after apply)
      + name          = "test-aws-user"
      + path          = "/test/"
      + tags          = {
          + "createdby" = "terraform"
        }
      + tags_all      = {
          + "createdby" = "terraform"
        }
      + unique_id     = (known after apply)
    }

Plan: 2 to add, 0 to change, 0 to destroy.

Do you want to perform these actions?
  Terraform will perform the actions described above.
  Only 'yes' will be accepted to approve.

  Enter a value: ▌
```

Figure 3.5 – terraform apply console output

Terraform will use the installed providers to create the final execution plan on how the resources need to be created. You may notice that some of the parameters are set to (known after apply), which means the actual value will be set when the resources are created and it is not a known value. You may also notice that additional parameters such as arn and create_date are displayed. These parameters are not actually coded in the configuration scripts and are specific to the resources being created.

A user prompt is also given in the output, which needs to be set to yes if you wish to proceed and apply the configuration. If any other value is specified, the apply operation will be terminated. Please enter yes if you are happy to proceed, and you will see the resources are created in the configured AWS account.

```
aws_iam_user.test_user: Creating...
aws_iam_user.test_user: Creation complete after 1s [id=test-aws-user]
aws_iam_access_key.user_access_keys: Creating...
aws_iam_access_key.user_access_keys: Creation complete after 0s [id=                    ]

Apply complete! Resources: 2 added, 0 changed, 0 destroyed.
```

Figure 3.6 – resource creation from terraform apply

When the resources are created, Terraform creates the terraform.tfstate state file and stores all details about the resources, such as IDs and resource types, so it can update and destroy the resources going forward. Since there is no specific backend configuration, the state file is stored locally inside the working directory and can be inspected with the terraform show command.

Terraform also has the terraform state command for advanced state management, and the list option can be used to list the resources created with the current configuration:

```
$ terraform state list
aws_iam_access_key.user_access_keys
aws_iam_user.test_user
```

Terraform Settings

The first step in using the Terraform tool for infrastructure resource provisioning has now been completed successfully and you have a better idea of how to write a simple configuration script based on the requirements using the relevant provider.

Take a look at each of the blocks in detail now. This section will particularly cover the different configuration settings available for use inside the terraform {} block, and subsequent sections will discuss the provider, resources, and data sources blocks.

The terraform {} configuration block is mainly used to configure the behaviour of the Terraform tool itself, such as the minimum Terraform version required to run the scripts.

This block has the following nested blocks, each with its own purpose, and they are not mandatory:

- HCP Terraform configuration using the `cloud {}` block
- Terraform backend configuration using the `backend {}` block
- The `required_version {}` block
- The `required_providers {}` block
- Experimental features using the `experiments []` block
- Providers metadata using the `provider_meta {}` block

HCP Terraform Configuration Using the cloud {} block

HCP Terraform is a special offering from HashiCorp for teams to work on infrastructure provisioning together without any conflicts. HCP Terraform is a hosted service, accessible from `https://app.terraform.io`, with the primary intention of providing a consistent and reliable environment for shared access, and additional features such as a private registry, security, and change approvals.

Small teams can use HCP Terraform for free and run Terraform in a remote environment. Its CLI-driven workflow is easy to adopt and you can start using it without any hassle.

If there is a requirement to use HCP Terraform instead of using the OSS version, the `cloud {}` nested block can be used within the `terraform {}` block to configure the settings pointing to the specific organization and workspaces under the organization. These concepts will be covered in detail in a later chapter covering HCP Terraform.

> **Note**
>
> Please note that HCP Terraform and the backend configurations cannot be used at the same time.

A sample `cloud {}` nested block is given for your reference, and you can look at each of the arguments inside the block at a high level:

```
terraform {
  cloud {
    organization = "test-cloud-org"
    hostname = "app.terraform.io"

    workspaces {
      project = "accounting-team"
      tags = ["accounting", "source:cli"]
    }
  }
}
```

The arguments used are as follows:

- organization: The name of the organization containing the workspaces that the configuration script should use.

- hostname: The hostname of a Terraform Enterprise installation. If it is not provided, then default to the HCP Terraform **app.terraform.io** hostname. (Terraform Enterprise is not the same as HCP Terraform; it is a self-hosted Terraform environment for organizations with tighter security requirements and statutory constraints.)

- workspace: This is another nested block that has details on the remote workspaces to be used for the configuration. The workspace block can contain only one argument – either name or tags – not both:

  - tags: This can contain a set of HCP Terraform tags and the current working directory can be used with any workspace that has the specified tags. The different workspaces can be switched using the terraform workspace select command. This cannot be used if name has already been specified.

  - name: This contains the name of the workspace to be used for the current working directory. It is optional like the tags argument.

- project: The name of the HCP Terraform project that contains the workspace. With the terraform workspace list command, the workspaces that will be listed in the output will be filtered with this project name.

- token: The authentication token to be used for HCP Terraform access. The right way to authenticate is by either using the terraform login command or supplying the credentials via the CLI config file.

Terraform Backend Configuration Using the backend {} Block

The terraform {} block also has a backend nested block to support different backend configurations to store the state file remotely in a secure manner.

In the previous section, with the first Terraform script, you saw that terraform.tfstate was created in the working directory because no backend configuration was available. But if you wish to store the Terraform state file remotely so the team can access and point to the same state file when multiple people work with the same configuration script, the backend configuration will help.

The backend nested block is optional, like the other nested blocks; you can configure it if it is applicable to your setup.

There are multiple backend types available for use; you can select the appropriate ones that work with your design. For example, if the team primarily works with AWS services, the s3 backend type is a natural option, and if microservices are being deployed in Kubernetes clusters, the Kubernetes backend can be selected to store the state as a Kubernetes Secret.

Unlike the cloud {} nested block, the backend {} block will vary based on the actual backend type selected. This is because the different backend types will have their own custom configuration and the user is expected to pass the relevant values for them.

A sample s3 backend is given here for your reference. It has arguments such as bucket, region, and key that are specific to AWS:

```
terraform {
  backend "s3" {
    bucket = "mybucket"
    key    = "path/to/my/key"
    region = "us-east-1"
    dynamodb_table = "terraform-s3-backend-xyz"
  }
}
```

There are different considerations while working with the Terraform backend. They are listed as follows:

- If there is no backend block specified, the default local backend will be used. In this case, the state file will be stored in plain text in the current working directory.

- The Terraform configuration script can contain one backend block only.

- The Terraform backend {} block cannot contain references to named values such as variables, locals, and data sources.

Initialization

When the remote backend configuration is added for the first time, the terraform init command must be rerun to validate the settings.

If the command execution is successful, the Terraform tool will create the .terraform directory locally and store the most recent backend setup and any associated credentials inside it. This directory should not be committed into your version control tool, such as Git or Bitbucket, as it may contain credentials.

When there are changes again to the backend configuration, Terraform gives the option to migrate the state to the new backend to avoid duplication and any conflicts.

Partial Configuration

Partial configuration is helpful to the user when working with dynamic values or when the backend configuration is not possible in the first stage. You can now try to understand this with an example.

A software developer writes Terraform scripts with the s3 backend that work for the setup of different lower environments, such as DEV and QA. They like to use the same bucket to store the state files with different values for key or region arguments.

But environment values such as DEV and QA will be known only during the time of `apply` command execution and it is not possible to code them beforehand. In this scenario, partial configuration will help with not setting the value in the backend block, and this can be configured while using the `terraform init` command.

The `terraform init` command has the option of setting the backend config with the `-backend-config` option to set the value for the `key` or `region` argument, as follows. This sets values such as key-value pairs. You can also do the same with the config file, even in an interactive manner:

```
$ terraform init -backend-config="key=DEV/data/"
$ terraform init -backend-config="region=us-east-1"
```

The required_version Setting

The `required_version` {} nested block accepts a version constraint string that enforces a minimum version of Terraform CLI that must be used to run the scripts.

This ensures that everyone working with the same configuration script has the required Terraform CLI version or the minimum version expected to run the scripts in a collaborative environment.

The `required_version` {} nested block version constraint is applicable only for Terraform CLI, and the resources created by the script are not applicable because each Terraform provider follows their own release timelines, independent of the Terraform CLI versions.

A sample `terraform` block with the `required_version` nested block is given for reference:

```
terraform {
. . .
required_version = "~> 1.4"
}
```

The required_providers {} Block

The `required_providers` nested block is used to specify all the providers required by the current configuration script. It maps the local provider name to the source address and the version constraint.

The provider configuration will be discussed in detail in the upcoming sections of this chapter. A sample provider configuration for AWS is given here for reference:

```
terraform {
  required_providers {
    aws = {
      version = ">= 5.17.0"
      source = "hashicorp/aws"
    }
  }
}
```

Experimental Features

The Terraform team has also introduced experimental features that the community can try and share feedback on before it becomes a backward compatibility constraint.

The experimental features can be opted for using `experiments` with a list of features to try out. Experimental features usage is generally not recommended for scripts intended for production use. Check out the following `terraform` block:

```
terraform {
. . .
experiments = [feature1, feature2]
}
```

In this example, `feature1` and `feature2` have been enabled in this configuration.

Provider Metadata

The provider metadata block, `provider_meta`, aids a provider in offering an interface to pass information unrelated to the resources in the module. This topic is particularly technical and is more related to the provider setup.

You can focus on the configuration of other nested blocks covered so far since they are commonly used in different scenarios and are useful for creating production-grade scripts for infrastructure provisioning.

You can now move on to understand more about providers and their importance in the Terraform ecosystem.

Terraform Providers

As you saw earlier in this chapter, Terraform depends on plugins called providers to interact with cloud providers, SaaS providers, or any other APIs. Before you use them, you need to download and install them in the local working directory so that Terraform can use them. The required providers are declared in the `terraform {}` block. It is always suggested to declare them explicitly.

If you have previously worked with languages such as Java or Python, you can assume that providers are equivalent to the Java packages or Python libraries used with the `import` statements.

Terraform will look for the declared providers in the configuration scripts and try to download them when the `terraform init` command is executed for the first time. Without the providers, Terraform cannot manage any kind of infrastructure.

Basically, if you pick any Terraform provider, the provider will have a set of **resources** and/or **data sources**. In most cases, the resources will be the real-world infrastructure components you are interested in creating and the data sources will be used to fetch/retrieve the information about the real-world resources.

Terraform providers are listed on the Terraform Registry page, `https://registry.terraform. io/browse/providers`, for the infrastructure platform you use. Some of the most common ones are as follows:

- AWS
- Azure
- Google Cloud Platform
- Kubernetes
- HTTP

Types of Terraform Providers

Some of the providers listed in the Terraform Registry are developed and published by HashiCorp and some are created and maintained by partners. There are also providers maintained by users and volunteers. Special badges are available to identify the provider type and know who maintains it:

Official Providers

These are the providers created and maintained by HashiCorp and are available under the HashiCorp namespace. At the time of writing this book, there are 35 official providers available for use.

For the AWS Terraform provider, you can see the **Official** badge in *Figure 3.7*.

Figure 3.7 – Official provider: aws

Partner Providers

These are providers written, validated, and published by third-party companies for their own APIs. Companies must first register and become a HashiCorp partner before they can publish any providers.

For the **Oracle Cloud Infrastructure** (**OCI**) Terraform provider, you can see the **Partner** badge on their dedicated registry page.

Figure 3.8 – Partner provider: oci

Community Providers

Community providers are created and maintained by individual maintainers, a group of maintainers, or other members of the Terraform community.

Community providers do not carry any special badge; it is simply blank.

Figure 3.9 – Community provider: ansible

Archived Providers

- These are official or partner providers that are no longer maintained by HashiCorp or the Terraform community. This can happen if the underlying APIs are deprecated or user interest declines.

Provider Requirements

In the previous section, you would have noticed that the providers are declared inside the `required_providers` nested block in the `terraform {}` block.

A provider requirement consists of the following:

- `local name`
- `source location`
- `version constraint`

Here is the template for declaring a Terraform provider:

```
terraform {
  required_providers {
    local name = {
      source   = «source location»
      version = «version constraint»
    }
  }
}
```

Local Names

Local names are assigned when the required provider is declared. It has details on the source location and the version constraint. The local names are module specific and should be unique to a module.

Outside the `required_providers` block, providers are referred to by the local names only.

Users have the option to select a local name to use; there are no restrictions. But almost every Terraform provider has a preferred local name. For example, the AWS Terraform provider (`hashicorp/aws`) has the prefix `aws` for every resource it contains. In this case, you can use `aws` as the local name; this is recommended.

Source Addresses

The source address of the Terraform provider specifies the primary location where Terraform can download it.

The source address consists of three parts:

- `hostname`: The hostname of the Terraform Registry that hosts the provider. This is an optional parameter. If this part is omitted, it will be defaulted to the hostname of the public Terraform Registry (**registry.terraform.io**)

- `namespace`: The namespace is the organizational namespace in the Terraform Registry. In the case of a public Terraform Registry, this could be the organization that published the provider.

- `type`: The type is the platform or the system that the provider manages and should be unique within the namespace. This could also be the preferred local name for the provider in some cases.

If source addresses are omitted or not specified, Terraform will try to form the implicit source address with the hostname as `registry.terraform.io` and the namespace as `hashicorp` with the local name assumed as the type. The final source address that will be formed implicitly, then, is `registry.terraform.io/hashicorp/<LOCAL NAME>`.

Version Constraints

Each Terraform provider has its own version and release cycle. When declaring a provider, the version should be specified in the `version` argument so Terraform can select a single version and install it.

The `version` argument is optional, but it is always recommended to use the right version to avoid issues.

To ensure Terraform always installs the same provider version it was tested with, and to avoid being impacted by provider version upgrades, you can use the **dependency lock file** with the Terraform CLI. The file can also be committed in your version control tool.

You will learn more about the dependency lock file in an upcoming section.

Provider Configuration

Now that you have a good idea about declaring provider requirements in the `terraform` block, you can proceed with the provider configuration, which will vary based on the provider you want to configure.

For example, the AWS Terraform provider might expect the user to set the right access keys and region to create the AWS resources. On the other hand, other providers, such as Kubernetes, need details such as the API server endpoint details and the certificate to access it.

Generally, the provider configuration should be declared in the root module of the Terraform configuration and the sub-modules should get the details from the root module. If the sub-modules expect different configurations, they can override the default provider configuration with their own.

You can now take a look at the sample provider configuration:

```
provider "aws" {
  region      = "us-east-1"
  access_key = "my-access-key"
  secret_key = "my-secret-key"
}
```

There are a few things to note here:

- The value "aws" next to the provider keyword is the **local name** provided for the AWS Terraform provider in the terraform {} block.

- Inside the provider block, there are specific parameters, such as region, access_key, and secret_key, with values specific to this provider. It will vary for every provider based on their configuration setup before using it.

- For a few providers, the configuration parameters can also be set using the equivalent environment variables and Terraform will pick the configuration values automatically. In this example, the same access_key value can be set using the AWS_ACCESS_KEY_ID environment variable and the region can be set with the AWS_REGION or AWS_DEFAULT_REGION environment variable.

- Expressions can be used inside the provider configuration block, unlike the terraform {} block, and the parameters required by the provider are expected to be documented on the Terraform Registry page of the provider.

- There are providers such as hashicorp/random that do not need any explicit provider configuration. In this case, Terraform will assume a dummy configuration and no action would be required from the user. You can directly work with the creation of resources without any provider {} block.

Provider Meta-Arguments

Terraform will define two meta-arguments called alias and version that will be supported for all providers. The version meta-argument is not recommended as the version constraint parameter in the required_providers {} block will handle the different versions.

The alias Meta-Argument

To understand a real use case of the alias meta-argument, consider this scenario.

A cloud architect wants to design an architecture where the application microservices are deployed in EC2 instances running in one AWS region and the underlying databases are expected to run in a different region. This entire setup of the infrastructure will be provisioned via Terraform.

Here, if you look closely, the cloud architect needs to create AWS resources in two different regions. That also means there are two different sets of provider configurations needed. This is where `alias` comes into the picture. It allows the user to have two provider configurations for the same provider declared only once inside the `terraform {}` block.

Here is an example:

```
# Default provider configuration - 1
provider "aws" {
  region = "us-east-1"
}
# Additional provider configuration - 2
# This can be referenced "aws.west".
provider "aws" {
  alias  = "west"
  region = "eu-west-1"
}
```

The version Meta-Argument

This meta-argument is deprecated and so there currently isn't much that needs to be said about it. One important thing to note, however, is that the `version` meta-argument should be considered if the `required_providers` block does not contain the `version` parameter.

This will be removed in future Terraform versions, so it is better not to use it at all.

Dependency lock file (.terraform.lock.hcl)

When Terraform configuration scripts are created to provision resources, there are two types of dependencies that need to be tracked: providers and modules. They have their own life cycles, as discussed already. Hence, it is necessary to track the right versions for providers and modules to ensure that you always work with the compatible versions for the current configuration, so that it does not get impacted by future version upgrades from the provider.

With the current features, Terraform can only track and work with different versions of providers but not modules. For modules, it always downloads and uses the latest version available.

Terraform can remember the versions for each dependency with the dependency lock file (`.terraform.lock.hcl`). So, it can use the same version every time with the help of this file.

Modules will be discussed in the following chapters in more detail, but you can consider them to be remote scripts that can be used for specific tasks, rather than having to write the code on your own. For example, there is a specific Terraform module for Amazon **Elastic Kubernetes Service** (**EKS**) cluster setup that internally creates a variety of resources. In this case, it makes sense to use the module provided by AWS to create the resources relevant for getting your EKS cluster setup up and running.

The dependency lock file is updated every time you run the `terraform init` command and it is stored in the current working directory along with other files.

The following points will help you understand Terraform's behavior with the dependency lock file:

- When the provider versions are modified/updated in the configuration scripts, Terraform will always check the matching versions and update the lock file accordingly.

- If you want to upgrade the version of any provider after the initial `terraform init` command execution that locked the versions, you can use the `-upgrade` option with `terraform init` to override the locked versions.

- If any of the providers are no longer needed, the dependency will be automatically removed in the subsequent command executions when the configuration scripts do not contain any references.

Resources and Data Sources

Resources are the most fundamental building blocks of Terraform as they describe one or more infrastructure objects, such as virtual machines, storage buckets, and user entities or databases.

Terraform uses data sources to gather information about resources defined by Terraform or outside Terraform or any objects modified by functions. Say you want to create an S3 bucket and provide access to an AWS IAM user already available in the system. The data sources can then be used to get information about the user with some inputs, and the details can then be used to set up bucket access.

Resources Syntax

You can now check out this example `resource` block:

```
resource "aws_ebs_volume" "example_ebs_volume" {
  availability_zone = "us-east-1a"
  size              = 20
  tags = {
    Name = "HelloWorld"
  }
}
```

This `resource` block declares the resource of type `aws_ebs_volume` with the local name set as `example_ebs_volume`. Inside the block, you have configuration parameters specific to the resource type. In this case, it is an EBS volume (AWS service for block storage). In AWS, when an EBS volume needs to be created, the minimum configuration parameters expected are the Availability Zone and the storage size, which are specified here.

Tags are common for most resources that can be defined in AWS.

The local name `example_ebs_volume` can be used to refer to this resource anywhere inside the module but not outside. Like the parameters coded here, there are also other configuration values or parameters set for this resource, and those can be referred to with the syntax `<RESOURCE_ TYPE>.<RESOURCE_NAME>.<ATTRIBUTE_NAME>`.

More information about configuration parameters available for specific resource types and example usage and validations can be found in the provider documentation on the Terraform Registry page.

Resources Meta-Arguments

Like providers, resources also support the use of meta-arguments and can be used with all possible resource types.

The following are the meta-arguments supported at the resources level:

- `depends_on`
- `count`
- `for_each`
- `provider`
- `lifecycle`
- `provisioner` (not discussed in this chapter)

depends_on

The `depends_on` meta-argument is helpful for handling module dependencies or hidden resource dependencies that Terraform cannot automatically infer. To understand this better, say you are creating an AWS IAM user and attach permissions with an IAM policy. In this case, the configuration scripts will be written so that the IAM user is created first and then the IAM policy. The IAM user created in the first place will be referred to while creating the IAM policy to attach.

In this case, Terraform will ensure that the IAM policy is not created until the IAM user resource is successfully created. However, there will be special scenarios, such as when the resource dependencies are not explicit but there is a logical sequence of how it needs to be used, where there are no direct dependencies. Note that certain resources cannot be created if the prerequisites are not set up.

As per the Terraform documentation, the `depends_on` meta-argument has to be used as a last resort when there is no other option to handle hidden resources or module dependencies. Instead of `depends_on`, the expression references can also be considered.

Wherever possible, it is always a good practice to include the comment along with the `depends_on` meta-argument explaining why it is being used.

The following example illustrates the use of `depends_on`:

```
module "eks_cluster" {
    source                  = "./modules/eks_cluster"
    region                  = var.region
    azs                     = module.vpc.azs
    environment             = var.environment
}


module "vault" {
    source                  = «./modules/vault»
    environment             = var.environment
    region                  = var.region
    service_secret_path     = var.service_secret_path
# The eks-cluster module creates certain keys that needs to be # added
to vault and only when creation is successful.
    depends_on              = [module.eks_cluster]
}
```

count

The `count` meta-argument is used when you want to create more than one identical resource with the same resource definition. The default behavior of Terraform is to create one real-world infrastructure object. It can be overridden with this option.

The `count` meta-argument can be used with modules as well as for any resource type, and the specific instance can be referred to using the relevant index:

```
resource "aws_instance" "server" {
  count = 3 # create four similar EC2 instances

  ami             = «ami-exdswe123»
  instance_type   = «t2.micro»
  tags = {
    instance_count = ${count.index}
  }
}
```

This example creates three identical EC2 instances with the `t2.micro` instance type with the same resource definition.

for_each

The `for_each` meta-argument can be used to create multiple resources with the same definition, but the input values will be mapped using the map or set of strings. Please note that `count` and `for_each` cannot be used at the same time within the resource block.

When the resource block contains `for_each`, the values can be referenced using the `each` object, such as `each.key` and `each.value`. If `for_each` input is set, both `each.key` and `each.value` will be the same.

Take a look at an example with `for_each`:

```
resource "aws_iam_user" "account-user" {
    for_each = toset( ["Adam", "Bob", "Chris", "Dennis"] )
    name     = each.key
}
```

In this example, the AWS IAM user is created for each value in the set.

provider

The `provider` meta-argument is used to refer to the provider configuration to use for the resource. As discussed in the *Provider configuration* section, multiple provider configurations are possible when the scripts need to work with different regions or access key combinations.

If the `provider` meta-argument is omitted, the default provider configuration with the preferred local name will be picked:

```
provider "aws" {
    region = "us-west-1"
}

provider "aws" {
    alias = west
    region = "us-west-1"
}
resource "aws_instance" "server" {
    provider = aws.west
    ami             = "ami-exdswe123"
    instance_type = "t2.micro"
}
```

lifecycle

The `lifecycle` meta-argument is used to customize the default life cycle behavior of how the resources are managed by Terraform. This can also be used with modules or any resource type.

The following options are supported for `lifecycle`:

- `create_before_destroy`

  If the Terraform resource cannot be updated in place, Terraform will try to recreate the resource after destroying it. This option will force Terraform to create the replacement resource first and then destroy the previous instance.

- `prevent_destroy`

  This will prevent the accidental deletion of critical objects and cause Terraform to reject any plan that will result in the destruction of the resource.

- `ignore_changes`

  This will ignore future changes to the resource configuration. This is helpful for working with resources that are expected to change in the future but should not result in recreating/updating resources.

- `replace_triggered_by`

  This triggers resource recreation every time the attributes of the different resources are changed:

```
resource "aws_instance" "server" {
  ami           = "ami-exdswe123"
  instance_type = «t2.micro»
  lifecycle {
    create_before_destroy = true
  }
}
```

Data Sources

Data sources are essentially read-only subsets of resources. Each provider will come with a set of data sources along with the resources that are supported. Data sources with the filter criteria are used to fetch the information about the specific resources that are defined already.

Sometimes it might be necessary to fetch the information about **Amazon Machine Image** (**AMI**) IDs before you use them to create the EC2 instance, and data sources can be helpful in this scenario.

Here is an example data source block:

```
data "aws_ami" "my-amis" {
  most_recent = true
  owners = ["self"]
  filter {
    name    = "name"
    values = ["myami-*"]
  }
}
```

Here, you can see that the data block has the `data` keyword and it tried to query the `aws_ami` resource type and export the result into the local name `my-amis`. The local name must be unique within the given module and can be referenced with the following syntax: `DATA.<RESOURCE_TYPE>.<LOCAL_NAME>`.

The query parameters inside the `data {}` block are the query constraints that are specific to the resource type. More information can be found on the Terraform Registry page. The main difference between the resources and the data sources is that the `resources` block can create/update/delete the infrastructure resources, whereas the data sources can only read the information about the provisioned resources.

The meta-arguments supported by Terraform for the managed resources are also applicable to data sources, but there will be slight differences in the behavior, as follows:

- While using `depends_on` with the data sources, the behavior is exactly the same as with the providers and the data sources will wait until all the dependencies are resolved.

- The `count` and `for_each` meta-arguments also behave the same way, and individual resource instances can be referred to in the same way as resources.

- The `provider` meta-argument can also be used with data sources to work with multiple provider configurations.

- The only exception is `lifecycle`, which is not supported for data sources, and there might be changes with the future versions of Terraform.

Variables and Outputs

You started the chapter with a quick hands-on exercise using the Terraform language and continued with the Terraform settings for configuration scripts. You then covered providers followed by resources and data sources.

You can now proceed with variables and outputs, which help users customize module behavior without changing the source. The Terraform language supports the blocks listed here:

- Input variables
- Output values
- Local values

Input Variables

After providers and resources, input variables serve a unique purpose in the Terraform language when used with modules. With the use of input variables, Terraform modules can be shared across multiple configurations, and users can use different values to customize module behavior.

The input variables declared in the root module of the configuration can be set using the Terraform CLI as well as the environment variables. If they are declared in the child module, the input variables can be set inside the `module {}` block.

Declaring Input Variables

Input variables are declared using the `variable {}` block. You will learn about this further with an example `variable {}` block:

```
variable "availability_zone_names" {
  type    = list(string)
  default = ["us-east-1a"]
  description = «Availability zone names»
  sensitive = false
  nullable  = false
}
```

The `variable` block here has the `variable` keyword followed by the variable name. This name should be unique in the module and used to refer to the variable's value inside the module. As per the Terraform documentation, the variable identifiers can be anything except `source`, `version`, `providers`, `count`, `for_each`, `lifecycle`, `depends_on`, and `locals` because these are reserved for module configuration blocks.

The input variables declared can be referenced with the syntax `var.<NAME>` where NAME is the input variable name.

Supported Arguments

The following are the supported arguments for variable declaration:

- `default`: Variable declarations can include the `default` argument, and if they are present, that makes the input variable optional. If the value is not set, the default value will be used. The value passed should be a literal value and cannot refer to other objects in the configuration.

- `type`: This argument will help restrict the type of value that can be set for an input variable. When the variable declaration does not specify it, the variable can accept any type of value. But it is always recommended to specify the type that will help Terraform throw an error message if an incorrect value is set.

  The following are the supported keywords:

  - `string`

  - `bool`

  - `number`

  - `list(<TYPE>)`

  - `map(<TYPE>)`

  - `set(<TYPE>)`

  - `object`

  - `tuple`

- `description`: The `description` argument is used to provide a concise description of the input variable.

- `validation`: You can specify the custom validation rules for the variable with this argument and throw a custom error message if the validation fails.

- `sensitive`: If the variable declaration is marked as `sensitive`, the variable will not be printed in the console output. Please remember that the variable value will still be recorded in the Terraform state file. You will learn about handling sensitive values in a state file further in future chapters when covering state management.

- `nullable`: The variable cannot be set to `null` when the variable declaration indicates that it is not nullable (`nullable = false`).

Input Variables Assignment

Input variables can be assigned in a number of ways:

- With the -var command-line option
- Using the .tfvars files
- With environment variables
- With variables set in the HCP Terraform workspace (covered later)

If you are using the -var command-line option, individual variables can be set while executing the terraform plan and terraform apply commands.

A few examples are given here to understand the usage:

```
$ terraform apply -var="user_name=Bob"
$ terraform apply -var='az_list=["us-east-1a","us-east-1b"]'
```

Another option is to use the variable definition files with the .tfvars extension to set lots of variables. In this option, you can use the -var-file command-line option. If comfortable with the JSON format, you can use JSON as well and change the extension to .tfvars.json.

The .tfvars file will just contain the variable assignments. Here is an example:

```
user_name = "Bob"
az_names_list = ["us-east-1a", "us-east-1b"]
```

The last option is to use the environment variables to set the input variables and, in this case, Terraform will search the system environment variables to load the values before applying.

Here, the environment variable being set should follow a specific naming convention, which is the TF_VAR_<variable_name> prefix. For example, if the variable name is username, the environment variable that should be set is TF_VAR_username.

Input Variables Precedence

Terraform loads variables in the following order:

- Environment variables
- The terraform.tfvars file, if present
- The terraform.tfvars.json file, if present
- Any *.auto.tfvars or *.auto.tfvars.json file
- Any -var and -var-file options on the command line

  (this includes variables set by a HCP Terraform workspace)

Output Values

Output values are mainly used to expose information about the infrastructure to other Terraform configurations to use. This is similar to the return values in the case of programming languages.

Output values are declared using the `output {}` block mainly with the `value` argument. Here is an example output block:

```
output "iam_user_arn" {
  value = aws_iam_user.testuser.arn
}
```

In this block, the output name is `iam_user_arn`, which is used to output the `arn` attribute of the `aws_iam_user` resource type and the `testuser` resource name.

Like this, the output names of the child module can be accessed with the syntax `module.<child_module>.<output_name>`.

The output values support the following arguments. The usage is exactly the same as was explained in the *Provider configuration* and the *Input variables* section:

- `depends_on`
- `description`
- `sensitive`

Local Values

Local values are helpful when you want to use the same expression multiple times in the Terraform configuration and you can assign a name to the expression to be used. This is very similar to the local variables you use with the programming languages.

The local values are declared using the `locals {}` block, and local values are referenced with the syntax `local.<NAME>`.

An example local block is as follows:

```
locals {
  environment = "dev"
  team = "accounting"
}
```

Core Workflow

The core Terraform workflow has three steps. The general idea is that the core Terraform workflow process repeats every time there are changes to the configuration scripts. The three steps are as follows:

- Write

- Plan

- Apply

Write – Creating the Configuration Script

The first step is to create the configuration scripts in Terraform to provision infrastructure components. Once the initial scripts are created, the scripts can be added to a version-controlled repository to save the changes.

The scripts can be validated using the `terraform fmt` and `terraform validate` commands to ensure that the code is rightly formatted and that any syntax errors can be corrected.

If the team is working on the same configuration scripts rather than individuals, it is also recommended that different branches are created so that the work is not affected by other parallel changes. Automating the application of configuration can also be considered, since the scripts will be tested with the same workflow and the deployments streamlined.

Plan – Previewing the Changes

Once the scripts are validated and ready to be deployed, the final plan can be reviewed with the `terraform plan` command. This gives a clear picture of the resources that will be provisioned in the apply step.

This is the step to check whether the changes that are going to be applied match the requirements and if any further changes need to be considered.

Apply – Provisioning the Infrastructure

The final step is the actual application of the configuration scripts that will provision the resources in the cloud. As indicated earlier in the chapter, the apply step will also update the state file to record the changes being applied.

Summary

In this chapter, you have learned about the basics of the Terraform language and the CLI-based workflow and when to apply them. The different block types, configuration settings, and parameters such as input variables and outputs were discussed. You also saw the steps involved in the Terraform core workflow.

The next chapter will cover Terraform commands in detail, along with the options and the scenarios where they can be used.

Exam Readiness Drill – Chapter Review Questions

Apart from a solid understanding of key concepts, being able to think quickly under time pressure is a skill that will help you ace your certification exam. That is why working on these skills early on in your learning journey is key.

Chapter review questions are designed to improve your test-taking skills progressively with each chapter you learn and review your understanding of key concepts in the chapter at the same time. You'll find these at the end of each chapter.

> **How to Access these Resources**
>
> To learn how to access these resources, head over to the chapter titled *Chapter 11, Accessing the Online Practice Resources.*

To open the Chapter Review Questions for this chapter, perform the following steps:

1. Click the link – `https://packt.link/HCorp003Ch3`.

   Alternatively, you can scan the following **QR code** (*Figure 3.10*):

Figure 3.10 – QR code that opens Chapter Review Questions for logged-in users

2. Once you log in, you'll see a page similar to the one shown in *Figure 3.11*:

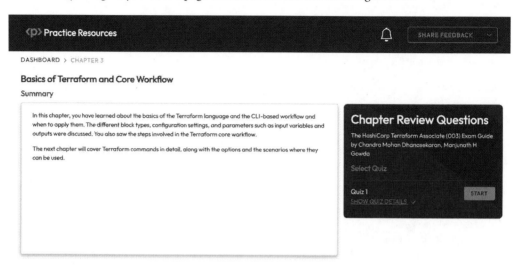

Figure 3.11 – Chapter Review Questions for Chapter 3

3. Once ready, start the following practice drills, re-attempting the quiz multiple times.

Exam Readiness Drill

For the first three attempts, don't worry about the time limit.

ATTEMPT 1

The first time, aim for at least **40%**. Look at the answers you got wrong and read the relevant sections in the chapter again to fix your learning gaps.

ATTEMPT 2

The second time, aim for at least **60%**. Look at the answers you got wrong and read the relevant sections in the chapter again to fix any remaining learning gaps.

ATTEMPT 3

The third time, aim for at least **75%**. Once you score 75% or more, you start working on your timing.

> Tip
>
> You may take more than **three** attempts to reach 75%. That's okay. Just review the relevant sections in the chapter till you get there.

Working On Timing

Target: Your aim is to keep the score the same while trying to answer these questions as quickly as possible. Here's an example of how your next attempts should look like:

Attempt	Score	Time Taken
Attempt 5	77%	21 mins 30 seconds
Attempt 6	78%	18 mins 34 seconds
Attempt 7	76%	14 mins 44 seconds

Table 3.1 – Sample timing practice drills on the online platform

> Note
>
> The time limits shown in the above table are just examples. Set your own time limits with each attempt based on the time limit of the quiz on the website.

With each new attempt, your score should stay above **75%** while your "time taken" to complete should "decrease". Repeat as many attempts as you want till you feel confident dealing with the time pressure.

4

Terraform Commands and State Management

In the previous chapters, you learned about the building blocks of the Terraform configuration language and the out-of-the-box capabilities it provides, such as multi-cloud support, extensive support for different providers, and state management. This chapter is all about the various commands you will use while working with Terraform CLI.

Each command has its own significance and purpose, and you may not use everything in regular scenarios. But there are a few commands (such as `terraform init`, `terraform apply`, and `terraform destroy`) that will be a part of almost every infrastructure workflow and are used as and when the need arises.

The following exam objectives will be covered in this chapter:

- Use the core Terraform workflow
- Implement and maintain state

You will start by looking at the aforementioned primary commands and then you will cover the various subcommands. This will then be followed by concepts around Terraform state management.

This chapter will cover the following topics:

- Basic workflow commands
- Commands for code management
- Special commands
- State management and the `terraform state` command and subcommands

Technical Requirements

In this chapter, you will deep dive into Terraform commands and try them out on Terraform CLI, installed on your workstation. Please ensure that you have the following installed and ready to use:

- An AWS account ID with administrator access credentials

- AWS CLI version 2.x.x

- Terraform CLI version 1.5.x or later

- Visual Studio Code or any text editor

The GitHub URL for the chapter will contain graphics and the sample scripts used in the chapter and can be referred to at the following link:

```
https://github.com/PacktPublishing/Hashicorp-Certified-Terraform-
Associate-003-Exam-guide-Second-Edition/tree/main/ch4/terraform-
commands-and-state-management
```

Basic Workflow Commands

In the previous chapter on Terraform basics, you used the following commands in the sample exercise to create an IAM user. You saw how it helps in different phases of project development. You will now take a closer look at the basic commands. The different options available to use are listed here and will be covered in detail in the subsequent sections:

- `init`

- `plan`

- `apply`

- `destroy`

Please note that all the preceding commands will be preceded by the keyword `terraform` when you actually use them in Terraform CLI. For every command, you will be look at the command syntax and options, followed by more details on the command usage in different scenarios.

As a general rule, the command syntax will be as follows:

```
$ terraform <command_name> <command_options>
```

The init Command

As you have seen in the previous chapter on Terraform basics, the `terraform init` command is the first command that should be run to initialize the working directory where the configuration scripts are stored. The `init` command will download all the required providers and modules needed to run the script.

Based on the configuration scripts, the `init` command will perform different activities in the background, but it is safe to say that you do not need to know the details. Suppose the provider or the module version is changed in the script; the `init` command needs to be rerun to allow the changes to take effect before the resource creation.

This is how the command is used:

```
$ terraform init <init_options>
```

Now take a look at some common options supported by the `init` command:

- `-input=true`: If you are setting this option, it will ask for an input to execute the `init` command if necessary. If this is set to `false`, the command will fail directly without the user prompt. The default value is `true`.

    This option is like using Amazon S3 as the backend to store the `terraform state` file and the partial configuration (not all inputs are provided for successful backend configuration) is used in the script.

    A backend for S3 would require a bucket name, region, and key name to store the file. If any of the inputs are missing, the default behavior is that it will be prompted when you run the `terraform init` command.

    If this option is set to `false`, the command will error out immediately.

- `-lock=false`: This option will disable the locking of state files; locking is enabled by default.

- `-lock-timeout=<duration>`: This option will override the duration of the state lock with the user-provided value; the default is zero seconds. It might help in scenarios where there are parallel processes running pointing to the same state file and it makes sense to wait for the lock to get released for the next process to use it.

- `-no-color`: This option will disable color codes in the output.

- `-upgrade`: This option will upgrade modules and providers to the latest version if applicable. If this option is used, the recorded versions in the dependency lock file will be ignored and the relevant modules and provider plugins will be upgraded to match the version constraints currently in the configuration.

- `-from-module=<module_location>`: This option will be used in special scenarios where your configuration scripts refer to a module that is not present in the local/current working directory.

  In this case, the module source location should be provided when running the `init` command, and this option helps achieve providing the module source location. Take a look at a scenario.

  You have created a new Terraform configuration and it has a module block that refers to the code available in GitHub and not available on your local machine. When you run the `init` command with the `-from-module` option, in this case, the given module will be copied to the local working directory before the initialization steps are performed.

- `-reconfigure`: If the Terraform script is configured with the `backend` block, the `init` command execution will configure the backend settings accordingly. However, there might be cases where the current backend configuration is not relevant, and changes have been made to use a different backend. This is when this option needs to be specified along with the `terraform init` command, once again, to reflect the latest changes to use the new backend.

- `-migrate-state`: This option is used to migrate the state file to the new backend, and, based on the setup, there will be additional prompts for the user to enter values to complete the state migration.

- `-force-copy`: The use case for this option is exactly the same as the `-migrate-state` option but the difference is that there will not be prompts and `yes` will be automatically assumed for state migration.

- `-backend=false`: This option is used to skip the backend configuration with the current execution of the `init` command.

- `-plugin-dir=<plugin_location>`: This option is used to provide the alternate path to search for plugins, and is primarily used in the development stages when you create new modules or develop a new provider plugin.

- `-get=false`: This option will disable downloading the modules referenced.

- `-lockfile=MODE`: This is used to set the dependency lock file mode; the only value supported now is `readonly`.

- `-lock=false`: This option will not hold the state file during the backend migration, and should be used very cautiously, especially when there will be other developers who can run the same configuration referring to the same workspace. State locking is enabled by default.

The plan Command

You now have a better idea about using the `terraform init` command that primarily deals with the initialization of the working directory. You can continue with the commands that form the core part of the Terraform provisioning workflow. The `terraform plan` command is the first one before the `apply` and `destroy` commands.

The main purpose of the `plan` command is to evaluate the configuration scripts and determine the desired state of the resources declared. Then, it will compare the desired state with the state of the real infrastructure objects using the state file and figure out the changes to achieve the desired state.

Once the changes needed are figured out, the `plan` command presents the execution plan. Please note that the `plan` command does not make any changes to real-world infrastructure objects. The responsibility of making actual changes is given to the `terraform apply` command, which usually follows next.

The plan output from the command can also be saved with the `-out` option, which can be directly given as input to the `apply` command to proceed with making the changes.

In some cases, it is also possible that the real-world infrastructure objects are in sync with the desired state of the declared resources, which means no change is needed. If you run the `terraform plan` command in this case, the command output will clearly indicate that no infrastructure change is needed.

This is how the command is used:

```
$ terraform plan <plan_options>
```

Now you can take a look at some of the options supported by the `plan` command:

- `-destroy`: This option with the `plan` command is to clean up all the resources provisioned so far, and this will result in an empty state file. The `plan` command with the `-destroy` option will exhibit the same behavior as running the `terraform destroy` command, which will be discussed in the subsequent sections.

- `-refresh-only`: This option has two purposes: updating the Terraform state file and output values from the root module to sync with the changes made outside Terraform.

  Now, when might this be useful? Assume that you have created a resource in AWS such as an IAM user or RDS database instance, initially using Terraform, and the `terraform.tfstate` state file has been updated. You also went ahead and made changes directly on the AWS Management Console.

  It is important to sync the state file with the changes made from the console, and that is when the `-refresh-only` option can be used.

- `-refresh=false`: This option will disable the refresh of the Terraform state file before applying the configuration changes. In the default scenario, the `plan` command will also check the remote objects and refresh the Terraform state to figure out the changes needed to achieve the desired state. This indirectly means Terraform will issue API calls to the respective providers and get the details, which can consume more time.

  With this option, the refresh part is disabled, and hence, the plan will run faster; this can be considered only in special scenarios because the state file can go out of sync.

  This option cannot be used along with the `-refresh-only` option since the refresh behavior will not happen at all.

- `-target=<RESOURCE_ADDRESS>`: This option is used to target particular resources or a set of resources for planning rather than for the entire configuration. This will be helpful to provision the resources that you would like to test first before completing the entire development.

- `-replace=<RESOURCE_ADDRESS>`: This option is used to replace the resources that match the given address; this is similar to the target option to focus on a particular resource or a set of resources that have been manipulated and need replacement. The earlier version of Terraform had a separate command, `terraform taint`, for this purpose, but it is deprecated now.

- `-var "VARIABLE_NAME=VALUE"`: Use this option to set a value for the variable declared in the main configuration. If there are multiple variables, the option can be used for each variable name.

  Here is a sample command:

  ```
  $ terraform plan -var "region=us-east-1"
  ```

- `-var-file=<FILENAME>`: This option is used to set the values of multiple input variables usually using the `*.tfvars` file. The option can also be used multiple times to pick the values from more than one file.

- `-detailed-exitcode`: This option changes the exit codes and meanings to provide more information on the output plan. The possible values are zero (0), one (1), and two (2) according to the execution result:

  `exitcode 0`: Success with no changes in the plan

  `exitcode 1`: Error condition

  `exitcode 2`: Success with changes in the plan

- `-generate-config-out=<PATH>`: If there are `import` blocks available in the configuration, this option will help generate Terraform resource blocks in the HCL language in the path specified. The concept of using `import` blocks is an advanced topic and will be covered in later chapters when applicable.

- `-input=false`: This option exactly works the same as we have seen with the `init` command, and it disables the default prompt for any input variable with the value missing.

- `-lock=false`: This disables the state file lock operation, which is not generally recommended if there is a possibility of multiple concurrent runs.

- `-json`: This can be set to enable the JSON formatted output and is very helpful when the Terraform execution happens in an automated fashion and the JSON format is machine readable.

- `-lock-timeout=<duration>`: This option will override the duration of the state lock with the user-provided value; the default is zero seconds. It might help in scenarios where there are parallel processes running pointing to the same state file and it makes sense to wait for the lock to get released for the next process to use it.

- `-no-color`: This option is used to disable color codes in the output.

- `-parallelism=<COUNT>`: This option can be used to override the maximum number of parallel operations on the machine running Terraform. This can be used when you want to intentionally decrease/increase the load on the host machine to have better control. The default value is ten (10).

- `-out=<FILENAME>`: As already mentioned earlier, the `terraform plan` command can also include the `-out` option to save the plan output, which can be used directly with `terraform apply`.

  One important thing to note here is that Terraform can accept any filename, but the file should not have any suffix or file extension. If a suffix is present, Terraform will consider it as a different file format and the `.tf` suffix will also result in Terraform treating it as a regular configuration file.

  Here is a sample command:

```
$ terraform plan -out=tfplan -input=false
```

Some of these options are also supported by the `terraform apply` command, and you will read about this in the next section.

The apply Command

In the core workflow, the next command is the `apply` command and its responsibility is to make the changes proposed in the Terraform execution plan. The `terraform apply` command has two ways of operating: auto plan mode and saved plan mode.

In the auto plan mode, you cannot expect the `terraform plan` file to be saved already, and when the `apply` command is executed, it automatically creates an execution plan for you. This will be followed by a user prompt to confirm the plan and take the necessary actions. In automation cases, the prompt can be disabled with the `-auto-approve` option.

In the case of the saved plan mode, `terraform plan` was executed previously, and you have the plan already. In this mode, the `apply` operation will run and it does not need any user inputs. In this mode, additional plan options cannot be specified.

This is how the command is used:

```
$ terraform apply <apply_options>
```

The following options are also supported in the `terraform apply` command. Since you have already read about this in the previous topic, the options are just listed here:

- `-destroy`
- `-refresh-only`
- `-refresh=false`
- `-replace=<RESOURCE_ADDRESS>`
- `-target=<RESOURCE_ADDRESS>`
- `-var "VARIABLE_NAME=VALUE"`
- `-var-file=<FILENAME>`
- `-input=false`
- `-lock=false`
- `-lock-timeout=<DURATION>`
- `-parallelism=n`
- `-no-color`

Please remember that all the preceding options are applicable when the `apply` command is executed without a saved plan file.

Other options supported for `apply` are as follows, and the last three options are applicable when using the local backend:

- `-auto-approve`: Setting this option will allow the process to proceed without the user prompt to provision the resources and update the state file.
- `-compact-warnings`: This option will compact the warning messages.
- `-state=<PATH>`: This option is used to read and save the state file path; if not set, this will default to the `terraform.tfstate` file in the current working directory.

- `-state-out=<PATH>`: This option is used to save the state file in a different location, so the old state is not impacted by the latest execution.

- `-backup=<PATH>`: This is used to back up the state file in the specified path before modifying the state file.

The destroy Command

The `destroy` command is used to destroy all the real-world infrastructure objects managed by a particular configuration. As we have seen in this chapter, the `destroy` command will have the same behavior as the `terraform apply` command with the `-destroy` option. So, most of the options supported by the `apply` command can also be used with `terraform destroy`.

This is how the command is used:

```
$ terraform destroy <destroy_options>
```

Before the actual execution of `destroy`, you can also review the plan by running the following command:

```
$ terraform plan -destroy
```

This is helpful in scenarios where the applied configuration will not be used further, and the resources provisioned can be cleaned up.

Commands for Code Management

In this section, you will quickly look at a couple of commands – `terraform fmt` and `terraform validate` – used in the development stages. There will be no harm to the configuration if these are not used. The intention, however, is to check that it is the right code and is formatted properly, and to check whether there are syntactical errors.

The fmt Command

The `terraform fmt` command is used to rewrite/update the Terraform configuration scripts to a canonical format and style. This is based on the style conventions opinionated of HashiCorp itself to ensure consistency across all the files.

For example, you can generate a Terraform configuration using the `-generate-config-out` option with the `plan` command and the resulting configuration will follow the Terraform styling conventions. You also might write scripts manually for other resources, but using the `terraform fmt` command will ensure that the code is formatted consistently.

At the end of the day, it is up to the developer to choose the styling conventions, and there is no problem with the approach. It is not enforced by any means. There will be no change in the result, irrespective of the formatting approach you use.

This is how the command is used:

```
$ terraform fmt <fmt_options> <TARGET>
```

Running this command will format the files in the current working directory by default. If the <TARGET> option is used, the command will scan the file/directory passed in the input. If a hyphen is specified for <TARGET>, the command will read the input from standard input (STDIN).

The following are the options supported by this command and it is not mandatory to use them. Just running the terraform fmt command will also work if you expect the default behavior:

- -list=false: Setting this option will not list the files that are not properly formatted.
- -check: This option will just check whether the input files are formatted as per the styling conventions and the exit code will be set accordingly. It will be zero (0) if all input files are formatted properly and non-zero if there are any inconsistencies.
- -rewrite=false: This option will not overwrite the input files and can be used along with the -check option if you are just going to validate the configuration or input files.
- -diff: This option lists differences in the formatting changes.
- -recursive: This option is used to format the input files in the current working directory as well as in subdirectories. The default behavior is that the command will format the files in the current working directory only.

Take a look at a simple example of how terraform fmt will reorganize a simple resource block that will create an Amazon S3 (AWS storage service to store files as objects) bucket. You will notice that the Name key and value alignment are formatted according to the other tag in the tags { } inner block.

This is before running the terraform fmt command:

```
resource "aws_s3_bucket" "testbucket" {
  bucket = "fmt-test-bucket"


  tags = {
    Name = "Test bucket"
    Environment = "testing"
  }
}
```

This is after running the terraform fmt command:

```
resource "aws_s3_bucket" "testbucket" {
  bucket = "fmt-test-bucket"

  tags = {
    Name           = "Test bucket"
```

```
    Environment = "testing"
  }
}
There are few additional
```

The validate Command

The terraform validate command is used to validate the configuration files in the directory, checking whether the configuration is syntactically correct and that there are no inconsistencies with the variable names or any attributes. This command does not access the state file or call the provider APIs, and it works within the directory only.

The command requires the current working directory to be initialized with the terraform init command.

This is how the command is used:

```
$ terraform validate <validate_options>
```

The following are the options supported:

- -json: This option produces the machine-readable JSON output and this can help with automation scenarios.

- -no-color: The output will not have any color if this option is specified.

Special Commands

So far, you have read about the core Terraform workflow commands and then followed this up with the code reformatting commands that will be used in most cases. In this section, you will see some special commands in appropriate scenarios.

The login Command

The terraform login command is used to obtain and save an API token for HCP Terraform, Terraform Enterprise, or any other compatible host. In the case of HCP Terraform and Terraform Enterprise, the user will be interacting with the host with the API token as the authentication mechanism and it is applicable to use in interactive scenarios.

This is how the command is used:

```
$ terraform login <HOSTNAME>
```

In case HOSTNAME is not specified, it will default to the HCP Terraform host at app.terraform.io.

If the command execution is successful in CLI, the API token retrieved will be stored locally in the file named credentials.tfrc.json by default. But there is also an option to change this behavior and save the API token in a different location when you run the login command.

The logout Command

The terraform logout command is used to remove the API token stored by the login command. With this command, the API token will be removed from the local file storage only and the token stored in the remote server has to be manually revoked.

This is how the command is used:

```
$ terraform logout <HOSTNAME>
```

In case HOSTNAME is not specified, it will default to the HCP Terraform host at app.terraform.io.

The console Command

The terraform console command is used to start an interactive console to try out and experiment with expressions. For example, if you would like to try out expressions or any functions before using them in the actual configuration, this console-based command will help. This command has two ways of operating based on the state file content.

If the state file is empty, you can use this command as usual to try out the expressions; if the state file is not empty and you already have the configuration in place, the command will place a lock on the state file during the operation.

For configurations such as the local backend, the -state command-line option can be used to point to a different state file than the terraform.tfstate file in the current working directory.

Shortcuts such as Ctrl + C or Ctrl + D can be used to exit the console, and the exit command can also be used.

This is how the command is used:

```
$ terraform console <console_options>
```

Look at a simple string function, replace() and uuid(), to print a **Universally Unique Identifier (UUID)** in the terraform console command:

```
$ terraform console
> replace(«ec2_instances», «_», «-»)
"ec2-instances"
```

```
> uuid()
```

```
"b00bdca8-7e54-0f08-7127-3184926735f7"
```

The output Command

The `terraform output` command is used to extract the values of the output variables from the Terraform state file.

This is how the command is used:

```
$ terraform output <output_options> OUT_VARNAME
```

If OUT_VARNAME is not specified, the command will extract all the output values, and when specified, it will extract the value of that output variable.

The following options are supported by the `terraform output` command to interact with the output values stored in the state file:

- `-json`: This option produces the output in JSON format.
- `-raw`: This option can be used to produce the output values in string format without any special formatting and it helps when the Terraform execution is integrated with shell scripts. This option only supports string, number, and Boolean values; complex data types will not work.
- `-no-color`: This option is used to disable color codes in the output.
- `-state=<PATH_TO_STATE_FILE>`: This is used to point to a state file in a different location and is not applicable for remote backends.

Another important consideration with this command is that the command will display any sensitive value in the state file as plain text when using the `-json` or `-raw` option and should be used cautiously to avoid exposing sensitive data.

Take a look at the `output.tf` file in this configuration that has a couple of output values, such as the access key ID and the **Amazon Resource Name** (**ARN**) of the IAM user the script creates:

```
output "access_key" {
  value = aws_iam_access_key.user_access_keys.id
}

output "user_arn" {
  value = aws_iam_user.test_user.arn
}
```

After the Terraform configuration is applied, you can try the `terraform output` command, which will show the values from the state file. A few examples follow:

Example 1 shows `terraform output` with no output variable names:

```
$ terraform output
access_key = "AKIAEXAMPLETESTVALUE"
user_arn = "arn:aws:iam::123456789012:user/test/test-aws-user"
```

Example 2 shows `terraform output` in JSON format:

```
$ terraform output -json
{
  "access_key": {
    "sensitive": false,
    "type": "string",
    "value": "AKIAEXAMPLETESTVALUE"
  },
  "user_arn": {
    "sensitive": false,
    "type": "string",
    "value": "arn:aws:iam::123456789012:user/test/test-aws-user"
  }
}
```

Example 3 shows `terraform output` with an output variable name:

```
$ terraform output user_arn
"arn:aws:iam:123456789012:user/test/test-aws-user"
```

The show Command

The `terraform show` command is used to read the state file or the plan output file and show the output in human-readable format. This command can also be used in automation cases with the `-json` option flag.

This is how the command is used:

```
$ terraform show <show_options> <STATE_OR_PLAN_FILE>
```

If `STATE_OR_PLAN_FILE` is not specified, the state file in the default location will be referenced.

The following command options are supported by the `terraform show` command:

- `-json`: This option produces the machine-readable JSON output.
- `-no-color`: The output will not have any color if this option is specified.

Like the `terraform output` command, sensitive information will be displayed in plain text if the `-json` option is specified.

The graph Command

The `terraform graph` command is used to create a graph with the dependency relationships of the resources and data blocks for a given configuration as per the conventions in the **DOT language**. The DOT language saves the graph with `.gv` or `.dot` extensions and these are outside the scope of this book.

By default, the `graph` command results in a simple graph of resources and dependencies, and with the `-type` option, different types of graphs can be created with more detail and are helpful when you work with complex configurations.

This is how the command is used:

```
$ terraform graph <graph_options>
```

The supported command options are listed here:

- `-plan=tfplan`: This option creates the graph for the given plan that implies `-type=apply`.
- `-draw-cycles`: This option can be used to highlight the cycles in the graph with colored edges, and this is helpful for debugging any cycle errors.
- `-type=<operation_type>`: This option is used to specify the operation type for which the graph has to be created. The possible values are `plan`, `apply`, `plan-refresh-only`, and `plan-destroy`.

For the sample configuration you have in this chapter, the `terraform graph` command produces the following output. Please note that the command needs the Graphviz tool to be installed on your local workstation. Here is the download link: `https://graphviz.org/download/`

Here is an example command:

```
$ terraform graph | dot -Tpng > ch4_graph.png
```

Figure 4.1 shows the resource dependencies in graph format:

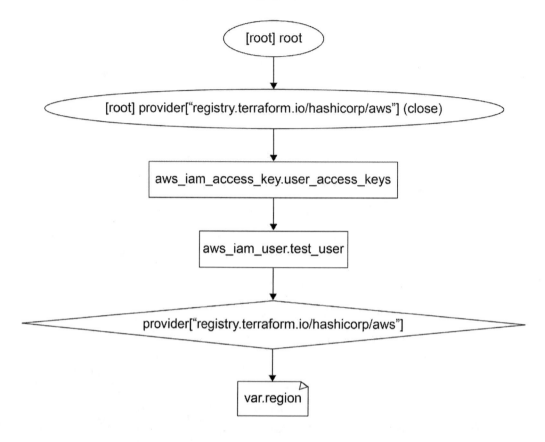

Figure 4.1: The graph command output

The import Command

The terraform import command is used to import the existing real-world infrastructure resources into your configuration state so it can be managed by Terraform.

The import command expects a resource configuration block to be written manually for the resource and then you can run the import command in Terraform CLI. This command itself will not generate any configuration.

If you would like Terraform to generate the configuration, the import block functionality can be used (available with Terraform v1.5.0 or later). The terraform import command can import only one resource at a time and the import block can import more than one resource at the same time.

This is how the command is used:

```
$ terraform import <import_options> RESOURCE_ADDRESS RESOURCE_ID
```

This command will import the resource with the specified Resource ID at the given Resource Address. If the resource is defined inside the module, the module name with the keyword should be appended before the resource address.

Here is an example:

```
$ terraform import module.foo.aws_s3_bucket.testbucket test-bucket-
qwi02
```

The resource ID can vary based on the resource type you intend to import. In the example configuration you are using in this chapter, the resource ID refers to the access key ID in the case of IAM access keys. So, if you are trying to import an IAM access key resource into Terraform, the import command would look like this:

```
$ terraform import aws_iam_access_key.user_access_keys
AKIAEXAMPLETESTVALUE
```

Take a look at the options available for this command:

- `-config=<PATH>`: This option can be used to specify the alternate location that contains the configuration scripts. If not specified, Terraform will look for configuration scripts in the current working directory.

- `-input=true`: Setting this option will ask for input to execute the init command if necessary. If this is set to false, it will cause an error if the input is not provided.

- `-lock=false`: This option will disable the locking of state files.

- `-lock-timeout=<duration>`: This option will override the duration of the state lock with the user-provided value. The default is zero seconds. It might help in scenarios where there are parallel processes running pointing to the same state file and it makes sense to wait for the lock to get released for the next process to use it.

- `-no-color`: This option is used to disable color codes in the output.

- `-parallelism=<COUNT>`: This option can be used to override the maximum number of parallel operations on the machine running Terraform.

- `-var "VARIABLE_NAME=VALUE"`: Use this option to set a value for the variable declared in the main configuration. If there are multiple variables, the option can be used for each variable name.

- `-var-file=<FILENAME>`: This option is used to set the values of multiple input variables, usually using the `*.tfvars` file. The option can also be used multiple times to pick the values from more than one file.

- `-provider=provider`: This option is used to override the default provider configuration while importing the object. By default, Terraform uses the provider specified in the configuration for the target resource. This option is deprecated.

> **Note**
>
> For configurations using the local backend only, `terraform import` also accepts the legacy options of `-state`, `-state-out`, and `-backup`. For more details on these options, please refer to the **Options** section under the `terraform apply` command.

State Management and the terraform state Command

As you have, the Terraform state file, `terraform.tfstate`, is critical to the core workings of a Terraform tool. The individual entries in the Terraform state file map directly to real-world infrastructure. This allows Terraform to sync the resources whenever there are changes to the configuration.

The state file is managed and updated automatically when commands such as `plan` and `apply` are executed. Sometimes, there might be a need to interact with the state file and make some adjustments to accommodate the changes made outside Terraform. This is where the `terraform state` command plays a vital role.

You can start with the `terraform state` command and the options associated with it. There are also subcommands within the `state` command that help in different scenarios, which will be discussed further in this topic.

The state Command

As discussed previously, the `terraform state` command is used mainly for state management. This command will modify the state file seamlessly without you having to work directly with the state file and editing it.

This is how the command is used:

```
$ terraform state [subcommand] <state_options> <ARGUMENTS>
```

The `terraform state` command will work the same way with both the local and remote backends. In the case of a local backend, the command will run faster, as there are no network hops, and remote backends take some time and the turnaround time will be delayed. Remote backends have their own advantages, such as security, backup management, and restricted access control.

The state command output can also be integrated with other tools, such as jq, and can be automated. The subcommands will also take a backup of the state file before it is modified by them. There are also subcommands such as terraform state list and terraform state show that are read-only and will not take any backups.

Subcommands of terraform state

The following section will cover the subcommands of the terraform state command; each has its own use case that will be discussed in detail.

The terraform state list Command

The terraform state list command will list all the resources within the state file.

This is how the command is used:

```
$ terraform state list <list_options> <RESOURCE_ADDRESS>
```

If RESOURCE_ADDRESS is not specified, the command will list all resources available in the state file. When specified, the command will list only the resources matching the criteria.

There could be situations where you might be dealing with a large number of resources and listing everything in one go may not be required. In that case, you can choose to list only specific resources, all resources belonging to a specific module, all instances created by the same resource group, and so on.

The options supported by this command are as follows:

- -state=<PATH>: This option is used to specify the state file to be considered. If not provided, it will default to the terraform.tfstate file in the current working directory.
- -id=<ID>: This option is used to filter the resource by ID.

For a better understanding, a few examples are provided here:

Example 1 lists all resources in the state file:

```
$ terraform state list
Output:
aws_iam_access_key.user_access_keys
aws_iam_user.test_user
```

Example 2 lists resources by resource address:

```
$ terraform state list aws_iam_user.test_user
Output:
aws_iam_user.test_user
```

In this case, if multiple instances of the same resource type are provisioned, all of them will be listed with the index. In your case, you only have one, so it displays the same resource.

Example 3 filters resources by resource ID:

```
$ terraform state list -id=AKIAEXAMPLETESTVALUE
Output:
aws_iam_access_key.user_access_keys
```

The terraform state show Command

The `terraform state show` command is used to display the attributes of a single resource in the state file.

This is how the command is used:

```
$ terraform state show RESOURCE_ADDRESS
```

In this command, RESOURCE_ADDRESS is not optional, and hence, needs to be provided always. Upon successful execution, the attributes of the matching resource will be displayed.

The resource address format can be in any valid form that can be accepted by Terraform, and the supported command option is as follows:

-state=<PATH>: This option is used to specify the state file to be considered. If not provided, it will default to the terraform.tfstate file in the current working directory.

You can now run this command with the available configuration:

```
$ terraform state show aws_iam_user.test_user
Output:
# aws_iam_user.test_user:
resource "aws_iam_user" "test_user" {
    arn           = "arn:aws:iam::123456789012:user/test/test-aws-
user"
    force_destroy = false
    id            = "test-aws-user"
    name          = "test-aws-user"
    path          = "/test/"
    tags          = {
        "createdby" = "terraform"
    }
    tags_all      = {
        "createdby" = "terraform"
```

```
    }
    unique_id       = "AIDAEXAMPLEUSERIDKHNJ"
}
```

You can see that this command lists all the possible attributes for the given resource from the state file and it is meant for human interaction. If there are any automation scenarios, the `terraform show -json` command can be used to get the same output in machine-readable JSON format, which we already discussed.

The terraform state mv Command

The default behavior of Terraform is that if you change the configuration after provisioning the resources already, it will track the changes and ensure that the remote objects match the current configuration settings.

How does this work? During the `apply` stage, Terraform destroys the resource provisioned with the previous snapshot of the configuration and a new resource will be provisioned with the latest changes.

But there will be rare scenarios where you do not want to destroy the remote object that's already active and want to track it with the new resource address. This command will help in this case.

This is how the command is used:

```
$ terraform state mv <move_options> SOURCE DESTINATION
```

Even here, SOURCE and DESTINATION should follow the resource-addressing conventions. When valid values are provided, Terraform will look at the specific resource address and see whether the object exists. If successful, it will move the resource to the new destination resource address.

The options supported are as follows:

- `-dry-run`: This option will report all resources in the state matching the source address but will not move/make any changes. It can be used for testing purposes before making the actual change.

- `-lock=false`: This option will disable the locking of state files; the default behavior is state locking will be enabled.

- `-lock-timeout=<duration>`: This option will override the duration of the state lock with the user-provided value and the default is zero seconds. It might help in scenarios where there are parallel processes running pointing to the same state file and it makes sense to wait for the lock to get released for the next process to use it.

A simple example to understand this command would be renaming the IAM user resource in the current configuration as follows.

This is the code before changes:

```
resource "aws_iam_user" "test_user" {
  name = "test-aws-user"
  path = "/test/"
  . . .
}
```

This is the code after changes:

```
resource "aws_iam_user" "preprod_user" {
  name = "test-aws-user"
  path = "/test/"

  . . .
}
```

In this case, the `terraform state mv` command will help us track the IAM user resource under the new address. The command to be used is as follows:

```
$ terraform state mv aws_iam_user.testuser aws_iam_user.preprod user
```

> **Note**
>
> For configurations using the local backend only, the `terraform state mv` command also accepts the legacy options of `-state`, `-state-out`, and `-backup`.

The terraform state rm Command

The `terraform state rm` command will help remove the remote object from the state file so it can continue to exist without destroying it. This also means that if the same configuration is reapplied, the new resources will be created again for the removed instances to be in sync.

This is how the command is used:

```
terraform state rm <remove_options> RESOURCE_ADDRESS
```

The supported command options are the same as the `terraform state mv` command:

- `-dry-run`: This option will report all resources in the state matching the source address but will not move any resources/make a change. It can be used for testing purposes before making the actual change.

- `-lock=false`: This option will disable the locking of state files.

- `-lock-timeout=<duration>`: This option will override the duration of the state lock with the user-provided value and the default is zero seconds. It might help in scenarios where there are parallel processes running pointing to the same state file and it makes sense to wait for the lock to get released for the next process to use it.

> **Note**
>
> For configurations using the local backend only, the `terraform state rm` command also accepts the legacy options of `-state`, `-state-out`, and `-backup`.

The terraform state replace-provider Command

If there are scenarios to replace the provider currently used in the configuration with the new provider configuration, the `terraform state replace-provider` command can be used. This command will also take a backup of the state file before the update and the backup option cannot be disabled.

This is how the command is used:

```
$ terraform state replace-provider FROM_PROVIDER TO_PROVIDER
```

Upon successful execution, resources from `FROM_PROVIDER` will be moved to `TO_PROVIDER`. The supported options are listed here:

- `-auto-approve`: This option will execute the changes without waiting for any approvals.
- `-lock=false`: This option will disable the locking of state files.
- `-lock-timeout=<duration>`: This option will override the duration of the state lock with the user-provided value and the default is zero seconds. It might help in scenarios where there are parallel processes running pointing to the same state file and it makes sense to wait for the lock to get released for the next process to use it.

> **Note**
>
> For configurations using the local backend only, the `terraform state replace-provider` command also accepts the legacy options of `-state`, `-state-out`, and `-backup`.

The terraform state pull Command

The `terraform state pull` command downloads the state file from its current location, upgrades it so that it is compatible with the locally installed Terraform, and prints the raw output to the console.

This is how the command is used:

```
$ terraform state pull
```

This command can also be used in cases where the information from the state should be retrieved when paired with other third-party tools such as jq. It is not recommended to use this command with the state file stored in the remote backend.

The terraform state push Command

The terraform state push command is used to manually upload a local state file to the remote backend and should be used very rarely, when there are no other alternatives.

This is how the command is used:

```
$ terraform state push <push_options> PATH
```

The state file from the specified path will be pushed to the currently configured backend.

Before the state file is pushed, Terraform performs safety checks to ensure the changes are completely secure. To disable the checks, the -force option can be used but is not recommended.

> **Note**
>
> To use the state pull and state push commands, Terraform expects the file to be in UTF-8 format without the **byte order mark (BOM)**.

Summary

In this chapter, you read about the core Terraform workflow commands. This was followed by explanations of special-purpose commands such as console, graph, and import, used as and when the need arises. The terraform state command was then discussed in detail with the subcommands. You also looked at how each command helps the developer interact with and manage the state file beyond infrastructure provisioning.

Now, you can proceed with the next chapter, on how to use the commands with Terraform CLI with full confidence. This will help in increasing productivity and the seamless transition to advanced concepts such as Terraform modules, HCP Terraform, and so on.

Exam Readiness Drill – Chapter Review Questions

Apart from a solid understanding of key concepts, being able to think quickly under time pressure is a skill that will help you ace your certification exam. That is why working on these skills early on in your learning journey is key.

Chapter review questions are designed to improve your test-taking skills progressively with each chapter you learn and review your understanding of key concepts in the chapter at the same time. You'll find these at the end of each chapter.

> **How to Access these Resources**
>
> To learn how to access these resources, head over to the chapter titled *Chapter 11, Accessing the Online Practice Resources.*

To open the Chapter Review Questions for this chapter, perform the following steps:

1. Click the link – `https://packt.link/HCorp003Ch4`.

   Alternatively, you can scan the following **QR code** (*Figure 4.2*):

Figure 4.2 – QR code that opens Chapter Review Questions for logged-in users

2. Once you log in, you'll see a page similar to the one shown in *Figure 4.3*:

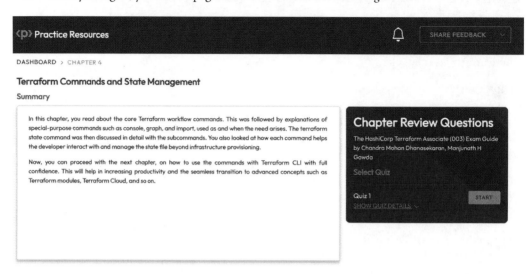

Figure 4.3 – Chapter Review Questions for Chapter 4

3. Once ready, start the following practice drills, re-attempting the quiz multiple times.

Exam Readiness Drill

For the first three attempts, don't worry about the time limit.

ATTEMPT 1

The first time, aim for at least **40%**. Look at the answers you got wrong and read the relevant sections in the chapter again to fix your learning gaps.

ATTEMPT 2

The second time, aim for at least **60%**. Look at the answers you got wrong and read the relevant sections in the chapter again to fix any remaining learning gaps.

ATTEMPT 3

The third time, aim for at least **75%**. Once you score 75% or more, you start working on your timing.

> Tip
>
> You may take more than **three** attempts to reach 75%. That's okay. Just review the relevant sections in the chapter till you get there.

Working On Timing

Target: Your aim is to keep the score the same while trying to answer these questions as quickly as possible. Here's an example of how your next attempts should look like:

Attempt	Score	Time Taken
Attempt 5	77%	21 mins 30 seconds
Attempt 6	78%	18 mins 34 seconds
Attempt 7	76%	14 mins 44 seconds

Table 4.1 – Sample timing practice drills on the online platform

> Note
>
> The time limits shown in the above table are just examples. Set your own time limits with each attempt based on the time limit of the quiz on the website.

With each new attempt, your score should stay above **75%** while your "time taken" to complete should "decrease". Repeat as many attempts as you want till you feel confident dealing with the time pressure.

5
Terraform Modules

Imagine that your company's **Quality Assurance** (**QA**) team needs a test environment to be spun up in a very short interval and the dependency on your team is causing delays.

The best way to handle this is to facilitate a self-service option for the QA team where they can create the required environment themselves by passing some unique inputs for each environment. This can be achieved using a module.

Modules are one of the core concepts of Terraform because of their extensive use in the production environment. You will rarely find a production environment where modules are not used. A good understanding of modules is required not just from a certification perspective but also for day-to-day operations while managing a Terraform-based setup. The following are the key topics that will be covered in this chapter:

- Why do we need modules?
- What is a module in Terraform?
- Advantages of modules
- Types of modules
- Module structure
- Module syntax
- Key points to consider before creating modules
- Key points to consider while using a module
- Drawbacks of modules

Once you complete these topics, you will find exercises where you will learn how modules are used in the real world in a practical way:

- Using a root module to provision resources

- Using a local module to provision resources

- Using a remote module to provision resources

By the end of this chapter, you will have a good understanding of modules and some of the key considerations from a design point of view. Operationally, you will also be able to write your own modules for any requirement and will be able to use a public module and customize it for your needs.

Technical Requirements

This chapter has three exercises. The following are the pre-requisites for you to get started with the exercises:

- An AWS account and an IAM user with required permissions (or an SSO user if your organization is using AWS SSO). Refer to the following URL for steps on how to create an IAM user in AWS: `https://docs.aws.amazon.com/IAM/latest/UserGuide/id_users_create.html`.

- The AWS CLI installed (version 2.0 and above preferred). For detailed instructions on installing the AWS CLI, go to `https://docs.aws.amazon.com/cli/latest/userguide/getting-started-install.html`.

- Terraform installed (version 1.4.0 and above preferred).

- The code required for the exercise is present in our GitHub repository.

- Here is the URL for the GitHub repository: `https://github.com/PacktPublishing/Hashicorp-Certified-Terraform-Associate-003-Exam-guide-Second-Edition/tree/main`

- Clone the GitHub repository to your local machine by running the following command:

```
git clone https://github.com/PacktPublishing/Hashicorp-
Certified-Terraform-Associate-003-Exam-guide-Second-Edition.git
```

- Navigate to *Chapter 5* by running the following command:

```
cd Hashicorp-Certified-Terraform-Associate-003-Exam-guide-
Second-Edition/ch5
```

- You should find the README.md file along with three folders, each of which contains an exercise.

- Refer to README.md for instructions on the exercises.

> **Note**
>
> The exercises launch real resources in the AWS cloud. Almost all the resources are free except for the EC2 instance, which gets charged till you delete it. It should not cost you more than a dollar if you complete the exercise within three to four hours. Please make sure you delete the resources to avoid getting charged.

Why Do We Need Modules?

When you start using Terraform, you start by creating a few infrastructure objects by writing code in a single configuration file. As your requirements grow, you start adding additional configurations to the same file or adding new files to the same directory. Theoretically, you can even keep using this approach. However, is this the right approach that is recommended by HashiCorp?

Before answering this question, take a look at the drawbacks of this approach:

Complexity

When you start copy-pasting the code for similar requirements or multiple resources of the same configuration, the complexity (imagine having 50 blocks of code to create 50 instances) will increase with the growth in the number of resources. It becomes very difficult for the team managing Terraform to understand the code and navigate it for either changes or troubleshooting.

Duplication of Code

You use the same block of code with minor changes for similar resources. One of the key principles of software development is **Don't Repeat Yourself** (**DRY**). When you are trying to adopt the best practices of software development in **Infrastructure as Code** (**IaC**), duplicating the code goes against one of the important principles of software development. For example, if you want to launch three EC2 instances of the same configuration but with different names, you end up copying the same code thrice and changing a single argument for the **name**.

Segregation

The segregation of different layers of infrastructure resources is important to assign ownership to different teams. Imagine a situation where the network team wants to create code for all the networking requirements and the application team wants to write code for app-related requirements. How are you going to segregate and delegate the ownership?

Misconfiguration

When you want to make changes, apart from knowing what exactly the Terraform command does, you also need to know the whole environment to gauge the impact a simple change will have on your setup. The chance of a misconfiguration and its impact on the environment is very high.

So, how can you solve these problems? What is the recommendation from HashiCorp? What is being followed by the industry? Terraform modules are the answer. By the end of this chapter, you will understand how Terraform solves all these problems.

What Is a Terraform Module?

In non-technical terms, a Terraform module is a template using which you can launch logically grouped resources as per your requirement even without knowing its inner workings.

You define the template once and use it any number of times to launch resources. For example, you can create a module for the launch of a test environment of your product and your QA team can use this module any number of times to launch the test environment.

HashiCorp calls the module a set of configuration files in a single directory that helps you organize and re-use Terraform configuration. In other words, any directory with Terraform configuration files to create a certain resource(s) can be called a module.

Terraform uses modules to package resource configurations, and the user can reuse these modules whenever there is a requirement to launch resources packaged in a module.

Advantages of Modules

In this section, you will look at some advantages of modules:

Reduces Complexity

Modules group logical components, making them easy to manage and update when required. This makes it easy for the team that manages Terraform to understand the code and make the required changes.

Reduces Code Duplication

You write modules once (or use public modules) and these get used to launch resources. There is no duplication of code here. You only pass values to the variables to decide the number of resources or the configuration of the resources.

This not only prevents the duplication of code but also saves time by reducing the effort required for the same task.

Segregation

Modules inherently support segregation because you can build one layer on top of another. A root module is the place where a child module gets referenced in one of the configuration files. The child module variable's value gets passed and the required outputs are defined. The output of one module can be used as input to another resource's configuration. Hence, you can create a separate layer for each infrastructure tier. For example, in a typical three-tier architecture, there will be a web layer (presentation layer), an app layer, and a database layer.

To deploy this three-tier-based application, you also need a network layer, which is managed by the network team.

The network team will be responsible for creating the networking components that will be used by other teams to deploy their respective layers. The app/web/DBA team will have their own modules for the launch of respective resources. They will own these modules but when they launch the infrastructure objects, they will consume the outputs of the networking layer to make sure these run within the defined network.

Reduces Misconfigurations

It is only human to err. You have likely experienced a situation where you or one of your colleagues made changes in an environment/file/resource that were not meant to be made. When you use individual files, you define every single parameter, and hence, the chance of human error is higher. With modules, you standardize most of these configurations and only allow a few important configurations to be modified via variables. This automation helps in reducing the chance of misconfigurations.

Self-Service

If you want to allow people to create resources on their own without spending too much time learning about Terraform, modules can help. You can just publish a module and the variables whose values need to be passed by the respective team to create the resource.

All the complex configurations are hidden under the hood. The end user just needs to understand the inputs and outputs. Inputs can be passed as input variables and the outputs of the modules need to be accessed using standard syntax.

Apart from these key advantages, modules help in quick deployments and maintain a consistent environment where the best practices of the industry can be tested once and deployed to environments via modules.

Types of Modules

Depending on the criteria one uses, modules can be classified in multiple ways. *Figure 5.1* shows the classification of modules based on two important criteria:

- Based on the entry point for the module (i.e., where `terraform plan/apply` is run):

  - Root module

  - Child module

- Based on where the configuration files are stored/installed:

  - Local module

  - Remote module

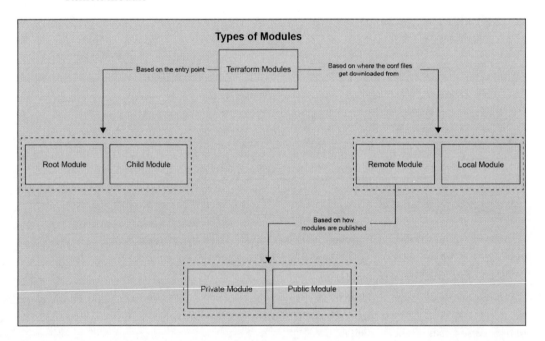

Figure 5.1: Types of modules

Now that you have seen the types of modules, it is time to take a look at each module type in detail in the following section.

The Root Module

Any folder with a set of Terraform configuration files to create infrastructure objects can be called a root module.

If the Terraform module is a template, someone must instantiate it, that is, make a copy of the infrastructure objects using the template. This is where the root module comes in.

The root module is the primary entry point for the module. This is the directory with the configuration files where the user will run `terraform plan` or `terraform apply`.

A root module can have a few configuration files to create the infrastructure and/or it can call the child modules as shown in *Figure 5.2*.

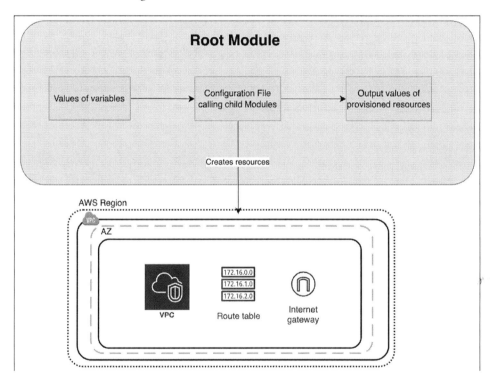

Figure 5.2: Root module

A typical root module's files are shown in *Figure 5.3*.

When you call the child module from the current directory (i.e., the root module), it loads the configuration files of the child module and replaces the variable value with the one you defined in the current directory.

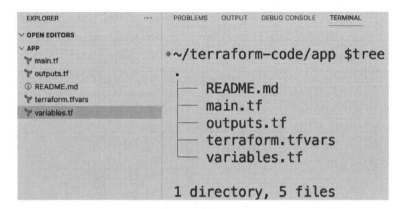

Figure 5.3: Root module file structure example

The Child Module

A module is called a child module when it gets called by the root module using a module block, as shown in *Figure 5.5*.

Once you have created the child module, you can call it any number of times within the configuration files in your root module. It can also be called from multiple root modules, provided they have access to this child module. When you run `terraform get` or `terraform init` from the root module, the child module gets downloaded if it's a remote module. If it is a local module, the `modules.json` file under `.terraform/modules` will contain the path of the modules in the local filesystem.

> **Note**
>
> When people talk about modules, most of the time it is in the context of a child module. If it is a root module, it is normally specified.

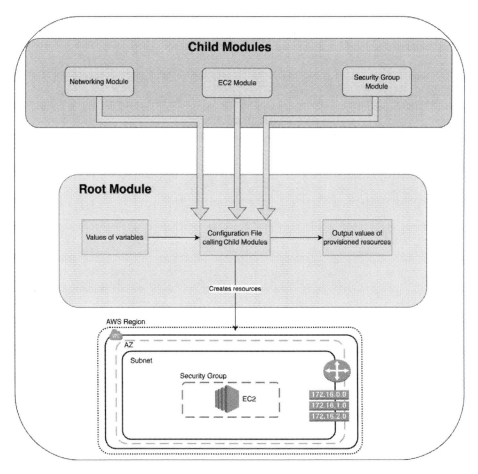

Figure 5.4: Child module called by root module

While *Figure 5.4* is a pictorial representation of the child module's work, the following *Figure 5.5* shows the code/file representation of the module.

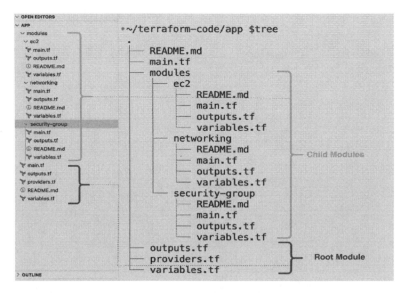

Figure 5.5: Child module and root module file structure example

> **Note**
>
> Some child modules have their own child modules. Such a module is called a nested module.

Local Modules

As explained earlier, a module is a bunch of configuration files and needs to be stored somewhere before it gets called by anyone who wants to use it.

If you store these configuration files on your local filesystem, it is called a local module.

When you are calling a local module, it must begin with ./ or ../ to indicate that the module is present in the local filesystem, as shown in *Figure 5.6*.

HashiCorp recommends using the relative filesystem paths to refer to the local Terraform modules instead of the absolute filesystem paths. Using the absolute path tightly couples the configuration file path to the specific computer's filesystem layout.

You will be able to understand this well with the following example, where you will try both the full path and relative path to call the child module from the root module.

This is the child module's path:

```
/Users/manju/Desktop/terraform/vpc-module
```

This is the root module where the execution is happening:

```
/Users/manju/Desktop/terraform/example
```

Within the `main.tf` file of the root module, you will call the child module.

If you use the full path as follows, your code will not be able to run on your colleague's laptop as the path where they run Terraform will be different:

```
module "vpc"{
    source = "/Users/manju/Desktop/terraform/vpc-module"
    ---- Truncated ----
}
```

Instead, you should use a relative path, as follows. This should work on any computer provided the operating system is Linux:

```
module "vpc"{
    source = "../vpc-module/"
    ---- Truncated ----}
```

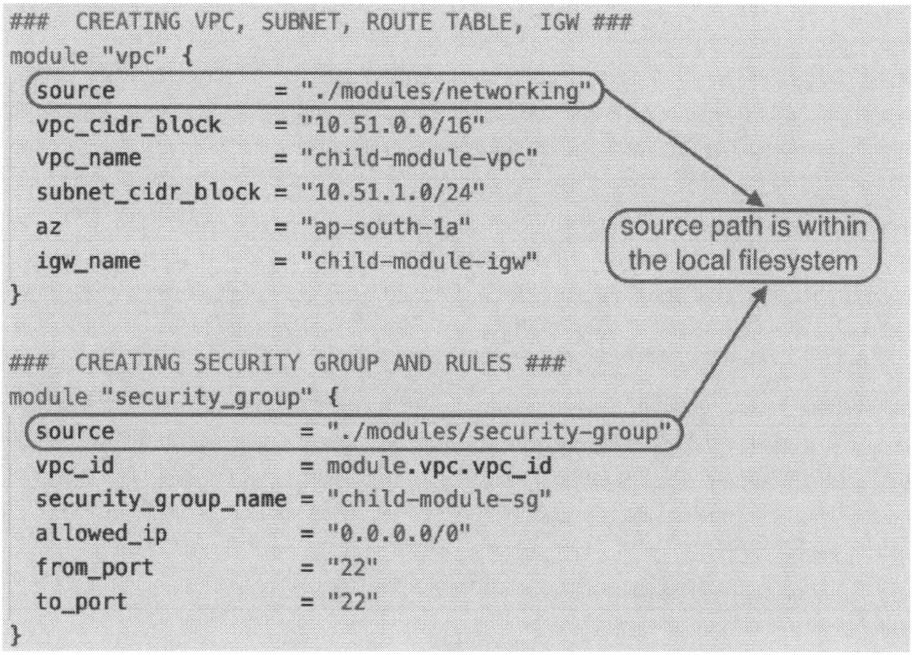

```
### CREATING VPC, SUBNET, ROUTE TABLE, IGW ###
module "vpc" {
    source             = "./modules/networking"
    vpc_cidr_block     = "10.51.0.0/16"
    vpc_name           = "child-module-vpc"
    subnet_cidr_block  = "10.51.1.0/24"
    az                 = "ap-south-1a"
    igw_name           = "child-module-igw"
}

### CREATING SECURITY GROUP AND RULES ###
module "security_group" {
    source               = "./modules/security-group"
    vpc_id               = module.vpc.vpc_id
    security_group_name  = "child-module-sg"
    allowed_ip           = "0.0.0.0/0"
    from_port            = "22"
    to_port              = "22"
}
```

source path is within the local filesystem

Figure 5.6: Example code for local module implementation

While *Figure 5.6* shows a local child module's path, *Figure 5.7* illustrates the local child module's initialization.

```
~/terraform-code/app $terraform init

Initializing the backend...
Initializing modules...
- ec2_instance in modules/ec2
- security_group in modules/security-group    Local child modules
- vpc in modules/networking                     getting initialized

Initializing provider plugins...
- Finding hashicorp/aws versions matching "5.34.0"...
- Installing hashicorp/aws v5.34.0...
- Installed hashicorp/aws v5.34.0 (signed by HashiCorp)

Terraform has created a lock file .terraform.lock.hcl to record the provider
selections it made above. Include this file in your version control repository
so that Terraform can guarantee to make the same selections by default when
you run "terraform init" in the future.

Terraform has been successfully initialized!
```

Figure 5.7: Local child modules getting initialized

When installing a local module, Terraform will not download the module, but will instead refer to the source directory using the path of the modules as specified in the modules.json file under .terraform/modules.

Storing the configuration on a local filesystem limits the ability to share the modules and work as a team. But this works great for testing modules before pushing them to a version control system or the Terraform Registry to make it a remote module.

Remote Modules

If a module's configuration files are stored and downloaded from a remote system like the Terraform Registry, a version control system (for example, GitHub, Bitbucket, etc.), HTTP URLs, an S3 bucket, or a GCS bucket, then these are called remote modules.

When installing a remote module, Terraform will download the module into the .terraform directory in your configuration's root directory. Any changes in the remote module will be reflected only after you upgrade the modules by running the terraform init -upgrade command.

A remote module can be public (Terraform Registry) or private (HCP Terraform private registry).

The Terraform Registry is the native way of distributing modules. It is integrated directly into Terraform, so a Terraform configuration can refer to any module published in the registry using the `<NAMESPACE>/<NAME>/<PROVIDER>` syntax: for example, `hashicorp/consul/aws`.

A registry is an index of modules and is the easiest way to find public modules that are created by the community.

Unless you specify a specific version using the **ref** argument, Terraform will choose the default branch of the selected repository. If you want to use a different version, you can use the **ref** argument with the tag name, branch, or SHA-1 hash.

Remote modules can be further divided into two, depending on the availability of the modules to the user:

- Private modules
- Public modules

Private Modules

Private modules are modules that are available only to members of your team/organization based on how you have set them up.

You can store your modules in the version control system and decide who has access to this repository. Another option is to use the organization's HCP Terraform private registry that is integrated with your version control system. Apart from keeping modules private, HCP Terraform offers other features that will be discussed in *Chapter 9, Understanding HCP Terraform's Capabilities*.

The private registry modules have the following syntax for their name:

```
terraform-<PROVIDER>-<NAME>
```

Examples are `terraform-gcp-vault` and `terraform-aws-vpc`.

Public Modules

Public modules are those that can be downloaded by everyone. The most popular place for hosting a public module is the Terraform Registry. A registry exposes some additional information that is very helpful in deciding whether you can use a module or should try others.

Some of these modules are uploaded by vendors themselves and are validated by HashiCorp. These are trusted to be good ones.

You can also see individuals/teams upload modules, allowing everyone to consume them.

An example of downloading a remote module from the Terraform Registry is shown in *Figure 5.8*:

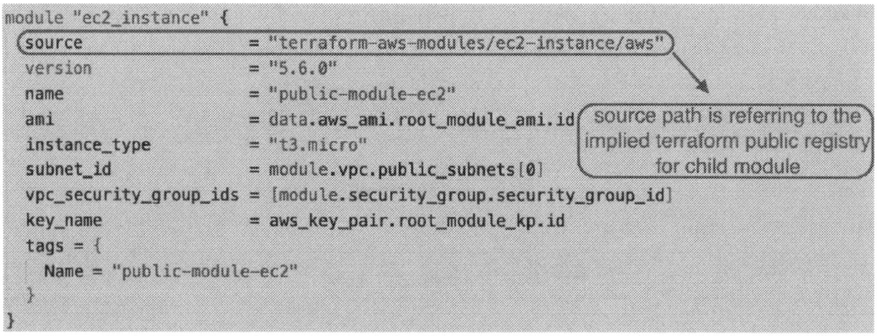

```
module "ec2_instance" {
  source                 = "terraform-aws-modules/ec2-instance/aws"
  version                = "5.6.0"
  name                   = "public-module-ec2"
  ami                    = data.aws_ami.root_module_ami.id
  instance_type          = "t3.micro"
  subnet_id              = module.vpc.public_subnets[0]
  vpc_security_group_ids = [module.security_group.security_group_id]
  key_name               = aws_key_pair.root_module_kp.id
  tags = {
    Name = "public-module-ec2"
  }
}
```

source path is referring to the implied terraform public registry for child module

Figure 5.8: Example code for a public (and remote) module (Terraform Registry)

An example of downloading a remote module from GitHub's public repository is shown in *Figure 5.9*:

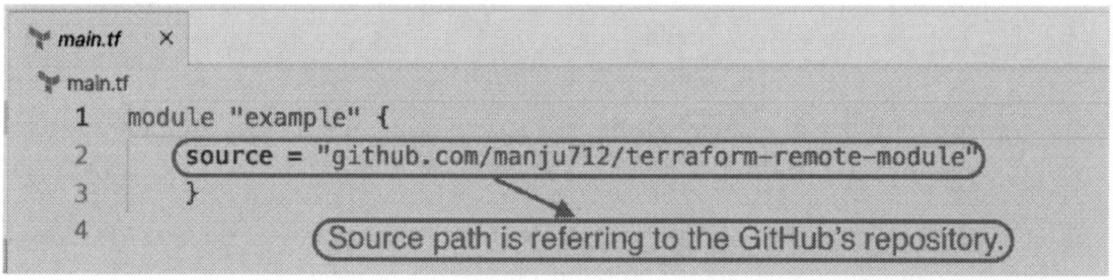

```
main.tf     ×
main.tf
1    module "example" {
2        source = "github.com/manju712/terraform-remote-module"
3    }
4
```

Source path is referring to the GitHub's repository.

Figure 5.9: Example code for public (and remote) module (GitHub)

You must always verify public modules before using them. Since anyone can contribute to the public modules on the Terraform Registry, you will not know whether the code is of high quality, free from security issues, or whether it follows best practices without verifying the code yourself. There is enough information about these modules that can help you decide whether you should use them. They are scattered between the Terraform Registry and GitHub.

Key parameters to verify a module in the Terraform Registry are the following:

- How old is the module?
- How active is the module? (How many times has it been downloaded in the last week/month?)
- Versions

Key parameters to verify a module in GitHub are the following:

- Is it getting frequent updates in terms of commits and versions?

- Does it have a good number of active contributors and stars?

- Are the license terms compatible with your organization's policies?

- Does it have pull requests and issues raised by the community? How has the response been for previous issues?

- Take a look at the code to rule out any undocumented resources or features.

Module Structure

There is no mandatory structure for modules. However, HashiCorp recommends following their standard module structure, since Terraform tools are designed to understand this structure in order to generate documentation and index modules when you upload modules to the Terraform Registry.

HashiCorp adds a root module as the mandatory component of the module structure. However, the focus here is mostly on the child module's structure. Hence, you will not see the root module as one of the requirements in the structure given here.

These are the key files that make up a module:

- `main.tf`: This is the main configuration file that defines the resources that need to be launched.

- `variables.tf`: Hardcoding the configuration value in the module's code makes it difficult to reuse it. You parameterize (define the variable but pass the value of the variable during execution) the arguments of the resources as variables and pass the value of these variables when you call this module from the root module. All the variables corresponding to the module are defined in the `variables.tf` file.

- `README.md`: This is a helper file to be written in the Markdown format. This gives information to the user on what the module is used for and how the module should be used.

- `outputs.tf`: All the resources created by the module are encapsulated and the attributes cannot be accessed from the root module unless they are exported in the child module as outputs. This is typically defined in the `outputs.tf` of the child module.

For example, if a security group is created using a child module, the ID of the security group will be available in the root module only if it is exported as an output in the child module and is also defined as an output in the root module – preferably, in `outputs.tf`.

You can use these outputs as input to other configurations or modules.

You typically refer to output values as module.MODULE_NAME.OUTPUT_NAME.

Most modules follow the preceding structure, and it is recommended that you use at least these files in a module.

Figure 5.10 shows the module with the minimum number of files as per the standard structure recommended by HashiCorp:

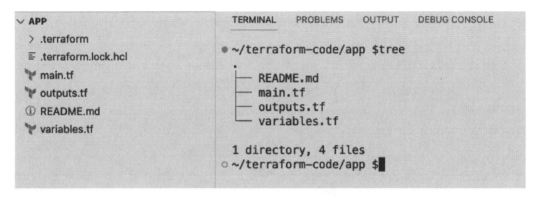

Figure 5.10: Module structure with minimal files

Some people also prefer to share more information about the module by adding additional files like changelog.md (key changes with version increment), folders like examples (with sample code for users), and modules with child modules. This is optional and you can add required files/folders based on your requirements.

The following URL is a good example for the module files. It has the changelog.md, LICENSE, and README.md file, along with main.tf, variables.tf, and outputs.tf:

https://github.com/terraform-aws-modules/terraform-aws-vpc/tree/master

The Module Block's Syntax

When you want to use child modules in the root module, there is a particular syntax you need to make use of. This syntax is part of the module block and is shown in *Figure 5.11*. Module blocks document the syntax for calling a child module from a parent module, including meta-arguments like for_each:

```
### GENERIC SYNTAX OF MODULE ###
module "local-name-for-the-module" {
  source    = "Local/Remote location of the child module"
  version   = "Version number of the module to be downloaded from the above source"
  VARIABLE1 = Value1
  VARIABLE2 = Value2
}


### EXAMPLE OF A MODULE ###
module "key_pair" {
  source  = "terraform-aws-modules/key-pair/aws"
  version = "2.0.2"

  key_name           = "my-keypair"
  create_private_key = true
}
```

Figure 5.11: Syntax and example of a module block

The name specified within " " after the module keyword is considered the local name. This is used by other modules to refer to this module.

The content within { } is called the module body.

This module body contains four arguments:

- source: This is a mandatory argument. This can be a path of a local filesystem or a remote one (Terraform Registry, GitHub, and more). This has to be a literal string, and expressions or variable interpolations are not allowed here.

- version: This is used to constrain the version of the modules that can be downloaded. It is recommended to pin the version number in production. By default, the latest version gets downloaded when you pull the module. This can cause compatibility issues and break some functionalities. By pinning the versions, you can perform testing for the newer version separately, iron out issues, and then do an upgrade of this module. Here are the other aspects of this argument:

  - Terraform supports various operators (=, !=, > , >=, <, <=, ~>) to help you pin versions.

  - version is not useful in the local modules as these are referenced directly in the local filesystem using the path specified in the modules.json file. Hence, the local modules used are always the latest ones.

- **Input variables**: Input variables are used to customize the resources of Terraform modules without altering the module's own source code. This helps to keep the module's code generic while allowing people to pass the specific values based on their requirements. Here are the other aspects of this argument:

  - These input variables can be declared in both the root module and the child module.

  - While the values for the root module can be passed via the CLI, environment variables, or a `.tfvars` file, the values for the child module should be passed by the calling module in the module block.

- **Additional meta-arguments**: Apart from `source` and `version`, there are a few more meta-arguments used with modules:

  - `count`: Used to create multiple copies of the infrastructure objects defined in a single module block. It is typically an integer that indicates how many times the module needs to be instantiated to launch infra objects.

  - `for_each`: Though `for_each` is also used to create multiple copies of infrastructure objects, it is used when the argument needed is a distinct value that is present in a map or set. Here, there is no definite number of iterations but it depends on the number of distinct values present.

  - `depends_on`: Terraform understands the implicit dependency (created when the graph gets created during `terraform plan/apply`). However, if there are any explicit dependencies that need to be configured, you can make use of this meta-argument.

Note

`~>` `operator`: This operator is called the pessimistic constraint operator. You use this operator to allow the upgrade of only the rightmost version component.

For example, if you define `version` `~>` `1.4.1`, the upgrade process is allowed to change to the new version starting from 1.4.1 to 1.4.10, but not 1.5.0.

If you define `version` `~>` `1.2`, the upgrade process is allowed to change the version from 1.2 to 1.10 but not 2.0.

As you will notice from the two examples, only the last number is allowed to change when you use this operator.

Key Points to Consider When You Create a Module

Once you decide to create a module for a certain requirement, there are certain points to keep in mind:

- You need to decide whether you are going to create modules to encapsulate all the services required for a particular project or create modules for the resources that are then called by a root module of the project. This is an important consideration and has a long-term impact since you will be using these modules on a day-to-day basis. Hence, it is a good idea to brainstorm this with your team before deciding on the approach.

- An infrastructure object may need multiple arguments to be passed before it can be provisioned. For example, an EC2 instance would need `ami-id`, `instance-type`, `keypair`, `security group`, and a number of other details. You will have to decide which of these arguments should be exposed to users and which ones to hide (and pass default values). Exposing all the arguments will make it difficult for the user to use the module. These arguments can be exposed to the users as input variables for which a user will pass the value. It is recommended to keep the input variables to a minimum.

- An infrastructure object created by the module can have multiple attributes as output. Are all these important for your requirements? You will have to decide which ones are required and expose them as outputs. These outputs can be consumed by other modules or the user who runs the code.

- Always have different modules for long-lived objects and short-lived objects, for example, VPC in AWS will be present for a long time, unlike application servers, which can be created and destroyed often. The same is true for the database servers, which should be around for a long time compared to a security group rule.

- If your organization allows it, share the module with the community via Terraform Registry. You will not only be helping the community but also helping yourself because the community shares feedback on bugs and new features that can be used to improve your module.

- Documenting the module is important as it helps the end user understand the purpose of the module and how to use the module. Documenting is done using the `README.md` file, which can be created either manually or using some automated tools. The following are some of the key details that will have to be present in the `README.md` file:

  - Resources created by the module

  - Example code usage

  - Inputs

  - Outputs

These are not exhaustive points but are key ones before you get started.

> **Note**
> terraform-docs is one of the tools used to generate documentation for modules. You may reference https://terraform-docs.io/ for more information.

Key Points to Consider While Using a Module

Whether you create a module yourself or use public modules, there are certain points you need to be aware of while using these. Though not exhaustive, the following points are a good starter:

- Modules call other modules using a module block.

- After adding or removing module blocks, you must run terraform init to enable Terraform to either download a module or delete a module.

- If you modify a module block, you will have to run terraform init –upgrade to enable Terraform to download the latest changes.

- When you are using a public module from Terraform Registry, go for verified modules unless there is not a verified module for your requirements. Verified modules are reviewed by HashiCorp for compatibility with the Terraform core. These modules also have active contributors from the providers (like AWS, GCP, and so on) to keep the module up to date. The verified badge appears next to modules that are published by a verified source. Public modules can be used in different ways:

  - You can download a whole module onto your filesystem and start referring to it from your root module. With this option, you will miss out on the latest updates of public modules.

  - You can directly refer to a public module in your root module.

  - You can create another abstraction and create a new module that refers to a public module. This newly created module is then called from the root module. This adds some flexibility and gives an option to add missing features.

Drawbacks of Modules

Though modules help in solving several problems, they also come with a few cons that you should be careful about. When you compare the pros and cons, the pros outweigh the cons by a huge margin, but still, you need to know about them. Even HashiCorp recommends using modules in moderation.

- When you start using module blocks, your configuration becomes hierarchical, where each module contains its own set of resources and could have its own child modules. This creates a deep, complex tree of resource configurations that make troubleshooting difficult.

- By default, Terraform downloads the latest version of the module from Terraform Registry. Over a period of time, you may end up having incompatibilities due to the untested version upgrade. You can avoid this issue by pinning the module to a certain version in the module block.

- Public modules are created to cover most generic use cases. If you have a use case that is very specific, you will either have to write your own module or create another abstraction (i.e., create another module) using the public module and make the required customizations. This customization helps when you want to add certain features but cannot modify the existing logic of a public module. If you need to do this, you will have to fork the code and modify it for your use case.

- Not every requirement needs a module; some use cases that need to be run only once are better done using resource blocks than writing a new module for them.

Summary

In this chapter, you learned about Terraform modules. Since there are multiple types of modules, it can be difficult to understand them without understanding the basics.

You started with a problem statement that the modules solve and then moved on to different ways of using modules.

With this understanding, you will be able to decide whether you should use a module or go for a one-time implementation via a resource block, create a module yourself, or use a public one, verify whether a public module is trustworthy to use, and so on.

Exam Readiness Drill – Chapter Review Questions

Apart from a solid understanding of key concepts, being able to think quickly under time pressure is a skill that will help you ace your certification exam. That is why working on these skills early on in your learning journey is key.

Chapter review questions are designed to improve your test-taking skills progressively with each chapter you learn and review your understanding of key concepts in the chapter at the same time. You'll find these at the end of each chapter.

> **How to Access these Resources**
>
> To learn how to access these resources, head over to the chapter titled *Chapter 11, Accessing the Online Practice Resources.*

To open the Chapter Review Questions for this chapter, perform the following steps:

1. Click the link – `https://packt.link/HCorp003Ch5.`

    Alternatively, you can scan the following **QR code** (*Figure 5.12*):

Figure 5.12 – QR code that opens Chapter Review Questions for logged-in users

2. Once you log in, you'll see a page similar to the one shown in *Figure 5.13*:

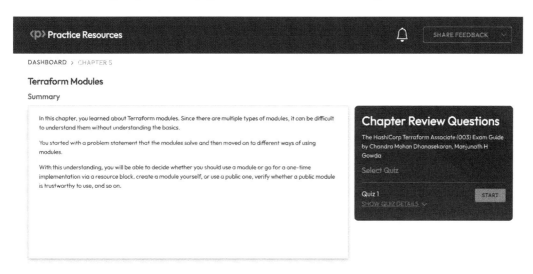

Figure 5.13 – Chapter Review Questions for Chapter 5

3. Once ready, start the following practice drills, re-attempting the quiz multiple times.

Exam Readiness Drill

For the first three attempts, don't worry about the time limit.

ATTEMPT 1

The first time, aim for at least **40%**. Look at the answers you got wrong and read the relevant sections in the chapter again to fix your learning gaps.

ATTEMPT 2

The second time, aim for at least **60%**. Look at the answers you got wrong and read the relevant sections in the chapter again to fix any remaining learning gaps.

ATTEMPT 3

The third time, aim for at least **75%**. Once you score 75% or more, you start working on your timing.

> **Tip**
>
> You may take more than **three** attempts to reach 75%. That's okay. Just review the relevant sections in the chapter till you get there.

Working On Timing

Target: Your aim is to keep the score the same while trying to answer these questions as quickly as possible. Here's an example of how your next attempts should look like:

Attempt	Score	Time Taken
Attempt 5	77%	21 mins 30 seconds
Attempt 6	78%	18 mins 34 seconds
Attempt 7	76%	14 mins 44 seconds

Table 5.1 – Sample timing practice drills on the online platform

> **Note**
>
> The time limits shown in the above table are just examples. Set your own time limits with each attempt based on the time limit of the quiz on the website.

With each new attempt, your score should stay above **75%** while your "time taken" to complete should "decrease". Repeat as many attempts as you want till you feel confident dealing with the time pressure.

6

Terraform Backends and Resource Management

Think of a scenario where you are part of a large enterprise-level DevOps team, primarily dealing with the provision of infrastructure resources from different cloud providers for multiple project teams. Your team maintains the Terraform configuration scripts and is responsible for end-to-end activities, such as state management and adding/updating resource attributes. There could be situations where you and your colleagues might have to collaborate and work on the same ticket, with the same set of configuration scripts.

This also means that everyone working on the same configuration needs to refer to the same state file. Terraform creates the state file and stores it locally with the `terraform.tfstate` filename by default. It is difficult to share the latest state file for every iteration within the team, and losing it completely due to workstation issues or an OS crash can be disastrous. This is where Terraform comes in, with the amazing idea of backends, which we will explore in the upcoming sections.

The exam objectives that will be covered in this chapter are as follows:

- Describe a default `local` backend
- Differentiate remote state backend options
- Describe a backend block and cloud integration in configuration

The high-level topics that will be covered in this chapter are as follows:

- Backend configuration
- Supported backends
- Resource addressing and dependencies
- Expressions and constraints

You can now proceed with the chapter, delving into backends and more.

What Are Backends?

Backends basically determine where a state file will be stored for a given configuration. Instead of locally, there are a couple of ways to use backend features:

- Integration with HCP Terraform

- Configuring the backend { } block to store the state file in a remote location

The Terraform paid offerings will be discussed in detail as part of *Chapter 9, Understanding HCP Terraform's Capabilities*. In this chapter, you will learn about remote backend configurations with supported backends and ways to configure them. The list of backends supported by Terraform will vary between different versions. Refer to the official documentation for the latest information. In the subsequent sections, you will cover the list of backends supported. The list is based on Terraform version 1.5.x at the time of writing.

Backend Configuration

As you have just seen, **backend configuration** can be done either using HCP Terraform or remote backend configuration, based on the type of backend we intend to use.

The backend configuration in both cases requires us to add the backend {} block to the configuration with the necessary parameters, which will be discussed in detail. Some of the backends will be used only to refer to the state file, and some might have advanced capabilities, such as state locking, that will help preserve the state file content when there is a possibility of simultaneous operations against the same state file.

If there is no explicit backend configuration, the default "local" backend will be used. The "local" backend does not need any parameters, and it simply stores the state file in the current working directory.

As per the Terraform 1.5.x documentation, the list of supported built-in backends is as follows:

- `local`

- `remote`

- `s3`

- `http`

- `Kubernetes`

- `azurerm`

- `consul`

- cos

- gcs

- oss

- pg

There were a few backends, such as `artifactory`, `etcd`, `etcdv3`, and `swift`, that were previously supported in Terraform versions prior to 1.3. So, it is always suggested to refer to the updated documentation for the list of backends that support the version you will use.

Configuring the backend {} Block

The `backend {}` block to configure the backend must be added as a nested block under the `terraform {}` block. A sample `backend {}` block looks like this:

```
terraform {
  backend "s3" {
    bucket = "tf-state-bucket-qu34y"
    key    = "dev/accounting/key"
    region = "us-east-1"
  }
}
```

In this example block, the `"s3"` label indicates the backend you are trying to use, and the parameter(s) inside the block is specific to this particular backend. This `"s3"` backend is useful when you want to store the state file in the bucket storage provided by AWS **Simple Storage Service (S3)**.

When using the remote backend configuration, Terraform stores the backend configuration settings inside `.terraform/terraform.tfstate` for the current working directory. This is also applicable when the plan is created via the `terraform plan` command, and it will ensure that the same backend settings will be used when the plan is actually applied.

Based on the type of remote backend, there could be situations where credentials need to be passed. This can be done in multiple ways:

- Directly specifying the credentials inside the `backend {}` block

- Using the `-backend-config` option in the `terraform init` command

- Using environment variables

- Out of these options, the use of environment variables is the preferred one because the credentials will not be stored in the state file, whereas using the two other options will result in storing the actual credentials in the state file, and that is risky.

- The backend configuration can also be changed at any time. After the changes, Terraform will automatically detect the changes, and you may be required to reinitialize based on the type of changes. A change could be the use of a completely new remote backend or switching back to the local backend from a remote one. When changing backends, Terraform also provides the option to migrate the existing state file to the new backend. However, it is always recommended to manually back up the current state file to a safe location before performing the migration.

There are a few limitations with `backend {}` blocks:

- Any terraform configuration can contain only one `backend {}` block
- Usually, the `cloud {}` block is used to configure the HCP Terraform, and if that is the case, the `backend {}` block cannot be used at the same time
- Input variables, `locals`, or data source attributes cannot be referred to in the `backend {}` block

Partial Configuration

In the previous section, the `path` parameter in the sample `backend {}` block is specified as `dev/accounting/key`, and this is where the remote state file will be stored. Assume that the value is not known at the time of writing the configuration and you want to keep that dynamic.

This means that it is possible to use the same configuration and the same backend, but there are parameters that can change based on the context. In such situations, Terraform allows us to write only the known parameters in the `backend {}` block and specify the dynamic parameters at the time of initialization. This capability is what you can call **partial configuration**.

With partial configuration, the following are the ways to specify the missing arguments:

- **File**: A file can be specified for the `-backend-config` option that will contain the arguments at the time of executing the `terraform init` command
- **Command key/value pairs**: The arguments can also be specified in the `-backend-config=KEY=VALUE` format to specify the arguments as part of the `init` command
- **Interactively**: If the previous options are not used, running the `terraform init` command only will prompt the user to enter the missing arguments in an interactive manner

It is also possible that there are no known arguments at the time of writing the configuration, and if so, an empty `backend {}` block can be specified:

```
terraform {
  backend "s3" {}
}
```

> **Note**
>
> If you are planning to use the configuration file option, the suggested naming convention is `*.backendname.tfbackend` as per the Terraform official documentation. Other names will not harm anything either.
>
> Valid examples could be `config.remote.tfbackend` or `config.http.tfbackend`.

Supported Backends

In this section, you will read about the list of supported backends and their actual usage. In most situations, you will stick to the type of backend that is closely associated with your system or application architecture and where it is currently deployed.

A few backends, such as "`s3`" and "`azurerm`", support a wide range of possible configurations that are specific to a cloud provider, but we will not cover every possibility and will stick to the scope of this book.

local

The "`local`" backend is the default option to store a state file when the remote backend is not configured. With this backend, the state file is stored in the local filesystem and the operations are performed locally.

A sample configuration for the local backend is given here:

```
terraform {
  backend "local" {
    path = "/path/to/terraform.tfstate"
  }
}
```

The "`local`" backend configuration accepts two parameters:

- `path`: The path to the location of the `terraform.tfstate` file. This is optional.
- `workspace_dir`: The path to the non-default workspaces. This is an optional parameter as well.
- Most commands, such as `terraform plan` and `terraform apply`, that work with the Terraform state file stored in the local backend accept the following command-line options to change the default behavior. However, they are not necessarily used in all scenarios:
- `-state=<FILENAME>`: Overrides the default state filename when the command intends to read the state file
- `-state-out=<FILENAME>`: Overrides the state filename with `FILENAME` when the command creates a new state file snapshot

- `-backup=<FILENAME>`: Overrides the default backup filename that the local backend will use to back up the state file

remote

The "`remote`" backend is special when compared to all the other available backends because it can support the default function, such as storing the state file, and also support remote operations, such as `plan` and `apply` with HCP Terraform.

HCP Terraform integration involves steps such as setting up workspaces, performing `terraform login` to log in to HCP Terraform, executing the `terraform plan` and `terraform apply` commands, and pointing to a remote workspace in HCP Terraform. You will look at the HCP Terraform configuration in a later chapter, but you should be aware of the `remote` backend capabilities in this section.

Another important consideration is that the HCP Terraform configuration can also be done using a `cloud {}` nested block inside the `terraform {}` block, and it's recommended to use it with the latest versions of Terraform because of its additional features.

This is a sample `remote` backend configuration:

```
terraform {
  backend "remote" {
    hostname = "app.terraform.io"
    organization = "mytestorg"
    workspaces {
      name = "payroll-dev"
    }
  }
}
```

Here, the label is set as `remote` to refer to the remote backend, and with HCP Terraform, the hostname will always be `app.terraform.io`, and the organization value will be set with the organization name defined in HCP Terraform.

This will refer to the `payroll-dev` remote workspace for the current configuration, and operations will affect the state file stored in this workspace.

You can now take a look at the configuration parameters in detail:

- `hostname`: The hostname for the remote backend to connect. This will default to `app.terraform.io` and is optional.

- `organization`: The name of the organization that contains the workspaces.

- `token`: The authentication token to connect to the host. This is optional. As per the Terraform documentation, using the token is not recommended, and instead, the `terraform login` command should be used before applying the configuration.

- `workspaces`: This block will have either `name` or `prefix`, which will help map the workspace to be used:

  - `name`: The `name` parameter can be used if we are going to work with a single HCP Terraform workspace, and a full workspace name can be specified.

  - `prefix`: The `prefix` parameter will help work with multiple workspaces, all with the same prefix, and you can switch the intended workspace with the `terraform workspace select` command.

- For example, if you have workspaces such as `billing-dev`, `billing-preprod`, and `billing-prod` for the same configuration, you can use the prefix value of `billing-` and the workspaces can be set dynamically.

- If you want to configure the remote backend with the configuration file rather than coding it directly, you can use the `-backend-config` option with `terraform init`. A sample config file is given here:

```
terraform {
   backend "remote" {}
}
```

Here is the config file content:

```
workspaces { name = "billing-test" }
hostname     = "app.terraform.io"
organization = "mytestorg"
```

s3

The "`s3`"backend is used to store the Terraform state file in the bucket created using Amazon **Simple Storage Service** (**S3**). This backend supports a state-locking feature with Amazon DynamoDB. It is optional. The S3 bucket and the DynamoDB table should exist already to use this backend, and one table can be used to lock multiple remote state files.

The recommendation with this backend is that the `S3 versioning` option should be enabled before using it with Terraform so that you can track the changes later, and you will retain the snapshots every time the state file is updated.

Here's a sample configuration:

```
terraform {
  backend "s3" {
    bucket = "my-tf-bucket-789ew"
    key    = "dev/acc/infra"
    region = "us-east-1"
  }
}
```

The credentials that have access to the bucket can be passed with the environment variable option, so it is not exposed in the configuration. There are AWS-specific IAM permissions to provide access to the S3 bucket and DynamoDB table, and those need to be mapped to the credentials before using them with Terraform.

The most common configuration parameters supported by the "s3" backend are given here:

- bucket: The name of the S3 bucket.
- key: The path in the bucket where the state file will be stored.
- dynamodb_table: The name of the DynamoDB table to be used.
- region: The AWS Region of the S3 bucket and the DynamoDB table that is applicable, which is required.
- access_key and secret_key: The AWS credentials to be used to access the bucket and the table. If these parameters are not set, the shared credentials file will be used.
- profile: The name of the profile to be used from the AWS shared credentials file.
- shared_credentials_file: The path location of the shared credentials file.
- endpoint: The custom endpoint of the S3 API.
- dynamodb_endpoint: The custom endpoint of the DynamoDB API.
- iam_endpoint: The custom endpoint of the AWS IAM API.
- sts_endpoint: The custom endpoint to retrieve the STS token from AWS **Security Token Service (STS)**.
- token: The session token to be passed if the temporary credentials option is used.

Some of the other supported parameters are as follows:

- acl
- encrypt
- force_path_style

- `kms_key_id`

- `sse_customer_key`

- `workspace_key_prefix`

This backend also supports the `Assume Role` option, where the AWS IAM role can be used in place of long-lived credentials with access. The environment variables option also can be used for most parameters discussed in this section, and the official documentation can be referred to for a complete list.

http

The "`http`" backend is used to store a state file via a REST client, and this supports state locking and unlocking.

When using the HTTP endpoint for this type of backend, there are a few requirements:

- The state file will be fetched with the `GET` method.

- The state file will be updated with the `POST` method.

- The state file will be deleted with the `DELETE` method.

- The valid HTTP status codes acceptable are as follows:

  - `423` – locked or `409` – a conflict when the state file is locked

  - `200` for success

A sample "`http`" backend configuration would look like this:

```
terraform {
  backend "http" {
    address = "http://myhttp-server.com/state"
    lock_address = "http://myhttp-server.com/lock"
    unlock_address = "http://myhttp-server.com/unlock"
  }
}
```

The following are the most common configuration parameters supported by the "`http`" backend:

- `address`: The address of the HTTP backend endpoint. This is a mandatory parameter.

- `update_method`: The HTTP method to be used to update the state file. The default value is `POST`.

- `lock_address` and `unlock_address`: The address for the state locking and unlocking, respectively.

- lock_method and unlock_method: The HTTP methods to use for locking and unlocking, respectively. The default values are LOCK and UNLOCK.

- username and password: The parameters to be used for HTTP basic authentication.

- Some other parameters supported are listed as follows – they will be discussed only in brief because they are outside the scope of this book:

- skip_cert_verification (flag to indicate whether the Transport Layer Security (TLS) verification should be skipped or not and the default value is false)

- retry_max (the maximum count of retries with a default value of two)

- retry_wait_min and retry_wait_max (the wait time between a retry – the default values are 1 and 30 seconds, respectively)

- The parameters for mutual TLS authentication:

  - client_certificate_pem

  - client_private_key_pem

  - client_ca_certificate_pem

Environment Variable Support

- All the preceding parameters can also be set with environment variables. The convention is TF_HTTP_ appended before the parameter. The parameter name should be uppercase.

- For example, the equivalent environment variable for the lock_method parameter is TF_HTTP_LOCK_METHOD.

pg

The word "pg" is an abbreviated version of **Postgres**, and this backend supports storing the state file in a Postgres relational table. The requirement to use it with Terraform is that the database version must be 10 or above.

This backend type also supports state locking via Postgres's native way, where the state file locks are automatically released when a connection is not active or aborted. The force-unlock command with LOCK_ID is not supported.

Here is a sample configuration:

```
terraform {
  backend "pg" {
    conn_str = "postgres://user:pass@my-tf-db.com/tf_backend"
  }
}
```

Here, the credentials along with the database address are provided in the connection string format. Another alternative could be setting the credentials in the environment variables, such as PGUSER and PGPASSWORD, and just using the database address as a value for CONN_STR.

The database must exist already before using this backend in the configuration. If using partial configuration or an empty pg {} block, the Postgres-supported environment variables can be used to pass the required values.

With this backend, Terraform will try to create a table called states, and each entry in this table will be mapped to the unique workspace we use. If no workspaces are used, the entry will be made with the default value.

The following are the parameters supported by this backend:

- conn_str: The connection string to connect with the postgres://<URL> format.

- schema_name: The name of the schema that will be managed by Terraform to track the state information. If not specified, the default value is terraform_remote_state. The ones given as follows are self-explanatory and can be used when you have a database managed by admin already:

  - skip_schema_creation

  - skip_table_creation

  - skip_index_creation

Environment Variable Support

This backend also supports using environment variables, and the convention is to append PG_ before the parameter. The parameter name should be uppercase.

For example, the equivalent environment variable for the connection string conn_str parameter is PG_CONN_STR.

Kubernetes

Kubernetes is a container orchestration tool that manages containers in the form of clusters, with features such as autoscaling, service discovery, load balancing, and automatic rollouts. This tool has become very popular recently because of its various capabilities and is widely used across different industries in various domains.

The "kubernetes" backend is also supported by Terraform and can manage the state with **Kubernetes Secrets**. This also supports state locking, but the restriction is that the **Secret** cannot be larger than 1 MB in size.

State locking is supported by provisioning a **Lease** resource in the given namespace.

This backend supports more than one way of doing configuration:

- Using `config_paths` or `config_path`
- Using `in_cluster_config`

If the configuration has both `in_cluster_config` or `config_paths` and `config_path`, `config_path` will take precedence.

The environment variables are different from the configuration parameters. Refer to the official Terraform documentation if you are opting to use environment variables.

A sample configuration block for the Kubernetes backend is given here:

```
terraform {
  backend "kubernetes" {
    secret_suffix    = "state"
    config_path      = "~/.kube/config"
  }
}
```

Here, the `config_path` option is used, and it points to the location of the `kubeconfig` file. `secret_suffix` is used when creating secrets in Kubernetes, with the naming convention `tfstate-{workspace-name}-secret_suffix`.

The following parameters are supported by this backend, and in most cases, a service account with `config_path` will do the job:

- `secret_suffix`: The suffix to be used while creating secrets.
- `labels`: The set of labels to be applied for a secret and the lease resource.
- `namespace`: The namespace to store the secret and the lease.
- `in_cluster_config`: If the authentication has to be done from one of the Pods already running in the Kubernetes cluster, this can be used.
- `config_path`: The path to the location of the `kubeconfig` file.
- `config_paths`: The list of paths to the `kubeconfig` files.
- `host`: The name of the Kubernetes master host. The default is `https://localhost`.
- `username` and `password`: The username and password to be used for HTTP basic authentication.
- `insecure`: A flag to indicate whether the connection should be tried without validating the TLS certificate.

- `client_certificate`, `client_key`, and `client_ca_certificate`: Parameters to be used for TLS authentication.

- `config_context`, `config_context_auth_info`, and `config_context_cluster`: The parameters to be used while picking specific context within a `kubeconfig` file that has more than one cluster config.

- `token`: The authentication token to be used for the service account.

- `exec`: The configuration block to use an exec-based credential plugin that will provide user credentials for authentication. The subparameters valid inside the `exec` block are listed here:

  - `api_version`: The API version to decode the user credentials

  - `command`: The command to execute

  - `args`: The list of arguments to pass

  - `env`: The list of environment variables to set for plugin execution

Consul

Consul is another offering from HashiCorp that primarily helps enterprises secure their applications running in production with identity-based networking policies. For example, a multinational financial company can choose to control the infrastructure access based on an employee's identity or role, the team, and the business unit or function, and that can be set up using Consul. This backend also enables other prominent features such as secure networking between applications, automated networking, and service discovery.

The "`consul`" backend manages the state information with the key-value store supported by Consul (commonly known as the Consul KV store).

Even here, the environment variables are different from the backend block configuration parameters. Refer to the official documentation for this backend.

Here is a sample configuration block for the "`consul`" backend:

```
terraform {
  backend "consul" {
    address = "myconsul.server.com"
    scheme  = "https"
    path    = "test/secret"
  }
}
```

The configuration parameters supported are as follows:

- `address`: The DNS name of the Consul server to use
- `scheme`: The type of HTTP protocol (HTTP/HTTPS) to use to connect to the server
- `path`: The path to the key-value store
- `access_token`: The access token
- `http_auth`: Credentials in the format of `user` or `user:password` to be used for authentication
- `gzip`: A flag to indicate whether the state file should be compressed using `gzip` or not
- `datacenter`: The data center to use for the connection
- `lock`: The flag to indicate the state locking – the default value is `true`
- `ca_file`, `cert_file`, and `key_file`: The parameters to use for the TLS authentication when applicable

azurerm

With the "`azurerm`" backend, you can manage the state file in Blob Storage provided by Azure, and state locking is supported natively.

This backend has multiple options to configure the backend block, but we will look at the most commonly used one in the following sample configuration:

```
terraform {
  backend "azurerm" {
    resource_group_name   = "Acc-ResourceGrp"
    storage_account_name  = "AzureAcctTest"
    container_name        = "tfstate"
    key                   = "prod.tfstate"
  }
}
```

The following configuration options are supported:

- `storage_account_name`: The name of the storage account.
- `container_name`: The name of the container within the storage account.
- `key`: The name of the Terraform state file inside the storage container. This is a mandatory parameter.
- `environment`: The possible values are `"public"`, `"china"`, `"german"`, `"stack"`, and `"usgovernment"`. The default value is `"public"`.
- `endpoint`: The custom endpoint for Azure Resource Manager.

- `metadata_host`: The hostname of the Azure Instance Metadata Service.

- `snapshot`: A flag to decide whether the state file snapshot has to be created before using it. The default value is `false`.

- Refer to the official Terraform documentation for more configuration options with this backend.

COS

The "`cos`" backend is used to store the state file in the **Cloud Object Storage** service provided by Tencent Cloud. The service is very similar to the S3 service provided by AWS.

This supports state locking. The bucket is expected to already exist to store the state file.

A sample configuration looks like the following:

```
terraform {
  backend "cos" {
    region = "ap-hongkong"
    bucket = "tf-bucket-yyitr"
    prefix = "terraform/state"
  }
}
```

The following configuration options are supported:

- `region`: The name of the region where the bucket is created.

- `bucket`: The bucket name to store the state file.

- `prefix`: The directory to store the state file inside the bucket.

- `key`: The file key or name for the state file. If not provided, it defaults to "`terraform.tfstate`".

- `secret_id` & `secret_key`: The credentials to access the bucket.

- `security_token`: The temporary credentials in the form of a token for bucket access.

- `encrypt`: This indicates whether the server-side encryption should be enabled or not.

- `acl`: The **access control lists** (**ACLs**) to be applied for the state file.

- `accelerate`: This indicates whether to enable global acceleration.

- This backend also supports authentication with the "`Assume Role`" option, where the role can be used for bucket access instead of supplying credentials, and the following options can be used to do the same inside the `assume_role` {} block:

- `role_arn`

- `session_name`
- `session_duration`
- `policy`

Here's an example configuration:

```
terraform {
  backend "cos" {
    region = "ap-hongkong"
    bucket = "tf-state-bucket-tpluy"
    prefix = "terraform/state"
    assume_role {
      role_arn = "qcs::cam::uin/xxx:roleName/yyy"
      session_name = "my-session-name"
      session_duration = 3600
    }
  }
}
```

Environment Variable Support

This backend also supports using the environment variables, and the convention is `"TENCENTCLOUD_"` appended before the parameter. The parameter name should be in uppercase.

For example, the equivalent environment variable for the `"region"` region parameter is `TENCENTCLOUD_REGION`.

gcs

If you use **Google Cloud Platform** (**GCP**) for your application hosting and deployment and plan to use Terraform, the "`gcs`" backend is the right option, as it provides backend support for state file storage in buckets created using the **Google Cloud Storage** (**GCS**) service.

A sample configuration is given here for reference:

```
terraform {
  backend "gcs" {
    bucket  = "terraform-state-bucket-ytr51"
    prefix  = "terraform/state"
  }
}
```

The Google account credentials that Terraform will use have to be set up properly with bucket access to manage the state files stored inside.

Take a look at the configuration parameters supported by this backend:

- `bucket`: The name of the GCS bucket to store the state file. This is a mandatory parameter.

- `credentials`: The path to the Google account credentials in the JSON format. If this parameter is not set, the application default credentials will be fetched from the default location if available.

- `prefix`: The prefix inside the bucket to store the state file.

- `access_token`: The OAuth token to pass for authorization. This is an alternative to the `credentials` option.

- `impersonate_service_account`: The service account to be used to access the GCS bucket.

- `impersonate_service_account_delegates`: Used in conjunction with the previous parameter if a delegation chain is used. This is specific to GCP.

- `encryption_key` & `kms_encryption_key`: The parameters to pass the customer-supplied encryption keys and customer-managed encryption keys to encrypt the bucket contents.

- The environment variables are different from the configuration parameters; refer to the official Terraform documentation if you are opting to use environment variables.

oss

The "`oss`" backend is used to store the state file in the Object Storage Service provided by Alibaba Cloud. It supports state locking with the OTS TableStore feature.

A sample configuration looks like the one here:

```
terraform {
  backend "oss" {
    bucket = "bucket-for-tf-state"
    prefix   = "tf/prod/statefile"
    region = "cn-beijing"
    tablestore_endpoint = "https://terraform-remote.cn-hangzhou.ots.
aliyuncs.com"
    tablestore_table = "statelock"
  }
}
```

The following configuration options are supported:

- `region`: The name of the region where the bucket is created.

- `bucket`: The bucket name to store the state file.

- `prefix`: The directory to store the state file inside the bucket.

- key: The file key or name of the state file.

- access_key and secret_key: The credentials to access the bucket.

- security_token: The temporary credentials in the form of a token for bucket access.

- endpoint: The custom endpoint to access the OSS API.

- encrypt: Indicates whether server-side encryption should be enabled or not.

- acl: The ACLs to be applied to the state file.

- shared_credentials_file: The path location of the shared credentials file.

- profile: The profile name in the shared credentials file to be used.

- ecs_role_name: The RAM role name to be used for API operations if applicable.

- tablestore_endpoint and tablestore_table: The parameters to set if the state locking feature is used.

This backend also supports authentication with the Assume Role option where the role can be used for bucket access instead of supplying credentials, and the following options can be used to do the same inside the assume_role {} block:

- assume_role_role_arn

- assume_role_policy

- assume_role_session_name

- assume_role_session_expiration

Resource Addressing and Dependencies

Now that you have seen the backends supported by Terraform, you can delve deeper into resource addressing and how to set and handle resource dependencies while you manage them with the state file.

Resource Addressing

When you write Terraform configuration scripts, they primarily consist of multiple resources that will support the overall infrastructure you try to deploy. So, it becomes necessary to refer to a particular resource or a set of resources, manipulating or recreating them if there are any issues.

This is where resource addressing becomes vital, and any resource address will consist of two parts:

- The module path

- Resource specifications

Resource specifications may not always be needed. If you would like to refer to all the resources created by a particular module, specifying the module path will suffice. You can read about each one of them in detail now.

Module Path

If there are multiple modules within the configuration, the module path will refer to the particular module, and if there are multiple module calls, it will refer to the particular instance.

The syntax is as follows:

```
module.module_name[module_index]
```

Here, the module keyword is static, and it is then followed by the module name. module_index is optional.

Resource Specifications

Similar to the module path, resource specifications also have three parts – resource_type, resource_name, and instance_index.

The syntax is as follows:

```
resource_type.resource_name[instance_index]
```

The resource type is the type of resource being provisioned, and resource_name is the user-defined value for the resource block. If there are multiple instances of the resource, instance_index will be used to refer to the particular instance.

For example, the Terraform configuration consists of a module with the name compute. It provisions the AWS EC2 instance with the resource name testinstance and the count parameter is set to 4.

Then, the first and third individual instances can be referred to as follows:

```
module.compute.aws_instance.testinstance[1]
module.compute.aws_instance.testinstance[3]
```

Addressing Resources with the for_each {} Block

There are possible scenarios where multiple instances of the same resource type are provisioned with the for_each block. If so, the resource address will slightly vary, with the index as the alphanumeric key. The following example will help you to better understand this.

Consider the following `resource` block:

```
resource "aws_instance" "web" {
  for_each = {
    "dev": "testinstance",
    "prod":  "prodinstance"
  }
}
```

In this case, the resource address will be based on the key inside the `for_each` block:

```
aws_instance.web["dev"]
aws_instance.web["prod"]
```

Resource Dependencies

With Terraform, the default behavior when applying the configuration is that the resources will be created in parallel. If some of the `resource` attributes are referenced in another `resource` block, Terraform will infer the dependency and ensure that the latter resource is created only after the prerequisite resource is provisioned successfully. This is known as **implicit dependency**.

This will work most of the time, but sometimes, Terraform will not be able to infer the dependencies on its own, and you need to explicitly specify the dependency with the `depends_on` argument.

Implicit Dependency

Take a look at how the implicit dependency approach works with this sample configuration:

```
provider "aws" {
  region = "us-east-1"
}
# Uncomment the below resource block to create default VPC with the
below command.
# terraform apply -target="aws_default_vpc.default"
#
# resource "aws_default_vpc" "default" {
#   tags = {
#     Name = "default-vpc"
#   }
#}

resource "aws_instance" "testinstance" {
  ami           = "ami-0cb06ac50a7eea4f2"
  instance_type = "t3.micro"
}
```

```
resource "aws_eip" "ip" {
  instance = aws_instance.testinstance.id
}
```

If you look at the configuration carefully, you can see that the `instance` attribute inside the `aws_eip` resource type block refers to the instance ID of the EC2 instance created in the same configuration.

In this case, the implicit dependency comes into effect, and Terraform will automatically wait for the EC2 instance to be created first and then assign the elastic IP address, as shown in *Figure 6.1*.

```
Do you want to perform these actions?
  Terraform will perform the actions described above.
  Only 'yes' will be accepted to approve.

  Enter a value: yes

aws_instance.testinstance: Still creating... [10s elapsed]
aws_instance.testinstance: Creation complete after 17s [id=i-                16]
aws_eip.ip: Creating...
aws_eip.ip: Creation complete after 4s [id=eipalloc-              c9]
```

Figure 6.1 – The terraform apply output – the implicit dependency

Explicit Dependency

As highlighted at the beginning of this section, an explicit dependency can be set with the `depends_on` argument inside the `resource` block.

To understand this, assume that you have an EC2 instance and your application is hosted inside the instance that internally uses an S3 bucket as part of the functionality. This dependency cannot be handled by Terraform, and hence, you can set the dependency explicitly that the S3 bucket has to be created first and then provision the EC2 instance to deploy the application.

In the following example, you can see that the `depends_on` argument is set for the EC2 instance `resource` block:

```
provider "aws" {
  region = "us-east-1"
}
#creates a S3 bucket with random name
resource "aws_s3_bucket" "appbucket" {}
resource "aws_instance" "testinstance" {
```

```
   ami              = "ami-0cb06ac50a7eea4f2"
   instance_type = "t3.micro"
   depends_on       = [aws_s3_bucket.appbucket]
}
```

When you apply the preceding configuration, you can see that the EC2 instance creation will wait for the S3 bucket because of the explicit dependency you added, as shown in *Figure 6.2*.

```
Plan: 2 to add, 0 to change, 0 to destroy.
aws_s3_bucket.appbucket: Creating...
aws_s3_bucket.appbucket: Creation complete after 7s [id=terraform-
aws_instance.testinstance: Creating...
aws_instance.testinstance: Still creating... [10s elapsed]
aws_instance.testinstance: Creation complete after 17s [id=i-
```

Figure 6.2 – The terraform apply output – the explicit dependency

Expressions and Constraints

In Terraform, expressions are computed values within the configuration. Terraform has rich support for different types of expressions, such as a reference to a data source, arithmetic evaluation, complex types, and built-in functions.

However, there are a few restrictions on the usage of an expression in specific places. For example, it is not allowed within the backend {} block. The official documentation of the Terraform language clearly indicates the scenarios where it can be used and cases where it is not applicable.

Data Types

The result of any expression is a value. Suppose that there is an expression such as 2 + 3; it will result in 5, which is the value.

In Terraform, there are different types of values supported, as follows:

- string: Any sequence of characters such as Hi, BobWilliams , or dev-team can be represented with this type.

- number: This can be used to represent numerical values such as 6 and 10.2 (both decimal numbers and fractional values).

- bool: A Boolean value – the possible values are true and false.

- list or tuple: A sequence of values enclosed within square brackets. Each item can be referenced by its index – for example, ["test", "dev", "prod"].

- set: A collection of unique values that do not have an index.

- `map` or `object`: A group of values with named labels – for example, `{ "environment" = "dev", "department" = "accounting" }`.

- `null`: This type represents the absence of a value, and if any attribute is set to `null`, Terraform will ignore it.

Data types such as `string`, `number`, and `bool` are termed **primitive types**, whereas `list`, `set`, and `map` are **complex types**.

Operators

An operator is another type of expression that works on one or more expressions to produce a result.

In Terraform, the following are the different types of operators supported:

- Arithmetic operators:

  - `+`: Addition

  - `-`: Subtraction

  - `*`: Multiplication

  - `/`: Division

  - `%`: The remainder operator

  - `-`: The negation operator when used with a single expression

- Logical operators:

  - `||`: The OR operator

  - `&&` The AND operator

  - `!`: The NOT operator

- Equality operators:

  - `==`: Returns `true` if the expressions are both equal and `false` if not equal

  - `!=`: Opposite of the `==` operator function

- Comparison operators:

  - `<`: Less than

  - `<=`: Less than or equal to

  - `>`: Greater than

  - `>=`: Greater than or equal to

Conditional Expressions

A conditional expression uses the Boolean result of an expression to choose between two values. A simple example would be wanting to return a `pass` or `fail` value based on the Boolean result of an evaluating mark.

The syntax is as follows:

```
condition ? value_if_true : value_if_false
```

If the condition is `true`, `value_if_true` will be returned, and if `false`, then `value_if_false` will be returned.

A requirement with conditional expressions is that both the return values should be of the same type, so Terraform will know what type of value will be returned without knowing the condition.

for Expressions

`for` expressions create the `complex type` value by transforming another complex type. The syntax is given here:

```
for <element> in <complex_type> : <expression>
```

Here, `element` refers to the individual element in the input complex type, and the expression on the right-hand side will create the new complex type. The resulting complex type depends on the enclosing brackets that contain the `for` expression.

If the `for` expression is enclosed in [ ] (square brackets), the new complex type will be a list. If it is ( ), it will create a set, and so on.

Here is an example:

```
vowel_list = ["a", "e", "i", "o", "u"]
{for item in vowel_list : item => index(vowel_list, item)}
```

The preceding example will create a map, with the key as the item in `vowel_list` and its position as the value.

splat Expressions

A `splat` expression is very similar to the `for` expression, but the only difference is the representation, and this is a more concise way to refer to all the elements in the input type.

Consider this example variable object that has two elements, and each has the `"id"` attribute:

```
obj_list=[{"id" = 1, "name" = "a"}, {"id" = 2, "name" = "b"}]
```

To retrieve only the id attribute from both elements, the following `for` expression can be used:

```
[for obj in  object_list : obj.id]
```

The `splat` expression can also be used in this case, and the syntax would be as follows:

```
var.obj_list[*].id
```

> **Note**
> The `splat` expression is applicable only to lists, sets, and tuples.

Type Constraints

We have already discussed the different data types to use in Terraform, and we will now look at the constraints applicable to them.

Automatic type conversion is applicable in Terraform, meaning a number or Boolean value can be automatically converted to `string` if needed.

`list` and `tuple` are similar, but `tuple` can contain different types of elements and `list` has elements of the same type:

- `["a", "b", "c"]:list`
- `["a", 1, true]:luple`

The any Type

There is also a special type called `any` that a developer can use as a placeholder if the variable type has not been decided upon yet. This type skips setting the right type and is not a recommended solution.

Here is an example:

```
variable "test_variable" {
  type = any
}
```

"*optional*"

When using complex types, you can set some attributes as "`optional`", and this will help when the user does not provide a value for the attribute. If the "`optional`" setting is not used, Terraform will throw an error.

If `default_value` is not set when using the `optional` modifier, Terraform will use `null`.

Here is the syntax:

```
optional(type, default_value)
```

Here is an example:

```
variable "optional_var_object" {
  type = object({
    name = string              # a required attribute
    age = number               # a required attribute
    birthplace = optional(string)# an optional attribute
  })
}
```

Version Constraints

Version constraints are helpful when you want to use specific versions of a module or a provider within your configuration, preventing the automatic use of newer versions in the future.

This can also be used in the `terraform {}` block to restrict the Terraform version that should be used to apply the configuration.

Here is the syntax:

```
version = "<condition>"
```

The condition has different variations with the operators used, and some of the examples are listed here:

- Only the exact version is allowed, and no other version can be accepted:

  ```
  version = "5.38.0"
  ```

- Not the specified version, but other versions can be used:

  ```
  version = "!= 3.14.0"
  ```

- The version can be in the range of specified version(s):

```
version = "> 2.1.0"
version = "< 5.1.0"
version = ">= 1.2.0, < 2.0.0"
```

- The last portion of the version can only increase:

```
version = "~> 2.1.0"
```

In the preceding example, Terraform will accept versions such as 2.1.1 and 2.1.2, but it will not use versions such as 2.0.0 and 2.2.0.

If Terraform does not have the acceptable versions, it will try to download the newest version as per the specified constraints. Also, if the acceptable version cannot be downloaded, Terraform will not allow for `plan` and `apply` operations.

Summary

In this chapter, you learned about the backend configuration syntax, and then you followed this up by reading about valid backends supported by Terraform and how to configure them with the limitations. Resource addressing and the concept of implicit and explicit dependency were also discussed. Finally, different types of expressions such as `splat` expressions and `for` expressions were looked at, with examples.

A backend configuration for any production-grade configuration script will help teams store the state file securely and interact with it in multiple executions, without any conflict. This is where Terraform stands out from other tools.

Exam Readiness Drill – Chapter Review Questions

Apart from a solid understanding of key concepts, being able to think quickly under time pressure is a skill that will help you ace your certification exam. That is why working on these skills early on in your learning journey is key.

Chapter review questions are designed to improve your test-taking skills progressively with each chapter you learn and review your understanding of key concepts in the chapter at the same time. You'll find these at the end of each chapter.

> **How to Access these Resources**
>
> To learn how to access these resources, head over to the chapter titled *Chapter 11, Accessing the Online Practice Resources*.

To open the Chapter Review Questions for this chapter, perform the following steps:

1. Click the link – `https://packt.link/HCorp003Ch6`.

   Alternatively, you can scan the following **QR code** (*Figure 6.3*):

Figure 6.3 – QR code that opens Chapter Review Questions for logged-in users

2. Once you log in, you'll see a page similar to the one shown in *Figure 6.4*:

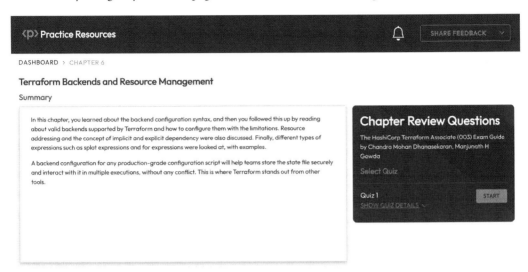

Figure 6.4 – Chapter Review Questions for Chapter 6

3. Once ready, start the following practice drills, re-attempting the quiz multiple times.

Exam Readiness Drill

For the first three attempts, don't worry about the time limit.

ATTEMPT 1

The first time, aim for at least **40%**. Look at the answers you got wrong and read the relevant sections in the chapter again to fix your learning gaps.

ATTEMPT 2

The second time, aim for at least **60%**. Look at the answers you got wrong and read the relevant sections in the chapter again to fix any remaining learning gaps.

ATTEMPT 3

The third time, aim for at least **75%**. Once you score 75% or more, you start working on your timing.

> **Tip**
>
> You may take more than **three** attempts to reach 75%. That's okay. Just review the relevant sections in the chapter till you get there.

Working On Timing

Target: Your aim is to keep the score the same while trying to answer these questions as quickly as possible. Here's an example of how your next attempts should look like:

Attempt	Score	Time Taken
Attempt 5	77%	21 mins 30 seconds
Attempt 6	78%	18 mins 34 seconds
Attempt 7	76%	14 mins 44 seconds

Table 6.1 – Sample timing practice drills on the online platform

> **Note**
>
> The time limits shown in the above table are just examples. Set your own time limits with each attempt based on the time limit of the quiz on the website.

With each new attempt, your score should stay above **75%** while your "time taken" to complete should "decrease". Repeat as many attempts as you want till you feel confident dealing with the time pressure.

7

Debugging and Troubleshooting Terraform

When Terraform fails or does not work as expected, how do you figure out what is wrong? Is it a configuration issue or is it the wrong version? Is it the authentication that is creating an issue or is the problem something else entirely?

This chapter talks about the issues you generally face while managing Terraform and how to either avoid, debug, or fix them.

The focus here will be on the general errors you might receive across key areas of Terraform and what steps need to be taken to resolve them. The following types of issues will be covered in the chapter:

- Configuration errors
- Variable-related issues
- State-related issues
- Core and provider errors
- Module-related issues
- Bug reporting
- Gotchas

Configuration Errors

Terraform configuration is defined in the **Hashicorp Configuration Language** (**HCL**), which is interpreted by Terraform Core.

When Terraform core processes the configuration files and finds an error, it will throw an error with additional information about the error along with the line number where it found the problem. These could be interpolation errors or malformed resource definitions.

The following example code shows a configuration error where a variable has not been defined but is being referred to in the code:

```
provider "aws" {
   region = "ap-south-1"
}

resource "aws_instance" "test" {
   ami                 = "ami-026255a2746f88074"
   availability_zone = "ap-south-1a"
   instance_type       = var.instance_type

   tags = {
     Name = "Test-EC2"
   }
}


~/terraform-troubleshoot:terraform plan
Error: Reference to undeclared input variable
on main.tf line 8, in resource "aws_instance" "test":
8:    instance_type       = var.instance_type
An input variable with the name "instance_type" has not been declared.
This variable can be declared with a variable "instance_type" {}
block.
```

In the preceding error message, you can clearly see the reference to the undeclared variable on line 8. At times, you will come across problems where there is no configuration issue but, still, the resource/resource's attribute that gets created is not the one you expected. The following section talks about one of the reasons for issues such as this.

override.tf File-Related Issues

The override.tf file is used very rarely in the production setup. It overrides specific portions of an existing configuration object that has been defined in the main configuration files.

The code defined in the following appserver.tf file is used to create an EC2 instance of the t3.small instance type. In this code, instance_type is an attribute that defines the type of EC2 instance to be created.

However, this attribute is overwritten by the code defined in the override.tf file and the instance type is changed to c5.large.

The `appserver.tf` file has the following code (truncated):

```
resource "aws_instance" "appserver" {
  instance_type = "t3.small"
}
```

The `override.tf` file has the following code:

```
resource "aws_instance" "appserver" {
  instance_type = "c5.large"
}
```

The final code executed by Terraform core will have the following code. Please note that this code is given for reference and you will not see this in any configuration file:

```
resource "aws_instance" "appserver" {
  instance_type = "c5.large"
}
```

As you can see, the instance type defined in the `aws_instance` resource block has changed from `t3.small` to `c5.large`. If you do not know about the presence of the `override.tf` file, you will not be able to understand why Terraform is creating the wrong instance type.

terraform validate

`terraform validate` can help solve the basic syntax issue in configuration files present in the current working directory. It checks whether the code in the configuration file is syntactically valid and the correctness of the attribute and values of the resource defined in the configuration file. Please note that it only refers to the configuration, does not access any remote services such as remote state or provider APIs, and requires an initialized working directory with any referenced plugins and modules installed. Terraform does not continue validating once it catches an error.

The following example shows the code used to launch an EC2 instance. However, it will throw an error when you run `terraform validate` since `instance_types` is not a valid attribute of the `aws_instance` resource:

```
provider "aws" {
  region = "ap-south-1"
}

resource "aws_instance" "test" {
  ami                = "ami-026255a2746f88074"
  availability_zone  = "ap-south-1a"
  instance_types     = "t3.micro"
```

```
  tags = {
    Name = "Test-EC2",
  }
}
terraform-troubleshoot:terraform validate
Error: Unsupported argument
    on main.tf line 8, in resource "aws_instance" "test":
    8:    instance_types      = "t3.micro"
  An argument named "instance_types" is not expected here. Did you
mean "instance_type"?
```

Variable-Related Issues

Variable-related errors are some of the most common errors you will find while working with Terraform. In the following sections, you will see the errors related to the variable type constraint, variable input validation, and variable precedence.

Type Constraint

- One of the issues you might come across while managing Terraform is incorrect input variable values that cause failures during `terraform run`.

- You can use the `type` argument in the variable block to restrict the type of the value accepted for the variable.

- An example is if the total number of instances to be launched by Terraform is controlled by the `ec2-count` variable, which is expecting a number, but the user inputs the string `Two` instead of the number 2. Terraform runs would fail in this case.

Input Validation

- At times, even though the value of the type matches the variable, it may not be in the format that is expected. For such use cases, you can use the `validation` option in the input variables as a proactive measure to prevent issues.

- This feature is supported in Terraform version 0.13 and above.

- You can specify custom validation rules for a particular variable by adding a `validation` block within the corresponding `variable` block. The following example checks whether the AMI ID has the correct syntax:

```
variable "image_id" {
    type        = string
    description = "The id of the machine image (AMI) to use for
    the server."
```

```
   validation {
      condition     = length(var.image_id) > 4 && substr(var.
   image_id, 0, 4) == "ami-"
      error_message = "The image_id value must be a valid AMI id,
   starting with \"ami-\"."
   }
}
```

- The following conditions are checked by the `validation` condition in the `variable` block. All the conditions need to evaluate to TRUE to pass the validation:

- The `length` function is used to determine the length of a string/map/list. In this code, it is used to determine the length of the `image_id` variable and then the `>` comparison operator is used to check whether this length is greater than 4.

- The `substr` function is used to extract a substring from a given string. In this code, it will extract the first four characters of the `image_id` variable (i.e., `image_id`) by offset (from the zero index) and maximum (the total characters to be selected) length and use the equality operator, `==`, to compare whether the value returned is equal to `ami-`: `substr (var. image_id, 0, 4) == ami-`.

- Finally, when the user inputs the value for the `image_id` variable, both conditions explained in the previous two points will be checked and the validation will pass only if both conditions return TRUE. Otherwise, the user will get an error message: `"The image_id value must be a valid AMI id, starting with ami-"`.

- Depending on your requirement, you can add the validation either for all your variables or the ones that are prone to wrong input from the users.

Variable Precedence

- At times, you will see that the variable has a different value than what you have defined. This is most prevalent during the authentication with cloud providers since there are multiple places from which the credentials can be taken.

- A variable's value can be defined at multiple places such as the command line, environment variable, `tfvars` files, and so on. If the variable is given different values in different places, Terraform picks only one value of the variable, and this value is dependent on the variable precedence. Terraform loads variables in the following order, with later sources taking precedence over earlier ones:

  - Environment variables

  - The `terraform.tfvars` file, if present

  - The `terraform.tfvars.json` file, if present

- Any `*.auto.tfvars` or `*.auto.tfvars.json` files, processed in lexical order of their filenames

- Any `-var` and `-var-file` options on the command line, in the order they are provided (this includes variables set by a HCP Terraform workspace)

While managing Terraform, you might get authentication errors or permission errors in the cloud despite using the right credentials and permissions. This could be because of the presence of multiple credentials in different locations with different permissions. The credentials with higher precedence would be used by Terraform, but you may be expecting credentials with lower precedence to be used.

For example, if you have `admin` credentials in the environment variables but `read-only` credentials in the `terraform.tfvars` file, `read-only` will take precedence as per the variable precedence order.

State-Related Issues

As you already know, the Terraform state file (`terraform.tfstate`) is a JSON document that maps your Terraform configurations to the resources that it is managing. This file tracks the metadata, resource relationships, and the actual state of resources.

The following sections talk about some of the state-related issues.

Configuration Drift

- There are times when you might have to make changes outside of Terraform. This could be because of a lack of knowledge of how to make these changes from Terraform or you may not have permission to modify the Terraform code. This could also be due to time constraints.

- While dealing with production issues where you are running against time, it is not uncommon to make the changes directly in the console. If you are managing too many resources in a single directory, Terraform can take a long time, and hence, a manual change may be warranted. Though this may not be the ideal way, this happens quite often in the real world. You can reconcile this in a few ways:

  - If you can afford to roll back the manual changes and apply this change via Terraform at a later time, this is recommended.

  - If you have created new resources manually, you will have to add the relevant code in the configuration file and import that resource using `terraform import`.

  - If you have changed the name of the resource manually, you can use the `moved` block of Terraform to give this file a new name in the state file.

- If you have deleted some resources manually, you can do one of the following:

  - You can remove that resource from the state using `terraform state rm resource` for versions prior to Terraform 1.7 or use the `removed` block for Terraform 1.7+ and delete the relevant code from the configuration file. (Make sure you understand the Terraform state command and its impact before making these changes. Also, take a backup of your state file before the activity.)

  - Alternatively, you can delete the relevant code in the configuration file (or change the attribute value) and use `terraform refresh` for Terraform versions prior to v0.15.4 and `terraform apply -refresh-only` for versions post v0.15.4. This updates the state file of your infrastructure with metadata that matches the physical resources they are tracking. This will not modify your infrastructure, but it can modify your state file to update metadata. `terraform refresh` is deprecated but is still available only for backward compatibility.

State Conflict

- Simultaneous Terraform runs can cause conflicts if you do not configure the state file locking. It is highly recommended to enable state file locking even if you are the only person using Terraform.

- Remote backends such as Consul, S3 with DynamoDB, Azure Blob storage, HCP Terraform, and a few others offer state locking to prevent such conflicts.

- When you enable state file locking, Terraform makes sure only a single process that has the key modifies the state file. Any other simultaneous process trying to acquire the key will get an error. This is the expected behavior to prevent potential state corruption.

- The following error shows the messages you will see when there is a state-locking error:

```
State locking error:
Acquiring state lock. This may take a few moments…
  Error: Error acquiring the state lock
  Error message: ConditionalCheckFailedException: The
conditional request failed
  Lock Info:
    ID:         a2324f3-x872-09fs-b216-g87ed071284
  ---- Truncated ----
```

- You get this error in different situations, and some of them are listed here:

- You run `terraform apply` while one of your colleagues has already run `terraform apply` and has the key that locks the state file. This is a genuine use case where you want Terraform to throw this error to prevent state corruption.

- You have run `terraform apply` by mistake and want to cancel it. You hit Ctrl + C (or Ctrl + Z) to cancel the run. Though the run gets canceled, you end up with a state lock. The state error will show up next time you run either `terraform plan` or `terraform apply` since Terraform has not released the lock properly.

- You have run `terraform apply` on your laptop and Terraform core is making the required changes. If the laptop shuts down during the operation or the session gets disconnected due to a network issue, you will end up with a state lock.

In the first situation, the lock will be automatically released once the process that holds this key is completed. However, the second and third situations need the lock to be released before you can use Terraform. The `terraform force-unlock` command is used to release the lock. This should be used only in genuine use cases where you have a state lock problem and not to kill the parallel Terraform runs from a colleague.

When you run `terraform plan` or `apply`, you will see the error message and an ID. You will have to supply this ID in the next command:

```
terraform force-unlock ID
terraform force-unlock a2324f3-x872-09fs-b216-g87ed071284
```

Migrating the State from One Backend to Another

- There are a number of reasons for migrating the state from one backend to another. It could be due to team collaboration where you want to migrate from the local to a remote backend or to move from the remote backend (such as S3 or Consul) to HCP Terraform.

- Terraform supports the migration of state between backends or from local to remote backends.

- Be very careful while migrating the state from one backend to another (local to remote or from one cloud storage to another).

- Make a backup of the state file before you attempt the migration.

- After adding the relevant backend code in the configuration file, you will have to run the following command to migrate the state:

    ```
    terraform init -migrate-state
    ```

- The following output shows the message and prompt you will receive when you are migrating your state from local to S3:

    ```
    Initializing the backend...
    Do you want to copy existing state to the new backend?
      Pre-existing state was found while migrating the previous
    "local" backend to the
      newly configured "s3" backend. No existing state was found in
    the newly
    ```

```
configured "s3" backend. Do you want to copy this state to the
new "s3"
  backend? Enter "yes" to copy and "no" to start with an empty
state.
  Enter a value:
```

- As the message says, entering `yes` will copy the state file from the local backend to a remote backend.

- If you enter `no`, an empty state file will be created in the remote backend.

> **Note**
>
> If you try running `terraform plan` or `terraform apply` before running `terraform init`, you will see the following error:
>
> ```
> Backend initialization required: please run terraform init
> Reason: Backend configuration block has changed
> ```

Core and Provider-Related Issues

- Terraform core interprets the configuration, manages the state file, constructs the resource dependency graph, and communicates with provider plugins. Errors produced at this level may be a bug. You will have to raise a GitHub issue with HashiCorp for such an error.

- The provider plugins handle authentication, API calls, and mapping resources to services. For any issues you find in the providers, you will have to directly raise a GitHub issue with the provider development team.

- To debug errors related to the core or provider, you will have to enable logging.

- To enable logging in Terraform, you will have to declare a specific environmental variable, `TF_LOG`, with one of the logging levels that is described in the following points. When you enable logging, the logs are sent to the console where you are running the Terraform commands. Since these logs can be too many to be captured within the console, it is also recommended to use another environment variable, `TF_LOG_PATH`, to store these logs in a file on the local filesystem.

- There are multiple log levels. You will have to choose the right log level depending on the verbosity of the logs you need. The following are the various log levels supported by HashiCorp:

  - TRACE: Setting the logging to this level provides the details of every step taken by Terraform during the execution. This is the most verbose log level.

  - DEBUG: This is less verbose than the TRACE level and helps developers debug the issues by providing a shorter description of the internal events when the terraform run happens.

- INFO: This provides information instructions similar to the contents of the README file. This is fine for the general logging to get the high-level messages during Terraform runs.

  - WARN: This provides information about the misconfigurations but is not a blocker that needs to be fixed immediately.

  - ERROR: Enable this level to get the logs only when something is severely wrong and is blocking the Terraform run. This does not generate too many logs.

- The TF_LOG environment variable logs all the components such as Terraform core, providers, and SDKs. If you want to get logs related to a specific component, you can use different environment variables for them.

- TF_LOG_CORE, only Terraform core binary logs are written.

- With TF_LOG_PROVIDER, logs related to all providers and SDKs used in the configuration file are written. To enable the TRACE logging level for all components (from Linux or macOS), run the following command:

```
export TF_LOG=TRACE
```

- To enable logging only for providers, run the command below:

```
export TF_LOG_PROVIDER=TRACE
```

- To enable logging only for Terraform core, run the following command:

```
export TF_LOG_CORE=TRACE
```

- To enable storing the logs in a specific file, run the following command (from Linux/macOS), run the command given below:

```
export TF_LOG_PATH=~/terraform-logs.txt
```

Module-Related Issues

You will be able to spot the errors related to modules when you have some basic understanding of child modules getting called from the root module. You will have to know whether the root module is using the local child module or remote child module, the mandatory input variables expected by the child module, and the outputs exposed by the child module to spot an error related to the module.

Most of the time, the errors are related to the unsupported argument, unable to get the expected output, version mismatch, missing features, and so on. These are discussed in more detail in the following sections.

Missing Features

- If you are writing modules yourself, this is easy to solve. You need to add additional code to the module to add the missing features. Once you add the new code for the feature, you will have to pull the latest changes of the child module in your root module by running `terraform init -upgrade` if there is no versioning. If you have versioned the modules, then you will have to pull the latest version of the child module in the root module.

- If you are using public modules, this can get tricky. Check whether there is a latest version of the module that adds this feature. If it does, then pull the latest version of the module in the root module.

- There are a couple of other ways to handle such issues:

- Fork this module and make the required changes. But you will have to manage this code yourself going forward.

- Create an abstraction layer where you create a new module using the public module as the source. This new module can be stored in the version control system. With this option, you will still be able to make use of the latest versions of the public module and still add the features that are not present in the public module.

- If you are using local modules, you do not have to upgrade the module. The `modules.json` file under `.terraform/modules` will contain the path of the modules in the local filesystem.

Output-Related Issues

- This is one of the most common issues while dealing with modules.

- When you call the child module via the root module, you need to make sure the outputs you are defining in the root module are exposed in the child module.

For example, if you are using the child module of EC2 to create the instance and have not defined output for the instance ID or the IP address, you will never be able to get these details from the calling module (i.e., the root module). First, you need to define this in the child module and then refer to it from the root module's outputs.

Unsupported Argument

- Take a look at the error given below. This error is similar to the output-related issue, where the particular argument is not defined in the child module, and hence, when you pass the value for that argument in the root module, you get an error:

```
Unsupported argument: An argument named "xxxxxxx" is not
expected here.
```

- Review the variables declared in the child module to troubleshoot this issue.

Version-Related Issues

- In the production environment, it is highly recommended to lock the versions of the modules.

- One con of this precaution is that you will not upgrade the module version regularly and will fall behind in terms of the features available with the modules.

- Always test the latest version of the module thoroughly before rolling it out to production setup.

Taking Help from the Forum

- After you run out of options, you may reach out to the community for help in the HashiCorp forum.

- Make sure you search the existing threads for your issue before raising a new one.

- You may access the Terraform forum using the following URL:

  `https://discuss.hashicorp.com/c/terraform-core/27`

- Go through the guidelines of the forum before you post a question:

  `https://discuss.hashicorp.com/t/guide-to-asking-for-help-in-this-forum/48571`

Bug Reporting

Once you eliminate the possibility of language misconfiguration, version mismatch, variable-related issues, or state discrepancies, consider bringing your issue to the core Terraform team or Terraform provider community as a GitHub issue.

If you would like input from the community before submitting your issue to the repository, consider submitting your issue as a forum topic in the **HashiCorp Discuss forum**.

You will have to provide the Terraform version when opening a GitHub issue. Enable Terraform logging by running `export TF_LOG_CORE=TRACE` and `export TF_LOG_PATH=logs.txt`.

Run `terraform refresh`, which generates the logs and stores them in the `logs.txt` file.

Before raising this issue, you will have to confirm whether it is a provider issue or a Terraform core issue. In your `logs.txt` file, find the final error message and trace it back to the source. It should contain `provider-terraform-<PROVIDER-NAME>` if it is a provider issue. Make sure you remove any confidential information that may be present in the logs.

When you determine where your error originated, navigate to the Terraform core GitHub repository or search the provider registry for your provider's GitHub repository.

First, navigate to the Terraform GitHub repository, choose Issues from the top tabs, and create one with all the information.

Gotchas

In this section, you will see some recommendations that are typically not covered in the Terraform documentation. These are not very obvious unless you go through them in your setup, hence the name "Gotchas." This section is followed by general tips.

Avoid Lists Where Possible

- When you are dealing with use cases that warrant using lists, try using maps or sets wherever possible.

- When you use a list, Terraform uses the index position to map it to the resource that gets created. Using the index position may be fine for use cases where you do not see many deletions of values in the list, but it should not be used for use cases where you expect the values to be deleted and added to the list in random order. This may sound confusing or may not make sense in the first read. Try reading this again after going through the following example.

- Say, for example, you are creating IAM users using the `list` type. The following code can be used to create users, and whenever you need a new user, all you need to do is add the username to the default argument in the `usernames` variable:

```
resource "aws_iam_user" "iam-user" {
  count = length(var.usernames)
  name = element(var.usernames,count.index)
}
variable "usernames" {
  type = list(string)
  default = ["manju","packt","chandru"]
}
```

- `terraform apply` will create three IAM users: `manju`, `packt`, and `chandru`.

- Now, you want to remove the `packt` user. While the `resource` block remains the same, you would remove the `packt` user from the `variable` block in the following manner:

```
variable "usernames" {
  type = list(string)
  default = ["manju","chandru"]
}
```

- When you run `terraform plan`, the expectation is to delete the `packt` user and for all the other users to remain as is. But the output of this modification is given here:

```
# aws_iam_user.iam-user[1] will be updated in-place
~ resource "aws_iam_user" "iam-user" {
      id         = "packt"
    ~ name       = "packt" -> "chandru"
      tags       = {}
      # (5 unchanged attributes hidden)
  }

# aws_iam_user.iam-user[2] will be destroyed
# (because index [2] is out of range for count)
- resource "aws_iam_user" "iam-user" {
    - arn        = "arn:aws:iam::123456789:user/chandru" ->
null
    - id         = "chandru" -> null
    - name       = "chandru" -> null
    - path       = "/" -> null
    - unique_id  = "AIDA3LH3Gxxxxxxxx" -> null
  }
Plan: 0 to add, 1 to change, 1 to destroy.
```

- As you can see, Terraform is trying to rename the `packt` user to `chandru` and delete the `chandru` user.

- From Terraform's perspective, index position 1 was occupied by the `packt` user previously, but now the `chandru` user is present in that position. Hence, it has to be renamed.

- There are only two users in the variable, hence `index [2]` is out of range (index starts from zero). So, the `chandru` user must be deleted.

- Alternatively, you can use the `for_each` option along with the `toset` function to solve this problem:

```
resource "aws_iam_user" "iam-user" {
  for_each = toset(["manju", "packt", "chandru"])
  name     = each.value
}
```

- This would create three users.

- When you delete the `packt` function and try running `terraform plan`, you will see only one deletion:

```
# aws_iam_user.iam-user["packt"] will be destroyed
# (because key ["packt"] is not in for_each map)
- resource "aws_iam_user" "iam-user" {
    - arn          = "arn:aws:iam::123456789:user/packt" ->
null
    - id           = "packt" -> null
    - name         = "packt" -> null
    - path         = "/" -> null
    - unique_id    = "AIDA3LH3Gxxxxxxxxxx" -> null
  }
Plan: 0 to add, 0 to change, 1 to destroy.
```

- Here, the list is converted to a set before `for_each` iterates over the values.

- The IAM user list does not need an ordered collection, and hence, it is fine to convert it to a set here. But if you need an ordered collection, then this may not be the right option.

Using -target in Terraform Runs

- Using the `-target` option for specific resources makes changes to the dependent resources too. Use the `-target` option only in exceptional circumstances such as recovering from a mistake or implementing a solution to overcome the limitations of Terraform.

- The code in the following example creates two resources – an EC2 instance and an elastic IP, which has an implicit dependency on the EC2 instance:

```
provider "aws" {
  region = "ap-south-1"
}
resource "aws_eip" "eip" {
  instance = aws_instance.test.id
  domain   = "vpc"
}
resource "aws_instance" "test" {
  ami                = "ami-026255a2746f88074"
  availability_zone  = "ap-south-1a"
  instance_type      = "t3.micro"
  tags = {
    Name = "Test-EC2"
  }
}
```

- When you try to delete just the EC2 instance using the -target option, you will see that Terraform tries to delete the elastic IP too:

```
$~/terraform-troubleshoot:terraform destroy -target="aws_
instance.test"
aws_instance.test: Refreshing state... [id=i-01c2645577c1b2b65]
Terraform used the selected providers to generate the following
execution plan. Resource actions are
indicated with the following symbols:
  - destroy
Terraform will perform the following actions:
  # aws_eip.eip will be destroyed
  - resource "aws_eip" "eip" {
      ---- TRUNCATED ----
  }
  # aws_instance.test will be destroyed
  - resource "aws_instance" "test" {
      - ami = "ami-026255a2746f88074" -> null
      ---- TRUNCATED ----
  }
Plan: 0 to add, 0 to change, 2 to destroy.
| Warning: Resource targeting is in effect
```

- To summarize, -target not only deletes the resource you are targeting but also the dependency. You need to be aware of this while using this option.

General Tips

Finally, here are some general tips to make things easier for you:

- If you do not lock the versions of modules and providers, they get updated during terraform init -upgrade. The updated version might break the compatibility and cause issues in your environment.

- Make sure that Terraform is also locked to a certain version, and that team members are asked to use the same version while dealing with Terraform. Changing the Terraform version that is incompatible with the version you have defined in the Terraform block will throw an error, but will not update the Terraform version in your state file, saving you a lot of pain.

- Whenever possible, try to create the resource manually (or go through the steps for the creation) before writing the Terraform code. Once you get a sense of the steps involved, you will be able to write efficient code or troubleshoot the issue.

- If you are not able to find the resources that you created, make sure you are in the right CLI workspace.

Summary

In this chapter, you learned about the key areas in which Terraform issues arise and how to handle those issues. The areas or the issues highlighted here are in no way exhaustive but should give you a good understanding of the frequent issues in Terraform.

You also learned how to enable logging, which is the most important step in troubleshooting issues or raising a bug report with the providers or with HashiCorp.

In the end, you saw some tips from real-world Terraform management. In *Chapter 8, Terraform Functions*, you will read about the use of Terraform functions that the Terraform language supports.

Exam Readiness Drill – Chapter Review Questions

Apart from a solid understanding of key concepts, being able to think quickly under time pressure is a skill that will help you ace your certification exam. That is why working on these skills early on in your learning journey is key.

Chapter review questions are designed to improve your test-taking skills progressively with each chapter you learn and review your understanding of key concepts in the chapter at the same time. You'll find these at the end of each chapter.

> **How to Access these Resources**
>
> To learn how to access these resources, head over to the chapter titled *Chapter 11, Accessing the Online Practice Resources.*

To open the Chapter Review Questions for this chapter, perform the following steps:

1. Click the link – `https://packt.link/HCorp003Ch7`.

   Alternatively, you can scan the following **QR code** (*Figure 7.1*):

Figure 7.1 – QR code that opens Chapter Review Questions for logged-in users

2. Once you log in, you'll see a page similar to the one shown in *Figure 7.2*:

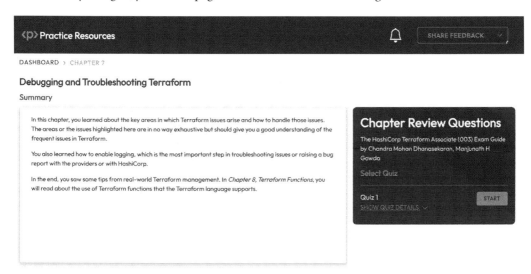

Figure 7.2 – Chapter Review Questions for Chapter 7

3. Once ready, start the following practice drills, re-attempting the quiz multiple times.

Exam Readiness Drill

For the first three attempts, don't worry about the time limit.

ATTEMPT 1

The first time, aim for at least **40%**. Look at the answers you got wrong and read the relevant sections in the chapter again to fix your learning gaps.

ATTEMPT 2

The second time, aim for at least **60%**. Look at the answers you got wrong and read the relevant sections in the chapter again to fix any remaining learning gaps.

ATTEMPT 3

The third time, aim for at least **75%**. Once you score 75% or more, you start working on your timing.

> **Tip**
> You may take more than **three** attempts to reach 75%. That's okay. Just review the relevant sections in the chapter till you get there.

Working On Timing

Target: Your aim is to keep the score the same while trying to answer these questions as quickly as possible. Here's an example of how your next attempts should look like:

Attempt	Score	Time Taken
Attempt 5	77%	21 mins 30 seconds
Attempt 6	78%	18 mins 34 seconds
Attempt 7	76%	14 mins 44 seconds

Table 7.1 – Sample timing practice drills on the online platform

> **Note**
> The time limits shown in the above table are just examples. Set your own time limits with each attempt based on the time limit of the quiz on the website.

With each new attempt, your score should stay above **75%** while your "time taken" to complete should "decrease". Repeat as many attempts as you want till you feel confident dealing with the time pressure.

8

Terraform Functions

In *Chapter 6, Terraform Backends and Resource Management*, you read about Terraform expressions and their different variations and took a look at some use cases. The Terraform language also supports the use of Terraform functions as part of these expressions.

The main use of Terraform's built-in functions is in expressions and to transform input values and create new values. For example, the `toset()` function can be used to convert an input value to a set (the input value type can be a list or map), and this can be used in places where the set type is expected.

In this chapter, you will learn about the different built-in functions and their syntax with examples. Not all functions are regularly used, but knowledge of different functions will help when there are special requirements that can be simplified by using functions.

Terraform functions are grouped based on the types of values or arguments they can act upon, and the configuration files are also created with the same approach.

Here is a list of topics that will be covered in this chapter:

- Function syntax
- Numeric functions
- String functions
- Date and time functions
- Collection functions
- Type conversion functions
- Filesystem functions
- IP network functions
- Encoding functions
- Hash and crypto functions

After finishing this chapter, it is recommended that you try out the most common functions in your own expressions with different use cases. This will help in the **HashiCorp Terraform Associate 003** certification journey as well as with your daily tasks.

If you only want to try out the functions, the `terraform console` command will be a good starting point. This feature is particularly useful for understanding the behavior of the different functions with the example inputs before actually using it in the configuration scripts.

Technical Requirements

Sample configuration files have been used in the chapter, and you can find them at the following link:

```
https://github.com/PacktPublishing/Hashicorp-Certified-Terraform-
Associate-003-Exam-guide-Second-Edition/tree/main/ch8/terraform-
functions
```

- To use the files, you need the following tools in your workstation:
- AWS account ID with administrator access credentials
- AWS CLI version 2.x.x
- Terraform CLI version 1.5.x or later
- Visual Studio Code or any text editor

Function Syntax

The functions in Terraform follow this common syntax:

```
FUNCTION_NAME(argument-1, argument-2, . . . . argument-n)
```

FUNCTION_NAME is the name of the function to be called, and the number of arguments it takes will vary from 1 to n based on the function.

Some of the functions have a definitive set of arguments that they can accept, and a few will accept any variable number of inputs. For example, the `endswith()` string function will accept only two arguments and return either `true` or `false`. The first argument is the string to check and the second is the suffix string.

But if you take the `max()` function, which gives the maximum number in the given list of input numbers, you can pass any number of input values and the result will be a single number.

Numeric Functions

In this section, you will look at some of the most common functions that work with numeric arguments. Numeric functions will help in cases where you might need to select the smallest value from the given list of values and process accordingly or convert the string representation of the given value to a number to perform some arithmetic operations using the same. It will be clearer once you go through the different functions supported by Terraform with sample inputs.

The examples used in this section will be available with the filename `1. numeric-functions. txt` in the GitHub link provided at the start of this chapter. You just need to take the specific command and try it with your sample inputs in the `terraform console` terminal.

The abs() Function

The `abs()` function always returns the absolute value of the given number, and it takes only one argument. If the input number is less than zero (0), the value will be multiplied by -1 and then returned. If the input number is greater than zero, the value will be returned with no changes.

Here is the syntax:

```
abs(argument-1)
```

Some examples are as follows:

```
$ abs(-5)
> 5
$ abs(100)
> 100
```

The ceil() Function

The `ceil()` function will return the whole number that is greater than or equal to the input number. If the input number is a whole number already, the output will be the same number. If the input number is a fraction, the next closest whole number will be returned.

Here is the syntax:

```
ceil(argument-1)
```

Some examples are as follows:

```
$ ceil(7)
> 7
$ ceil(10.4)
> 11
```

The floor() Function

The `floor()` function will return the whole number that is less than or equal to the input number. If the input number is a whole number already, the output will be the same number. If the input number is a fraction, the previous closest whole number will be returned.

Here is the syntax:

```
floor(argument-1)
```

Some examples are as follows:

```
$ floor(11)
> 11
$ floor(8.8)
> 8
```

The max() Function

The `max()` function will return the greatest number in the given inputs, and it can take any number of values as input. The function works with the individual arguments; if the input values are already in a complex type such as a list or set, use three dots (. . .) next to the input list or set to expand the collection.

If the three dots are not specified when the input is a complex type, the command will fail with the following error:

```
Error: Invalid function argument. Invalid value for "numbers"
parameter: number required
```

Here is the syntax:

```
max(argument-1, argument-2)
max([argument-1, argument-2]...)
```

Some examples are as follows:

```
$ max(10, 59, 23, 68)
> 68
$ max([10, -2, 3, 15]...)
> 15
$ max([10, -2, 3, 15])   --- without the three dots
> Error: Invalid function argument
|
|   on <console-input> line 1:
|   (source code not available)
```

```
| Invalid value for "numbers" parameter: number required.
```

The min() Function

The `min()` function will return the smallest number in the given inputs, and it can take any number of values as input. The function works with the individual arguments; if the input values are already in a complex type such as a list or set, use three dots (. . .) next to the input list or set to expand the collection.

The behavior is exactly the same when the three dots are not specified for a complex type input value.

Here is the syntax:

```
min(argument-1, argument-2)
min([argument-1, argument-2]...)
```

Some examples are as follows:

```
$ min(-2, 5, 11, 1)
> -2
$ min([13, 22, 76, 99]...)
> 13
```

The pow() Function

The `pow()` function will result in the exponent value based on the input arguments. The first argument will be raised to the power of the second argument, and it always only accepts two arguments.

Here is the syntax:

```
pow(argument-1, power-of-argument-2)
```

Some examples are as follows:

```
$ pow(2, 2)
> 4
$ pow(17, 0)
> 1
```

The log() Function

This function returns the logarithm of a given number and it takes two arguments. The first argument is the number, and the second argument is the base.

Here is the syntax:

```
log(number-argument-1, base-argument-2)
```

An example is as follows:

```
$ log(44,2)
> 5.459431618637297
```

The signum() Function

The `signum()` function will return the sign of the given number and the value will be between -1 and 1. If the input number is negative, then `-1` will be returned; the return value will be `1` in the case of a positive number. This function will return zero if the input value is zero (`0`).

Here is the syntax:

```
signum(number-argument-1)
```

Some examples are as follows:

```
$ signum(34)
> 1
$ signum(0)
> 0
$ signum(-24)
> -1
```

The parseint() Function

The `parseint()` function will return the number parsing the string representation of the input value in the specified base. The first argument is the input value in string format and the second argument is the base. The limitation of this function is that the base can only be between the values of 2 and 62.

If the input value cannot be parsed with the specified base, the function will return an error.

Here is the syntax:

```
parseint(input-argument-1, base-argument-2)
```

Some examples are as follows:

```
$ parseint("10110", 2)
> 22
$ parseint("EDA1", 16)
> 60833
```

With this function, we have covered the numeric functions supported in Terraform and we will proceed with the `string` functions in the next section. The functions supported might vary with the release of every new Terraform version and the latest documentation will help in those cases.

String Functions

The following section will cover the most common `string` functions supported by Terraform 1.5.x. `string` functions are primarily used for formatting the input values for different requirements and using the result in the subsequent workflow. The examples used in the section will be available with the filename `2. string-functions.txt` in the GitHub link provided at the start of this chapter. You just need to take the specific command and try it with your sample inputs in the Terraform console terminal.

The split() Function

The `split()` function will split the input string in all occurrences where the `separator` character is present. The resulting value will be of the `list` type, and if we are using the output values to initialize any variable, the variable should be of the `list` data type.

Here is the syntax:

```
split(separator-char, input-string)
```

Some examples are as follows:

```
$ split("-", "test-dev-prod")
> tolist([
  "test",
  "dev",
  "prod",
])
$ split(",", "Adam,Bob,William")

> tolist([
  "Adam",
  "Bob",
  "William",
```

The join() Function

The `join()` function joins the string elements in the input list and produces the final string with the specified separator. If the `separator` character is not specified (just double quotes), then the list elements will be just concatenated.

Here is the syntax:

```
join(separator-char, input-list)
```

Some examples are as follows:

```
$ join("-", ["h", "e", "l", "l", "o"])
> "h-e-l-l-o"
$ join("", ["c", "a", "t"])
> "cat"
```

The endswith() Function

The endswith() function will return either true or false based on whether the input string ends with the specified suffix string or not. The function takes two arguments.

Here is the syntax:

```
endswith(input-string-1, suffix-string)
```

Some examples are as follows:

```
$ endswith("test-app", "app")
> true
$ endswith("terraform-function", "func")
> false
```

The startswith() Function

The startswith() function will return either true or false based on whether the input string ends with the specified prefix string or not. The function takes two arguments.

Here is the syntax:

```
endswith(input-string-1, prefix-string)
```

Some examples are as follows:

```
$ startswith("test-app", "test")
> true
$ startswith("terraform-function", "test")
> false
```

The chomp() Function

This function will be very helpful when you read strings from any file that has newline characters at the end, and it takes only one argument. It does not remove the spaces at the end of the input string.

Here is the syntax:

```
chomp("input-string")
```

Some examples are as follows:

```
$ chomp("hello  \n\n")
> "hello  "
$ chomp("test string 01\n")
> "test string 01"
```

The substr() Function

The substr() function extracts the part of the string that starts at the specified offset and length. The function takes three arguments, which are the input string, the offset value (which starts from 0), and the length.

Here is the syntax:

```
substr(input-string, offset-value, length)
```

Some examples are as follows:

```
$ substr("Adam Williamson", 5, 7)
> "William"
$ substr("input-string", 0, 2)
> "in"
```

The strrev() Function

The strrev() function returns the reversed version of the input string and it takes one argument only, which is the input string.

Here is the syntax:

```
strrev(input-string)
```

Some examples are as follows:

```
$ strrev("olleh")
> "hello"
$ strrev("string")
> "gnirts"
```

The lower() Function

This function converts the input string to lowercase.

Here is the syntax:

```
lower(input-string)
```

Some examples are as follows:

```
$ lower("Language")
> "language"
$ lower("ALPHABETS")
> "alphabets"
```

The upper() Function

This function converts the input string to uppercase.

Here is the syntax:

```
upper(input-string)
```

Some examples are as follows:

```
$ upper(«document»)
> «DOCUMENT»
$ upper(«characters»)
> "CHARACTERS"
```

The trim() Function

The trim() function will remove the characters specified in the second argument from the start and end of the input string. Here, every character in the second argument will be replaced individually and does not have to be an exact match in the input string.

Here is the syntax:

```
trim(input-string, remove-chars)
```

Some examples are as follows:

```
$ trim("football", "fl")
> "ootba"
$ trim("sports", "s")
> "port"
```

The trimprefix() and trimsuffix() Functions

The `trimprefix()` and `trimsuffix()` functions will remove the specified prefix and suffix strings from the start and end of the strings, respectively. If the input prefix/suffix is not present in the input string, the output value will be the same with no change.

Here is the syntax:

```
trimprefix(input-string, prefix-to-remove)
trimsuffix(input-string, suffix-to-remove)
```

Some examples are as follows:

```
$ trimprefix("bridge", "b")
> "ridge"
$ trimsuffix("baseball", "ball")
> "base"
$ trimprefix("universe", "one")
> "universe"
```

The trimspace() Function

The `trimspace()` function will remove the newline characters from the start and end of the given string. This is different from the regular `trim()` function, which will remove the specified characters. In this function, newline characters mean \n, \r, and similar characters.

Here is the syntax:

```
trimspace(input-string)
```

Some examples are as follows:

```
$ trimspace("\n\r test string\n")
> "test string"
$ trimspace("    terraform        \n    \r")
> "terraform"
```

The indent() Function

The `indent()` function will be used to indent the strings in the specified multi-line string based on the input value except the first line.

Here is the syntax:

```
indent (number-of-spaces, input-string)
```

An example is as follows:

```
$ indent(2, "[\n  test-line-1,\n  test-line-2,\n]")

> <<EOT
[
    test-line-1,
    test-line-2,
  ]
EOT
```

The replace() Function

The `replace()` function is used to replace the specified character set from the input string with the replacement sequence provided. If the substring to be replaced is wrapped with forward slashes (/), then it is considered to be a regular expression.

Here is the syntax:

```
replace(input-string, string-to-replace, replacement-chars)
```

Some examples are as follows:

```
$ replace("This is a test string", " ", "-")
> "This-is-a-test-string"
$ replace("There are ten players", "/t.*n/", "10")
> "There are 10 players"
```

The strcontains() Function

The `strcontains()` function will return either `true` or `false` based on whether the specified substring is present in the input string or not. This function takes two arguments only.

Here is the syntax:

```
strcontains(input-string, string-to-search)
```

Some examples are as follows:

```
$ strcontains("The game is on", "is")
> true
$ strcontains("Apple is Red", "white")
> false
```

The title() Function

This function will convert the first letter of each word in the specified input string to uppercase and it takes one argument only.

Here is the syntax:

```
title(input-string)
```

Some examples are as follows:

```
$ title("this is amazing")
> "This Is Amazing"
$ title("one two three")
> "One Two Three"
```

The format() Function

The `format()` function is used to format the string with the specifications, and this is similar to the `printf` function in C.

Here is the syntax:

```
format(specification-string, input-string)
```

For the specification string, some of the commonly used parameters are the following:

- `%s`: For strings
- `%d`: For numbers in decimal representation
- `%b`: For numbers in binary representation
- `%f`: For fraction notation

Please refer to the Terraform documentation for more options available with this function.

Some examples are as follows:

```
$ format("%s has won the match", "Brazil")
> "Brazil has won the match"
$ format("Each team has %d players", 11)
> "Each team has 11 players"
$ format("The value of PI is %.2f", 3.14)
> "The value of PI is 3.14"
$ format("Binary value of 2 is %b", 2)
> "Binary value of 2 is 10"
```

The formatlist() Function

The formatlist() function uses the same syntax as the format() function except that this function produces the list of strings with the specifications provided.

Here is the syntax:

```
formatlist(specification-string, input-list-string)
```

An example is as follows:

```
$ formatlist("%s is a vowel", ["a", "e", "i", "o", "u"])

> tolist([
  "a is a vowel",
  "e is a vowel",
  "i is a vowel",
  "o is a vowel",
  "u is a vowel",
])
```

The regex() Function

The regex() function applies a regular expression to the input string and returns any matching substrings as the output. If the regular expression does not match with any substrings, the function will throw an error. If the pattern sequence itself starts with the backslash, another backslash must be added before use inside the function.

This function has several advanced features and possible sequences that cannot be covered in this topic. Therefore, please refer to the official documentation for more information.

Here is the syntax:

```
regex(regular-expression, input-string)
```

Some of the commonly used regular expression sequences are as follows:

- \d: Any ASCII digit from 0 to 9

- [a-z]: Any character between a and z

Some examples are as follows:

```
$ regex("\\d\\d",   "1234abc5678")
> "12"
$ regex("[a-z]",   "1234a5678")
> "a"
```

The regexall() Function

The regexall() function uses the same syntax as the regex() function, but this function produces a list of matching strings.

Here is the syntax:

```
regexall(regular-expression, input-string)
```

An example is as follows:

```
$ regexall("[a-z]+", "ab123cd")

> tolist([
  "ab",
  "cd",
])
```

With this function, you have completed the discussion on string functions and can now proceed with the date and time functions, which are helpful when handling the different date and time formats to use with the Terraform resources.

Date and Time Functions

The following section will cover the most common date and time functions supported by Terraform 1.5.x. The examples used in the section will be available with the filename 3. date-and-time-functions.txt in the GitHub link provided at the start of this chapter.

The timestamp() Function

The timestamp() function returns the current date and time in the UTC format as per RFC 3339 specifications. This is the same format used internally by Terraform where the timestamps are used; hence, this function also returns with the same syntax.

Here is the syntax:

```
timestamp()
```

An example is as follows:

```
$ timestamp()
"2024-03-09T17:03:03Z" ("YYYY-MM-DDTHH:MM:SSZ")
```

> **Note**
> The output will vary based on when the function was tried out.

The formatdate() Function

The formatdate() function converts the given timestamp into a different date and time format. For more details on the possible format sequences, please refer to the official documentation.

The date and time format sequences that are commonly used are as follows:

- YYYY: Year in four digits
- YY: Year in two digits
- MMM: Month in abbreviated form, such as Jan, Feb, and so on
- MM: Month in two digits
- DD: Date in two digits with padding, such as 01, 02, and so on
- D: Date without padding
- HH: Hour in two digits with padding (12-hour format)
- hh: Hour in two digits with padding (24-hour format)

Here is the syntax:

```
formatdate(format, timestamp)
```

Some examples are as follows:

```
$ formatdate("DD-MM-YYYY", timestamp())
> "09-03-2024"
$ formatdate("hh:mm", timestamp())
> "17:15"
```

> **Note**
>
> The output will vary based on when the function was tried out.

The plantimestamp() Function

The plantimestamp() function is like the timestamp() function but the result of the function will change with every plan operation.

This function is not available within the Terraform console and can be tested with a random terraform plan.

Here is the syntax:

```
plantimestamp()
```

The timeadd() Function

The timeadd() function will return the new timestamp adding the duration specified with the input timestamp. It is possible that the duration parameter can contain negative values as well.

The valid units are one of the following:

- ns (nanoseconds)
- us or μs (microseconds)
- ms (milliseconds)
- s (seconds)
- m (minutes) and
- h (hour)

Here is the syntax:

```
timeadd(timestamp-value, duration)
```

Some examples are as follows:

```
$ timeadd(timestamp(), "4h")
> "2024-03-10T10:09:20Z"
$ timeadd(timestamp(), "5m")
> "2024-03-10T06:15:06Z"
```

> **Note**
>
> The output will vary based on when the function was tried out.

The timecmp() Function

The `timecmp()` function compares the given timestamps and returns a number based on their ordering. This function only accepts two timestamps as arguments.

Here is the syntax:

```
timecmp(timestamp-1, timestamp-2)
```

If `timestamp-1` < `timestamp-2`, then the return value will be `-1`.

If `timestamp-1` = `timestamp-2`, then the return value will be `0`.

If `timestamp-1` > `timestamp-2`, then the return value will be `1`.

Some examples are as follows:

```
$ timecmp(«2024-03-10T06:15:06Z», «2024-03-10T10:09:20Z»)
> -1
$ timecmp("2024-03-10T10:09:20Z", "2024-03-10T10:09:20Z")
> 0
$ timecmp("2024-03-10T10:09:20Z", "2024-03-10T06:15:06Z")
> 1
```

The date and time functions have now all been discussed, so you can proceed with the collection functions in the next section.

Collection Functions

Terraform supports a huge number of functions that work with collection types such as `list`, `tuple`, `set`, or `map`. In this section, you will briefly look at the most common ones. The examples used in the section will be available with the filename `4. collection-functions.txt` in the GitHub provided at the start of this chapter.

Since these functions can work with different collection types, you will be skipping the syntax part and looking at the examples directly.

The alltrue() Function

The alltrue() function will return true (Boolean type) if all the input elements in the list/tuple are true (Boolean type value) or **true** (string value).

Some examples are as follows:

```
$ alltrue([true, true])
> true
$ alltrue([true, false])
> false
```

The anytrue() Function

This function returns true if any of the elements in the input collection has true (Boolean type value) or **true** (string value).

Some examples are as follows:

```
$ anytrue([true, false])
> true
$ anytrue([true])
> true
```

The chunklist() Function

This function splits a single input list into a list of lists based on chunk size.

An example is as follows:

```
$ chunklist([11, 22, 33], 1)

> tolist([
  tolist([
    11,
  ]),
  tolist([
    22,
  ]),
  tolist([
    33,
  ]),
])
```

The coalesce() and coalescelist() Functions

These functions return the first input element that is not `null` or an empty string. The `coalescelist()` function will take lists as input.

Some examples are as follows:

```
$ coalesce("", "", null, "a")
> "a"
$ coalescelist([], ["a", "b"])
> [
  "a",
  "b",
]
```

The compact() Function

The `compact()` function will take a list of strings as input and return the list without empty or `null` values.

An example is as follows:

```
$ compact(["a", "b", "", null, "c"])

> tolist([
  "a",
  "b",
  "c",
])
```

The concat() Function

The `concat()` function takes lists as input and produces a single list after concatenation.

An example is as follows:

```
$ concat(["1", "2"],["3"])
> [
  "1",
  "2",
  "3"
]
```

The contains() Function

The `contains()` function returns `true` or `false` based on whether the element is present in the list or not.

An example is as follows:

```
$ contains(["1", "2"], "2")
> true
```

The distinct() Function

The `distinct()` function will return the list without any duplicates, as in this example:

```
$ distinct(["1", "11", "111", "1", "11", "1111"])

> tolist([
  "1",
  "11",
  "111",
  "1111",
])
```

The element() Function

This function retrieves a single element from the list, as in this example:

```
$ element(["1", "11", "111"], 1)
> "11"
```

The flatten() Function

The `flatten()` function will take lists and replace the elements with the flattened sequence of the elements. If the list element is a nested list, that too will be flattened.

Here is an example:

```
$ flatten([["a", "b", "c"], ["d"]])
[
  "a",
  "b",
  "c",
  "d",
]
```

The keys() and values() Functions

The keys() and values() functions will return the keys and values of the map, respectively.

Some examples are as follows:

```
$ keys({one=1, two=2, three=3})
[
  "one",
  "three",
  "two",
]
$ values({one=1, two=2, three=3})
> [
  1,
  3,
  2,
]
```

The index() Function

The index() function will return the index of the search element if it is present, as in this example:

```
$ index(["a", "b", "c"], "a")
> 0
```

The length() Function

The length() function will return the length of the list, as in this example:

```
$ length(["a", "b", "c"])
> 3
```

The lookup() Function

The lookup() function will return the value from the map for the provided key, as in this example:

```
$ lookup({one=1, two=2, three=3}, "two")
> 2
```

The matchkeys() Function

The `matchkeys()` function will create a new list with the elements whose indexes match the corresponding indexes in the `keylist`. `searchvalue` is the third argument.

Here is the syntax:

```
matchkeys(valuelist, keylist, searchvalue)
```

An example is as follows:

```
$ matchkeys(["ec2", "lambda", "dynamodb"], ["server", "serverless",
"serverless"], ["serverless"])

> tolist([
  "lambda",
  "dynamodb",
])
```

The merge() Function

The `merge()` function will take a map or objects as input and create a merged map. If the same key is present in multiple maps, the last occurrence will take precedence.

Here is an example:

```
$ merge({a=1, b=2, c=3},{b=4},{d=5})
{
  "a" = 1
  "b" = 4
  "c" = 3
  "d" = 5
}
```

The one() Function

The `one()` function will take a list, a set, or a tuple with zero or one element. If the input has zero elements, the function will return `null` and if it has one element, the first element will be returned. If there is more than one element, the function will throw an error.

Some examples are as follows:

```
$ one([])
> null
$ one(["1"])
> "1"
```

The range() Function

The `range()` function generates a list of numbers with the specified start value, end value, and step value.

Here is the syntax:

```
range(max-value)
range(start-value, max-value)
range(start-value, max-value, step-value)
```

Some examples are as follows:

```
$ range(3)

> tolist([
   0,
   1,
   2,
])
$ range(11, 15)

> tolist([
   11,
   12,
   13,
   14,
])
$ range(2, 10, 2)

> tolist([
   2,
   4,
   6,
   8,
])
```

The reverse() Function

The `reverse()` function takes the input list and returns it in a reversed fashion.

An example is as follows:

```
$ reverse([1,2])
> [
   2,
   1,
]
```

Set Functions

Under collection functions, there is a special category of functions grouped together as set functions and there are four functions available in this category that are similar in syntax. You will now look at the examples directly.

These functions will work with the input values of the `set` type.

The setintersection() Method

This is the intersection result of the input sets:

```
$ setintersection(["adam", "bob"],["bob", "chris"])

> toset([
   "bob",
])
```

The setproduct() Method

This is the product result of the input sets:

```
$ setproduct(["adam"],["1", "2"])

> tolist([
   [
     "adam",
     "1",
   ],
   [
     "adam",
     "2",
   ],
])
```

The setunion() Method

This is the combined result of the input sets:

```
$ setunion(["adam", "bob"],["bob", "chris"])

> toset([
    "adam",
    "bob",
    "chris",
])
```

The setsubtract() Method

This is the result of the input sets when the common elements are removed from the first set. This takes two sets only as input:

```
$ setsubtract(["adam", "bob"],["bob", "chris"])

> toset([
    "adam",
])
```

The slice() Function

The `slice()` function extracts the elements from the specified starting index and last index. The result will not include the element in the last index. This is similar to the `substr()` function, but the `substr()` function will use the length attribute instead of the index.

Here is an example:

```
$ slice([11, 22, 33, 44, 55], 1, 4)
> [
    22,
    33,
    44,
]
```

The sort() Function

The sort() function sorts a given list.

Here is an example:

```
$ sort(["23", "12", "44", "09", "66"])

> tolist([
  "09",
  "12",
  "23",
  "44",
  "66",
])
```

The sum() Function

This function returns the sum of the elements in a given list.

Here is an example:

```
$ sum([11, 22, 33])
> 66
```

The transpose() Function

The transpose() function takes a map of strings and switches the keys and values.

Here is an example:

```
$ transpose({"s3" = ["aws", "service"]})

> tomap({
  "aws" = tolist([
    "s3",
  ])
  "service" = tolist([
    "s3",
  ])
})
```

The zipmap() Function

The `zipmap()` function creates a map with the specified list inputs as keys and values.

Here is an example:

```
$ zipmap(["a"], ["1"])
> {
    "a" = "1"
}
```

With the `zipmap()` function, you have completed the section on collection functions, and have read about the functions that are primarily used to manipulate the input values or derive new values from it. The next section will deal with type conversions such as changing sensitive values to non-sensitive values and converting an input value to a new type.

Type Conversion Functions

This section will cover type conversion functions, as highlighted previously. They will be useful to ensure that input values are always compatible with the written configuration scripts, so they can be handled with the right validations.

The examples used in the section will be available with the filename `5. type-conversion-functions.txt` in the GitHub link provided at the start of this chapter.

The can() Function

The `can()` function is mainly used to validate whether the expression will produce a valid result or not. If a valid result is possible, `true` is returned; otherwise, `false` will be returned.

You can now take a look at a couple of examples:

```
$ can(anytrue([true, false]))
> true
$ can(one([1, 2]))
> false
```

Here, the `anytrue()` function will always return a result, so the `can()` output is `true`. In the second case, the `one()` function will throw an error if the input list has more than one element, and hence the function returns `false`.

The sensitive() and nonsensitive() Functions

The sensitive() and nonsensitive() functions are used to create a copy of any value that will be marked as sensitive and non-sensitive, respectively, so Terraform can manage how to handle it.

These functions can be used in situations where you want to mark any variable value marked as sensitive to a non-sensitive value to print it, and vice versa.

In the following example in *Figure 8.1*, there are two variables (outval1 and outval2) but outval1 is set with a sensitive variable value:

```
main.tf > ...
1    variable "test-sensitive" {
2      type      = string
3      sensitive = true
4      default   = "test-string-1"
5    }
6
7    variable "test-nonsensitive" {
8      type      = string
9      sensitive = false
10     default   = "test-string-2"
11   }
12
13   output "outval1" {
14     value     = var.test-sensitive
15     sensitive = true
16   }
17
18   output "outval2" {
19     value = var.test-nonsensitive
20   }
21
```

Figure 8.1 – main.tf with sensitive and nonsensitive variables

When the `terraform plan` command is executed, you can see the `outval1` value is hidden and the `outval2` value is displayed in the terminal, as shown in *Figure 8.2*:

```
rm-functions-new\type-conversion-functions> terraform plan

Changes to Outputs:
  + outval1 = (sensitive value)
  + outval2 = "test-string-2"

You can apply this plan to save these new output values to the Terraform state, without changing any real infrastructure.
```

Figure 8.2 – The terraform plan terminal output

The try() Function

The `try()` function will take the argument expressions and return the first one that does not result in an error.

Here is an example:

```
$ try(one([1,2]), ["1", "2"], [])
[
  "1",
  "2",
]
```

The type() Function

The `type()` function determines the type of the given value.

Here is an example:

```
$ type(["1", "2"])
> tuple([
    string,
    string,
])
$ type(true)
> bool
```

Conversion Functions

The following functions convert the input value from one type to another:

- `tobool()`

- `tolist()`

- `tomap()`

- `tostring()`

- `tonumber()`

- `toset()`

Some examples are as follows:

```
$ tobool("true")
> true
$ tonumber("23")
> 23
$ tostring(100)
> "100"
$ toset(["1", "2", "3", "2"])

> toset([
  "1",
  "2",
  "3",
])
$ tomap({"one" = 1, "two" = 2})

> tomap({
  "one" = 1
  "two" = 2
})
$ tolist(["a", "b", 1, true])

> tolist([
  "a",
  "b",
  "1",
  "true",
])
```

Now that you have read about type conversion functions, you can proceed to learn about filesystem functions, which allow you to interact with file-based input handling, along with encoding capabilities.

Filesystem Functions

Filesystem functions are used when you work with files to pass configuration values or read the input content and so on. This is very helpful in real-life scenarios such as processing upstream files via automation or creating files to be passed to downstream systems with custom content and encoding. The examples used in the section will be available with the filename `6. filesystem-functions. txt` in the GitHub link provided at the start of this chapter.

Function outputs for the examples in this section will be based on Windows OS but similar outputs can be expected if you use a different operating system.

For the following examples, create a file with the name `test.txt` with the content as `testfile` before trying out these functions.

The abspath() Function

The `abspath()` function will convert the string with the file path to an absolute path.

Here is an example:

```
$ abspath("/terraform")
"C:/terraform"
```

The dirname() and basename() Functions

The `dirname()` and `basename()` functions will return the directory name, removing the filename at the end if present. The behavior of the function will vary based on the operating system.

Some examples are as follows:

```
$ dirname("C:\\Users\\chandru\\test.txt")
"C:\\Users\\chandru"
$ basename("C:\\Users\\chandru\\test.txt")
"test.txt"
```

The pathexpand() Function

The `pathexpand()` function will expand the file path that might begin with a tilde symbol (~) and replace it with the HOME directory. If the HOME environment variable is not set, the HOMEDRIVE or HOMEPATH value will be used; if that is also not available, the USERPROFILE value will be used to expand the path.

Here is an example:

```
$ pathexpand("~")
"C:\\Users\\chandru"
```

The file() and filebase64() Functions

The `file()` and `filebase64()` functions read the contents of the given file and return it in regular string format and string encoded in the `base64` format, respectively.

Here is an example:

```
$ file("C:\\Users\\chandru\\test.txt")
> "testfile"
$ filebase64("C:\\Users\\chandru\\test.txt")
> "dGVzdGZpbGU="
```

The fileexists() Function

The `fileexists()` function returns `true` or `false` based on whether the file exists or not in the specified path, as in this example:

```
$ fileexists("C:\\Users\\chandru\\test.txt")
> true
```

The fileset() Function

The `fileset()` function will return the set of filenames matching the specified pattern. Please refer to the official documentation for more information on valid patterns.

Here is the syntax:

```
fileset(path, match-pattern)
```

The templatefile() Function

The `templatefile()` function is useful to read the template file and dynamically set the content of the file using the template variables.

Here is the syntax:

```
templatefile(file-path, template-vars)
```

With this, you have finished learning about filesystem functions.

IP Network Functions

In this section, you will read about IP network functions supported in Terraform. These are helpful when you work with the setup of AWS resources such as VPC and are creating public and private subnets within the VPC and similar components to provision new infrastructure from scratch. Understanding these functions requires knowledge of network-addressing concepts.

The examples used in the section will be available with the filename 7. `ip-network-functions.txt` in the GitHub link provided at the start of this chapter.

The cidrhost() Function

The `cidrhost()` function returns the full IP address for a given host number within the given IP address prefix.

The function will accept both the IPv4 and IPv6 prefixes.

Here is an example:

```
$ cidrhost("192.168.1.1/16", 10)
> "192.168.0.10"
```

The cidrnetmask() Function

The `cidrnetmask()` function converts an IPv4 address prefix to a subnet mask address. This will throw an error if the IPv6 address prefix is given as input.

Here is an example:

```
$ cidrnetmask("192.168.1.1/16")
> "255.255.0.0"
```

The cidrsubnet() Function

The `cidrsubnet()` function calculates the subnet address for a given IP address prefix, and this function takes three arguments to extend the prefix. This function accepts IPv4 and IPv6 address prefixes.

Here is the syntax:

```
cidrsubnet(prefix, new-range, net-num)
```

An example is as follows:

```
$ cidrsubnet("192.168.1.1/16", 4, 2)
> "192.168.32.0/20"
```

The cidrsubnets() Function

This function returns the sequence of IP address ranges within the CIDR range.

An example is as follows:

```
$ cidrsubnets("192.168.1.1/16", 4, 4)

> tolist([
  "192.168.0.0/20",
  "192.168.16.0/20",
])
```

Encoding Functions

This section will cover the different encoding functions available in Terraform. You can use them to encode the files created in your own configuration or decode a given file in a specific scheme.

The examples used in the section will be available with the filename 8. encoding-functions. txt in the GitHub link provided at the start of this chapter.

The base64encode() and base64decode() Functions

These functions can encode a given string in base64 format, decode a base64 encoded string, and return the original string.

Here is an example:

```
$ base64encode("This is a string")
> "VGhpcyBpcyBhIHN0cmluZw=="
$ base64decode("VGhpcyBpcyBhIHN0cmluZw==")
> "This is a string"
```

The base64gzip() Function

This function compresses a string with gzip and then encodes it with base64 encoding.

Here is an example:

```
$ base64gzip("This is a string")
> "H4sIAAAAAAAA/wrJyCxWyCxWSFQoLinKzEsHAAAA//8BAAD//z9jdggQAAAA"
```

The csvdecode() Function

The `csvdecode()` function decodes a CSV string and produces a list of maps. The first line is considered as a header and the remaining lines are considered as data.

Here is an example:

```
$ csvdecode("1,2\na, b\n")

> tolist([
  {
    "1" = "a"
    "2" = " b"
  },
])
```

The jsonencode() and jsondecode() Functions

The `jsonencode()` and `jsondecode()` functions are used to encode the given string into JSON syntax, and vice versa.

The Terraform types are converted to the equivalent JSON types as per the predefined conversion rules.

Here is an example:

```
$ jsonencode({"one" = 1, "two" = 2})
> "{\"one\":1,\"two\":2}"
$ jsondecode("{\"one\":1,\"two\":2}")
{
  "one" = 1
  "two" = 2
}
```

The textencodebase64() Function

The `textencodebase64()` function encodes the given string using the specified encoding scheme.

Here is an example:

```
$ textencodebase64("This is a string", "UTF-8")
> "VGhpcyBpcyBhIHN0cmluZw=="
$ textencodebase64("This is a string", "UTF-16")
> "/v8AVABoAGkAcwAgAGkAcwAgAGEAIABzAHQAcgBpAG4AZw=="
```

The textdecodebase64() Function

The `textdecodebase64()` function decodes an already encoded `base64` string using the specified encoding scheme.

Here is an example:

```
$ textdecodebase64("VGhpcyBpcyBhIHN0cmluZw==", "UTF-8")
> "This is a string"
```

The urlencode() Function

The `urlencode()` function encodes a given string in the URL encoding format, as in this example:

```
$ urlencode("test url/resource")
> "test+url%2Fresource"
```

The yamlencode() and yamldecode() Functions

The `yamlencode()` function encodes the given string using the YAML syntax and the `yamldecode()` function performs the opposite.

Here is an example:

```
$ yamlencode({"one" = "1"})

> <<EOT
"one": "1"

EOT
$ yamldecode("one : 1")
{
    "one" = 1
}
```

You have learned about encoding functions in this section and can now proceed to the next section on hash and crypto functions, which can be used to generate unique UUIDs. Different hashing algorithm-based functions are also supported.

Hash and Crypto Functions

Hash and crypto functions are helpful to generate UUIDs in version 4 and version 5. There are more functions to compute different hashing methods such as SHA1, MD5, and so on, which have applicable use cases in the field of cryptography.

These functions can also be used to encrypt a file using different methods based on specific requirements. The examples used in the section will be available with the filename `9. hash-and-crypto-functions.txt` in the GitHub link provided at the start of this chapter.

The uuid() Function

The `uuid()` function generates a unique UUID identifier. The version 4 UUID generated by this function is random in nature and cannot be duplicated easily. This function will generate a new output every time it is tried out.

Here is an example:

```
$ uuid()
> "9e3eaa9e-5304-4077-7a9a-4f267e9319aa"
```

The uuidv5() Function

This function generates a version 5 UUID based on the `name` and `namespace` values. This is different from the `uuid()` function, where the generated UUID will be the same if the `namespace` and `name` values remain the same (not random in nature).

The valid values for `namespace` are `"dns"`, `"url"`, `"oid"` (object identifier), and `"x500"`.

Here is the syntax:

```
uuidv5(namespace-value, name)
```

Here is an example:

```
$ uuidv5("url", "https://www.google.co.in")
> "1040b910-63b8-53cb-ad98-8d28e9d9eb95"
```

Other functions under this category can be grouped into two categories – functions that work on the string and ones that work on files.

These are the functions with string input:

- `base64sha256()`
- `base64sha512()`
- `bcrypt()`
- `md5()`

- sha1()
- sha256()
- sha512()

Some examples are as follows:

```
$ sha1("test string")
> "661295c9cbf9d6b2f6428414504a8deed3020641"
$ md5("test string")
> "6f8db599de986fab7a21625b7916589c"
$ base64sha256("test string")
> "1VecRt/MfxggcBPmW0Tky04sIpj0rEV7qPgnQ/Mekws="
```

These functions use file input:

- filebase64sha256()
- filebase64sha512()
- filemd5()
- filesha1()
- filesha256()
- filesha512()

For the following examples, you can reuse the same test file created previously when filesystem functions were discussed:

```
$ filebase64sha256("./test.txt")
> "03uTlcK68Wj5d86f+ewAfXJw/ITL8VSTJL/I38NDM6k="
$ filemd5("./test.txt")
> "8bc944dbd052ef51652e70a5104492e3"
```

With this example, you have completed a thorough walk-through of all the available Terraform functions and you should be able to use them in your configuration scripts to make them more dynamic and flexible.

Summary

In this chapter, you looked at the different types of functions, starting with basic numeric and string functions, followed by collection functions to work with the complex types. Then, the type conversion functions were covered with file-based functions with encoding options and a few special utility functions.

From the exam perspective, these functions may not be directly asked about in the questions, but this knowledge will be helpful in other scenario-based questions.

Exam Readiness Drill – Chapter Review Questions

Apart from a solid understanding of key concepts, being able to think quickly under time pressure is a skill that will help you ace your certification exam. That is why working on these skills early on in your learning journey is key.

Chapter review questions are designed to improve your test-taking skills progressively with each chapter you learn and review your understanding of key concepts in the chapter at the same time. You'll find these at the end of each chapter.

> **How to Access these Resources**
>
> To learn how to access these resources, head over to the chapter titled *Chapter 11, Accessing the Online Practice Resources*.

To open the Chapter Review Questions for this chapter, perform the following steps:

1. Click the link – `https://packt.link/HCorp003Ch8`.

    Alternatively, you can scan the following **QR code** (*Figure 8.3*):

Figure 8.3 – QR code that opens Chapter Review Questions for logged-in users

2.   Once you log in, you'll see a page similar to the one shown in *Figure 8.4*:

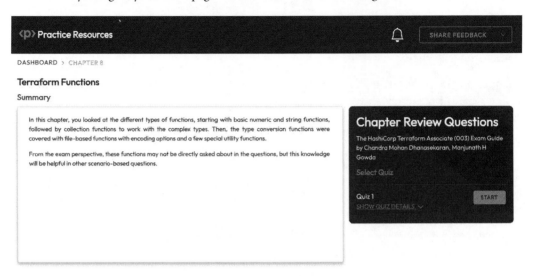

Figure 8.4 – Chapter Review Questions for Chapter 8

3.   Once ready, start the following practice drills, re-attempting the quiz multiple times.

Exam Readiness Drill

For the first three attempts, don't worry about the time limit.

ATTEMPT 1

The first time, aim for at least **40%**. Look at the answers you got wrong and read the relevant sections in the chapter again to fix your learning gaps.

ATTEMPT 2

The second time, aim for at least **60%**. Look at the answers you got wrong and read the relevant sections in the chapter again to fix any remaining learning gaps.

ATTEMPT 3

The third time, aim for at least **75%**. Once you score 75% or more, you start working on your timing.

> **Tip**
> You may take more than **three** attempts to reach 75%. That's okay. Just review the relevant sections in the chapter till you get there.

Working On Timing

Target: Your aim is to keep the score the same while trying to answer these questions as quickly as possible. Here's an example of how your next attempts should look like:

Attempt	Score	Time Taken
Attempt 5	77%	21 mins 30 seconds
Attempt 6	78%	18 mins 34 seconds
Attempt 7	76%	14 mins 44 seconds

Table 8.1 – Sample timing practice drills on the online platform

> **Note**
> The time limits shown in the above table are just examples. Set your own time limits with each attempt based on the time limit of the quiz on the website.

With each new attempt, your score should stay above **75%** while your "time taken" to complete should "decrease". Repeat as many attempts as you want till you feel confident dealing with the time pressure.

9

Understanding HCP Terraform's Capabilities

In this chapter, you will learn about HCP Terraform and Terraform Enterprise, the managed Terraform offerings by HashiCorp. While Terraform Community Edition is great, it does have some shortcomings that are fixed by HashiCorp with their HCP Terraform and Terraform Enterprise offerings.

It is important for you to understand the differences between the Community, HCP Terraform, and Enterprise editions. This knowledge will help you make an informed decision about which edition best serves your company's interests, not just from a technical perspective but also from a cost perspective.

The following are the key topics that will be covered in this chapter:

- Terraform editions
- Shortcomings of Terraform Community Edition
- HCP Terraform features
- HCP Terraform pricing
- Key concepts of HCP Terraform
- HCP Terraform sign-up
- Exercises on workflows, and execution modes in HCP Terraform
- Migrating to HCP Terraform
- Terraform Enterprise features

By the end of this chapter, you will have a good understanding of the difference between various Terraform editions, as well as the key features of HCP Terraform and Enterprise. This understanding will not only help answer the certification questions related to this chapter but will also help you decide which edition is suitable for your environment if you want to explore the paid options of Terraform.

Terraform Editions

HashiCorp provides the following editions of Terraform, which should cover a wide spectrum of customers:

- Community
- HCP Terraform
- Terraform Enterprise

The following figure shows the available Terraform editions:

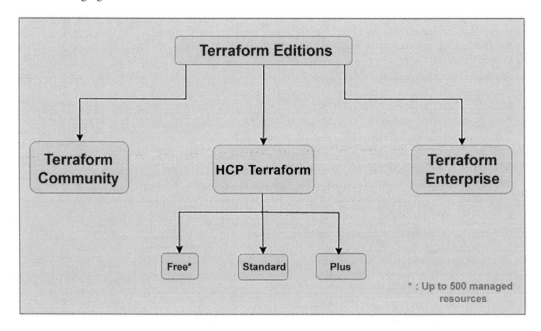

Figure 9.1: Terraform editions

> **Note**
>
> HashiCorp changed the name of **Terraform Cloud** to **HCP Terraform**. All the functionality provided by Terraform Cloud continues in HCP Terraform, with additional features expected to be added in the coming days.

Shortcomings of Terraform Community Edition

Imagine you are the only person managing your infrastructure using Terraform and you went with the default Terraform installation, which stored the configuration files and state file on your laptop (though it is not recommended even for a single user).

With the increase in the number of environments and the workload, you have been asked by your manager to hire additional members to handle the workload. Your new team members will not be able to access the state file and the configuration files as they are locally stored on your laptop. You realize that the default configuration of the Terraform Community Edition is not meant for team collaboration. However, you solve this by customizing Terraform by using version control system providers such as GitHub to store the configuration files, blob storage such as S3 for the state file, and a NoSQL database such as DynamoDB to enable locking for the state file.

You were able to solve this problem because you knew the shortcomings of the Community edition and how to address them. If you are a beginner with Terraform, you might not be able to get around problems such as this quite so quickly and confidently.

There are other challenges you will not be able to solve while using Terraform Community Edition. A few of them are listed here:

- If your company has a policy to have **Service-Level Agreement** (**SLA**)-based support for all third-party applications used in production
- The company's policy dictates using **Single Sign-On** (**SSO**) for all the third-party tools used in production
- Role-based access control
- Enforce a governance policy or cost policy using policy-as-code frameworks
- The team is comfortable using a **Graphical User Interface** (**GUI**)

Terraform Community Edition is great when you are the sole engineer working on infrastructure automation and management. However, you will soon notice the following:

- The state file, by default, gets stored in the local filesystem (in the default installation)
- No state file locking (in the default installation)
- No private modules
- No policy as code
- No GUI
- No SSO
- No production support

If these shortcomings are impacting your ability to manage the infrastructure, you should explore the paid offerings of HashiCorp, which address these problems and provide additional capabilities. Depending on your requirements, you can choose between HCP Terraform or Terraform Enterprise.

HCP Terraform Features

HCP Terraform is a SaaS application that runs Terraform in a stable, remote environment and securely stores state and secrets. HCP Terraform has a GUI that gives you a detailed view of the resources managed by Terraform and good visibility into each Terraform operation. It is available as a hosted service at `https://app.terraform.io`.

The key features of HCP Terraform are discussed in the following section.

Remote State Management

HCP Terraform acts as a remote backend to store Terraform state. It securely stores and versions Terraform state remotely, with encryption at rest. You also have access to the state file history since the state files are versioned.

> **Note**
> Please note that the sensitive data is still stored in the state file. Hence, access to the state file directly (via the `terraform state` command) or indirectly (by accessing the storage where the state is stored) should be tightly controlled.

Multiple Workflows

You can initiate Terraform runs (i.e. `terraform plan`, `terraform apply`, and any other Terraform commands) in any one of the following workflows:

- **The CLI-driven workflow**: As the name suggests, the workflow initiation happens with the user using the Terraform CLI tool but the runs happen in HCP Terraform. That is, the user will have the configuration files on the local system, and when they run `terraform plan` or `terraform apply`, the execution happens in HCP Terraform and the output gets streamed to the local system.

- **The UI/Version Control System (VCS) driven workflow**: Terraform configuration files are stored in the VCS repositories of providers such as GitHub. Any changes pushed to these repositories trigger runs in the respective workspaces.

- **The API-driven workflow**: This is an advanced use case. If you want to integrate Terraform directly into your application/workflows, you can trigger the Terraform run directly using its APIs.

Multiple Execution Modes

You can initiate Terraform runs in one of the following execution modes:

- **Remote**: The plan and apply commands occur on disposable virtual machines in HCP Terraform's infrastructure. You and your team will have the ability to review and collaborate on runs. You will be able to review the output of the Terraform runs of your colleagues.

- **Local**: The plan and apply commands occur on the machine where you are running Terraform CLI. HCP Terraform is used to store and synchronize the state only.

- **Agent**: Agents are used when you want to manage private isolated environments in the on-premises setup. These agents poll HCP Terraform/Enterprise for any changes in the configuration and apply them locally. As it works via a pull-based mechanism through the outbound connectivity, you do not have to allow any ingress traffic through the perimeter firewall. If you work in a highly restricted environment where inbound connectivity is not allowed, then the **Agent** execution mode can be used.

Version Control System Integration

Configuration files that are used by Terraform can be stored in a VCS. HCP Terraform supports integration with many VCS providers, such as GitHub, GitLab, and BitBucket. It watches for the changes in the repository and triggers a run when the new commits are merged. While using a VCS is strongly recommended, it is optional.

Private Registry

With Terraform Community Edition, you only get access to public modules. But what if you do not want to share your modules with anyone other than your team? A private registry is used in this situation. You can upload the provider and modules to it and share it only with the selected members/team. The user interface remains the same as the public Terraform registry. The modules can be published to the private registry in HCP Terraform and you can control access to these private modules via teams in HCP Terraform.

There are a few best practices to be followed while publishing a module to a private repository:

- You should be the admin of the repository where the code is residing (and is integrated with HCP Terraform).

- Module repositories should follow a standard naming convention: **terraform-PROVIDER-NAME** – for example, `terraform-aws-eip`, `terraform-gcp-vault`, and `terraform-aws-ec2-instance` (**NAME** can have additional hyphens to indicate the resources being managed).

- You must follow the semantic versioning convention for the release tag of the modules/providers. Semantic versioning follows the convention of MAJOR.MINOR.PATCH with an optional **v** at the beginning of the version, for example, v1.2.0, v3.8.2, and v5.4.1.

Notifications

HCP Terraform can send notifications about Terraform runs to other systems, such as Slack, or any other service that accepts webhooks.

Run Tasks

If you want to perform some actions using third-party tools at certain stages of the Terraform lifecycle, you can make use of the **run tasks** option in HCP Terraform. The stages where you can perform actions using such tools are before `terraform plan`, after `terraform plan`, before `terraform apply`, and after `terraform apply`.

Typical use cases of run tasks are cost management, policy compliance, and infrastructure drift detection.

Imagine you have a mandate to adhere to the **Payment Card Industry Data Security Standard (PCI-DSS)**, which is a security standard for data security in the payments industry, and you want to make sure all your infrastructure deployments are verified against the PCI-DSS compliance policies before they are provisioned.

run tasks can be utilized in such use cases where the policies related to the PCI-DSS are checked and, if they are successful, the resources will be provisioned, or the run will fail.

You can take a look at some of the run tasks available in the Terraform Registry at the following URL:

```
https://registry.terraform.io/browse/run-tasks
```

Role-Based Access Control

HCP Terraform supports role-based access control to ensure that only approved teams can access, edit, and manage infrastructure with HCP Terraform.

Policy Enforcement

Policies are rules that HCP Terraform enforces on Terraform runs. These policies are written using policy-as-code frameworks.

HCP Terraform supports the following policy-as-code frameworks:

- **Sentinel**: Policies are written in HashiCorp's Sentinel language.
- **Open Policy Agent (OPA)**: Policies are written in a high-level declarative language called Rego. This is not as intuitive as Sentinel.

Cost Estimation

HCP Terraform can estimate the cost you will incur when the resources you have defined in the configuration files are provisioned. By default, the cost estimation feature is disabled. You will have to enable this in the organization's settings. Once enabled, it will start showing the monthly cost you will incur for the resources that are provisioned in each run. Cost estimation is not supported by all the resources.

At the time of writing this book, HashiCorp has published the supported resources for AWS, Azure, and GCP. If you want to look at the supported AWS resources, check out the following URL:

```
https://developer.hashicorp.com/terraform/cloud-docs/cost-estimation/
aws
```

HCP Terraform Pricing

HCP Terraform has both free and paid offerings. The amount of features available to you depends on the plan you choose. HCP Terraform has three tiers:

- HCP Free (up to 500 managed resources)
- HCP Standard
- HCP Plus

Many key features, such as remote state storage, VCS connection, secure variable storage, private registry, a policy set of five policies (policy set is a collection of policies that can be applied at the individual workspace or all workspaces), and SSO are made available in the HCP Terraform Free edition.

Though the feature list is good for the free edition, it is very difficult to have a production environment as there is a limitation of 500 managed resources. This option is good for assessing whether the features of HCP Terraform suit your requirements.

Managed resource/**Resources Under Management (RUM)** is a resource in an HCP Terraform managed state file where **mode = managed**. HCP Terraform counts a resource as part of this count starting from the first `terraform plan` or `terraform apply` operation on the resource.

> **Note**
>
> HCP Terraform does not include resources defined as a `null_resource` or `terraform_data` in the total managed resource count.

RUM-based billing applies to the Free edition and the Standard edition. For the Free edition, you are limited to 500 managed resources. With the Standard edition, you get charged after 500 managed resources.

For more details on the pricing and features across different editions, refer to the following URL: `https://www.hashicorp.com/products/terraform/pricing`.

Key Concepts of HCP Terraform

When you compare Terraform Community Edition with the HCP Terraform edition, you will see several new concepts have been introduced. *Figure 9.1* shows the hierarchy of the concepts within HCP Terraform:

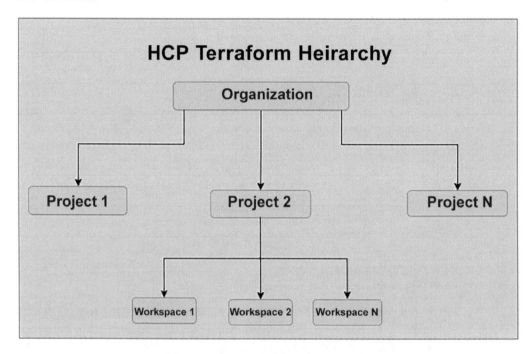

Figure 9.2: HCP Terraform concepts hierarchy

You will learn about some of the key concepts of HCP Terraform in the following section.

Workspaces

When you run Terraform locally, you have configuration files, a state file, and variables in a single directory (which is also your working directory). Terraform CLI always looks for configuration files ending with `.tf` or `.tf.json` for configuration, `.tfvars` files for the values of the variables, and the state file to know the current state of the infrastructure in the current working directory (it does not look at the subdirectories).

When you want to organize infrastructure resources into a meaningful group, you create different directories and have the relevant configuration files in these new directories.

For example, you could have all the VPC and subnet-related configuration files in the **network** folder and have all the config files of RDS and DynamoDB in the **database** folder.

Similarly, HCP Terraform manages the infrastructure collections with workspaces. You can equate the HCP Terraform workspace to the **directory** in the local Terraform CLI. A workspace contains the configuration file, a state file, and variables that are needed by Terraform to manage the infrastructure.

It is recommended that you create multiple workspaces instead of having one big workspace. This means Terraform runs and delegating permissions of different workspaces to different teams are quicker.

For example, you can delegate the management of the **network** workspace to your networking team, while an application team can manage the **application** workspace.

> **Note**
>
> Terraform CLI workspaces are different from HCP Terraform workspaces. CLI workspaces are used to deploy multiple environments using the same set of configuration files. Each CLI workspace in this context will have a different state file.
>
> For example, if you want to have a **testing** environment that is similar to the production environment, you do not have to duplicate the same code. You can just create two CLI workspaces named **production** and **testing** in the same directory. Any resources deployed in the production workspace will be tracked in a state file specific to the production workspace. Similarly, any resource deployed in the testing workspace will be tracked in a separate state file specific to the testing workspace. The production state file will not be visible when you are working in the testing workspace and vice versa. This is one of the features that is not well received by the community and is not recommended as there is a high chance of deleting resources due to confusion and difficulty in restricting access.

Projects

Projects let you organize workspaces into groups. Projects are typically used when you want to group a certain workspace based on a theme, such as business units, technology divisions, or subsidiaries.

Instead of assigning the same permissions to multiple workspaces that belong to the same business units or subsidiaries, you can group them into a single project and assign the permission to this project.

Each workspace must be part of exactly one project. Unless you create a new project, all the workspaces belong to a default project named **Default Project**.

Users

A user account is created for the individual user who has to log in to HCP Terraform to execute Terraform runs.

A user can be part of one or more teams that are granted permissions on one or more workspaces. These users can execute Terraform runs within their respective workspace. A user can be part of multiple organizations too.

Teams

A team is a group of HCP Terraform users and is used to grant permission on the workspace. The team management feature is available in HCP Terraform Standard.

Teams can only have permissions on workspaces within their organization, but users can belong to teams of other organizations too.

Owners team is the default team present in the organization (for all editions) and it cannot be deleted.

Permissions

The access a user or a team has in the organization/project or workspace is dictated by permissions. A permission is assigned to a team, and hence users who are part of the team will get these permissions. The permission model is split into organization-level, project-level, and workspace-level permissions. Most of HCP Terraform's permissions are focused on workspaces.

There are two ways to assign permission to a team in a workspace:

- **Fixed permission sets**: These are bundles of specific permissions for workspaces that you can use to delegate access to workspaces easily:

  - Workspace admins: Full permission over the workspace.

  - Write: Provisioning and modifying infrastructure.

  - Plan: For people who need to modify the configuration files to propose changes.

  - Read: For people who need to view the status and configuration of infrastructure.

- **Custom permissions**: If the fixed permission sets are too wide for your requirements, you can set fine-grained permissions to a team by using custom permissions.

Organizations

Organizations are a shared space for one or more teams to collaborate on workspaces. It is at the top of the hierarchy in HCP Terraform. To join an organization, you must be invited by one of its owners and must accept the emailed invitation.

Users who are part of the same organization can collaborate on workspaces and share private modules and providers.

Locking Workspaces

If you need to prevent Terraform runs on your HCP Terraform account due to production freeze or any other reason, you can lock a workspace. This prevents all applies (and many kinds of plans) from proceeding, and affects runs created via the UI, CLI, API, and automated systems.

To enable Terraform runs again, you must unlock the workspace.

Sentinel Policies

Sentinel policies are rules that are enforced by HCP Terraform on Terraform runs. It enables HCP Terraform to have granular control over the infrastructure using these policies.

A collection of these policies makes a policy set that can be applied at the organization level, the project level, or the workspace level.

Every time a Terraform run happens in the workspace, HCP Terraform checks the plan against the applicable policy, which can be either a Sentinel policy or an Open Policy Agent (OPA) policy.

As these policies can access the plan, state, and Terraform configurations during the plan stage, they are able to check for violations. Depending on the enforcement level configured, if there is a violation, the run will fail or will display an error message in the UI after allowing the run.

There are three enforcement levels with Sentinel policies:

- **Advisory**: The runs are not interrupted when the policy is violated but an error will be displayed in the HCP Terraform UI.
- **Soft mandatory**: The run is stopped when there is a policy violation, but the user can override it and allow the run to complete.
- **Hard mandatory**: The run is stopped until the user fixes the issue that caused this failure.

An important concept in Sentinel policy is **imports**. When you write a Sentinel policy, imports give the required information at the respective stage to compare them against the policy. There are four imports:

- `tfplan`: This import gives access to the plan created by Terraform core when the user runs `terraform plan`.
- `tfconfig`: This gives access to all the configuration present in the Terraform configuration files that describe the user's desired state.
- `tfstate`: This import gives access to the Terraform state, which has details of all the resources under Terraform's management and shows the current infrastructure state.
- `tfrun`: This import gives access to the data associated with a run in HCP Terraform.

The HCP Terraform UI displays policy results for each policy set you apply to the workspace.

Explorer

As your organization grows, keeping track of all your infrastructure objects will become increasingly complex.

Explorer helps you analyze your data to understand the organization's Terraform usage. It displays the information in two main sections: **types** and **usecases**.

Within the **types** section, you can get information about modules, providers, workspaces, and Terraform versions.

Within the **usecases** section, you can get details such as `top module versions` and `top provider versions`.

Clicking any of the options triggers the explorer to perform a query and display the results in a table of data.

HCP Terraform Sign-Up

You can use HCP Terraform by creating an account either with **HashiCorp Cloud Platform** (**HCP**) or by directly signing up with HCP Terraform.

If you use HashiCorp's other products, such as Boundary or Vault, then you can create an HCP account. The same account can be used for HCP Terraform too. If not, you can just create an account with HCP Terraform. The following sections cover both ways of creating an account to access HCP Terraform.

Creating an Account with HCP Terraform

The following steps explain how to create an account with HCP Terraform directly:

1. Navigate to this URL: `https://app.terraform.io/public/signup/account`.
2. Enter your username, email ID, and password, as shown in *Figure 9.3*.
3. Once you read the terms of use and privacy policy, you can select the checkboxes if you agree.
4. Click **Create account**.

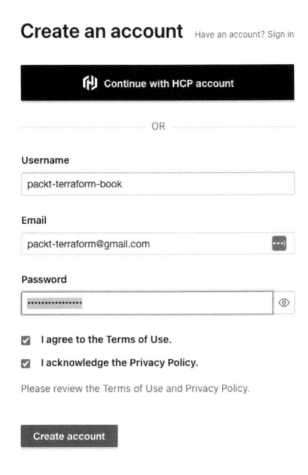

Figure 9.3: HCP Terraform account sign up

5.   A confirmation link will be sent to the email address you specified when creating the account. This is for verification. Once you click the link and complete the verification, you are ready to use the HCP Terraform account.

You have learned how to create an account with HCP Terraform.

The other way to create an account is by signing up with HCP. This is covered in the next section.

Creating an Account with HCP

The following steps explain how to create an account with HCP:

1. Navigate to this URL: `https://app.terraform.io/public/signup/account`.

2. Click on **Continue with HCP account**.

3. If you have a GitHub account, you can sign in to the HCP account by clicking on the **Sign in with GitHub** option.

4. If you do not have a GitHub account or want to create an account using a different email ID than the one you use for GitHub, look for the **Sign up** hyperlink at the bottom and click on it.

5. Enter the email ID and password, and you will be asked to agree to the terms of service and privacy policy on the next screen, as shown in *Figure 9.4*.

6. You may select them if you agree and click **Continue**.

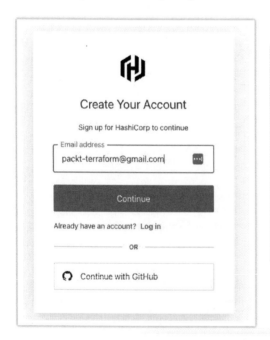

Figure 9.4: HCP sign-up screens

7. An email will be sent to validate the email address you have entered. Once validated, your account will be created in HCP.

8. Unlike the account with HCP Terraform, this account can be used to access other HashiCorp products, such as Boundary, Consul, and Vault. Within the HCP console, there is a hyperlink to take you to HCP Terraform. Once you have an account either with HCP or HCP Terraform, you can get started with your infrastructure management using HCP Terraform.

Exercises on Workflows and Execution Modes

In this section, you will perform three exercises to learn more about the **remote execution mode** and **local execution mode** on HCP Terraform. The other topics covered in these exercises are CLI-driven and VCS-driven workflows.

The following are the pre-requisites for the exercises:

- An AWS account and an IAM user with enough permissions to perform the exercises (or an SSO user if your organization is using AWS SSO). Refer to the following URL for steps on how to create an IAM user in AWS:

  `https://docs.aws.amazon.com/IAM/latest/UserGuide/id_users_create.html`.

- Terraform installed (version 1.4.0 and above preferred).
- HCP Terraform account.
- API token to configure Terraform CLI to access HCP Terraform API.

The following steps will help you create the API token and configure Terraform CLI:

1. Log in to HCP Terraform via the web browser, which is required to generate the API token.

2. Now, log in to HCP Terraform via the CLI by running the following command, which should prompt you for a confirmation to proceed, as shown in *Figure 9.5*:

```
terraform login
```

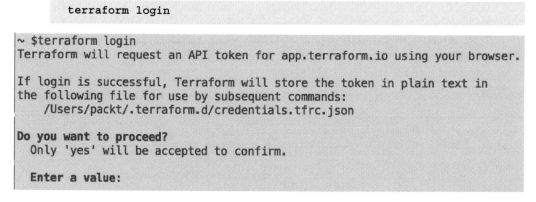

```
~ $terraform login
Terraform will request an API token for app.terraform.io using your browser.

If login is successful, Terraform will store the token in plain text in
the following file for use by subsequent commands:
    /Users/packt/.terraform.d/credentials.tfrc.json

Do you want to proceed?
  Only 'yes' will be accepted to confirm.

  Enter a value:
```

Figure 9.5: HCP Terraform login via CLI

3. Once you key in **yes** and hit **Enter**, a web page will be opened in your browser with a prompt to create an API token named **terraform login** with the expiration set to 30 days, as shown in *Figure 9.6*. (If you do not see this prompt, make sure you have logged in to HCP Terraform.)

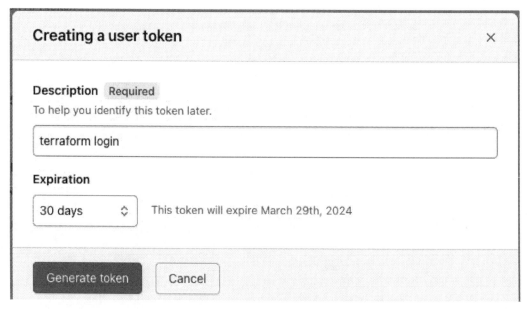

Figure 9.6: API token creation in HCP Terraform

4. Click **Generate token**, copy the API token displayed on the screen (this API token is displayed only once in HCP Terraform), and paste it into the CLI prompt, as you can see in *Figure 9.7* (as a security measure, the token will not be printed when you paste it in the CLI prompt).

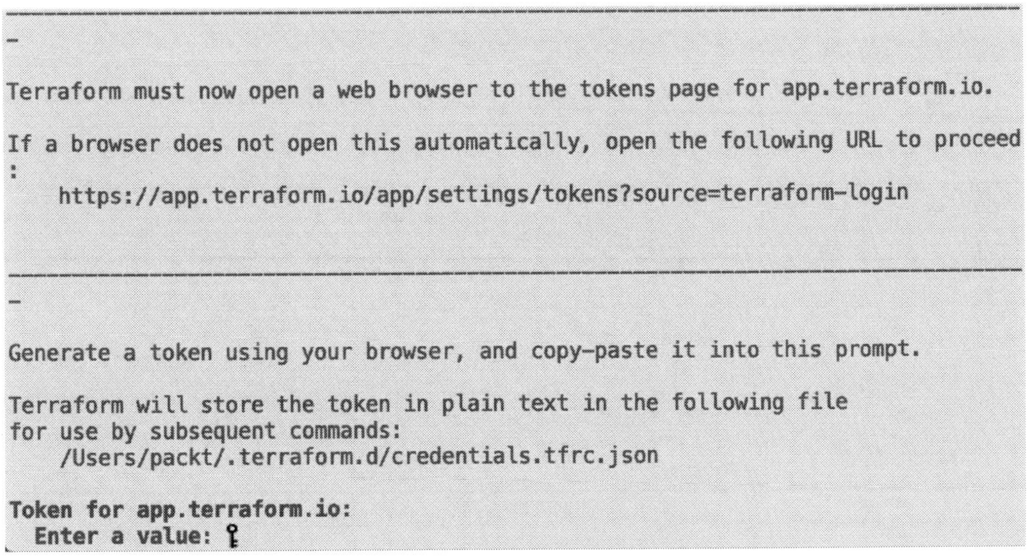

```
-

Terraform must now open a web browser to the tokens page for app.terraform.io.

If a browser does not open this automatically, open the following URL to proceed
:
    https://app.terraform.io/app/settings/tokens?source=terraform-login



-

Generate a token using your browser, and copy-paste it into this prompt.

Terraform will store the token in plain text in the following file
for use by subsequent commands:
    /Users/packt/.terraform.d/credentials.tfrc.json

Token for app.terraform.io:
  Enter a value: 
```

Figure 9.7: HCP Terraform login via CLI waiting for API token

5. This token is stored in the $HOME/.terraform.d/credentials.tfrc.json file, which is used to authenticate against HCP Terraform for future runs.

6. Once you have logged in successfully, you will see a message that says **Welcome to HCP Terraform** and a series of steps, as you can see in *Figure 9.8*:

```
Welcome to HCP Terraform!

Documentation: terraform.io/docs/cloud


New to HCP Terraform? Follow these steps to instantly apply an example config
uration:

    $ git clone https://github.com/hashicorp/tfc-getting-started.git
    $ cd tfc-getting-started
    $ scripts/setup.sh
```

Figure 9.8: Successful login to HCP Terraform via the CLI

Remote Execution Mode Using the CLI-Driven Workflow

In this exercise, you will learn how to run Terraform in remote execution mode in HCP Terraform using the CLI-driven workflow.

Make sure all the prerequisites highlighted in the preceding section are completed before you go to the next steps.

The code required for this exercise will be present locally on your system, but `terraform plan/apply` happens in HCP Terraform with the output being streamed to your local system.

Follow these steps to complete this exercise:

1. Clone the Git repository that contains the files required for this exercise. All the resources provisioned in this exercise use a fictitious cloud vendor called **Fake Web Services** that provisions fake VPC, servers, a load balancer, and a database. As these are not real resources that are provisioned in any cloud, you will not get charged for these resources.

    ```
    git clone https://github.com/hashicorp/tfc-getting-started.git
    ```

2. Navigate to the `tfc-getting-started` folder:

    ```
    cd tfc-getting-started/
    ```

3. Run the script by executing the `setup.sh` file:

    ```
    ./scripts/setup.sh
    ```

4. When prompted to press **any key**, hit *Enter* (or any other key) to confirm the execution.

5. Output like the following should be displayed on your screen too:

    ```
    ~/tfc-getting-started : ./scripts/setup.sh
    ----------------------------------------------------------
    Getting Started with HCP Terraform
    ----------------------------------------------------------
    HCP Terraform offers secure, easy-to-use remote state management
    and allows
    you to run Terraform remotely in a controlled environment. HCP
    Terraform runs
    can be performed on demand or triggered automatically by various
    events.
    This script will set up everything you need to get started.
    You'll be
    applying some example infrastructure - for free - in less than a
    minute.
    First, we'll do some setup and configure Terraform to use HCP
    Terraform.
    Press any key to continue (ctrl-c to quit):
    Creating an organization and workspace...
    Writing HCP Terraform configuration to backend.tf...
    ==========================================================
    Ready to go; the example configuration is set up to use HCP
    Terraform!
    An example workspace named 'getting-started' was created for
    you.
    You can view this workspace in the HCP Terraform UI here:
    https://app.terraform.io/app/example-org-64362c/workspaces/
    getting-started
    Next, we'll run 'terraform init' to initialize the backend and
    providers:
    $ terraform init
    Press any key to continue (ctrl-c to quit):
    ```

6. This script will create an **organization** (example-**org**-******) and workspace named **getting-started** in the HCP Terraform console.

7. It will try to run `terraform init`, `terraform plan`, and `terraform apply -auto-approve` in the next three steps. Each step will ask you to confirm the run by pressing **any key** to continue.

8. By the end of the **apply**, Terraform will create five resources: one VPC, two servers, a load balancer, and a database. These are all fake resources created using the **fakewebservices** provider.

9. Notice the execution mode set to **Remote**, as highlighted in *Figure 9.9*:

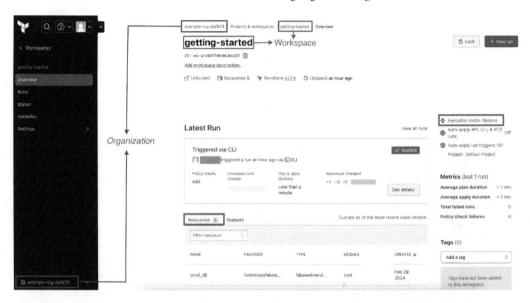

Figure 9.9: CLI-driven remote execution mode completion details

10. Now that you have learned how to run Terraform in remote execution mode and in the CLI-driven workflow, you can destroy the resources by running the following command:

```
terraform destroy –auto-approve
```

Do not delete the Terraform code, organization, and workspace used for this exercise. They will be used in the next exercise, which deals with the local execution mode.

Local Execution Mode Using the CLI-Driven Workflow

In this exercise, you will learn how to run Terraform in local execution mode using the CLI-driven workflow. This exercise uses the same Terraform code, organization, and workspace as the preceding exercise, *Remote Execution Mode Using the CLI-Driven Workflow*. Hence, the preceding exercise needs to be completed before you start this exercise.

When you select local execution mode, `terraform plan/apply` runs on your local system and the state file is stored in HCP Terraform.

You will not be able to check the details of the runs on HCP Terraform, but you can see the new state file being created on HCP Terraform after every local `terraform apply`.

Follow these steps to complete this exercise:

1. If you have already logged in to HCP Terraform, you may continue with this exercise. If not, log in to the HCP Terraform web interface via the browser.

2. Select the organization (example: **org-********) and workspace (getting-started) that were provisioned in the preceding exercise, *Remote Execution Mode Using the CLI-Driven Workflow*.

3. Navigate to the settings of the workspace (make sure you go to workspace settings and not the organization settings, which impacts all workspaces).

4. In the **General** workspace settings, you should find an option to change **Execution Mode**.

5. You should see **Organization Default** mode selected. Change this to **Local** (custom) execution mode as highlighted in *Figure 9.10*.

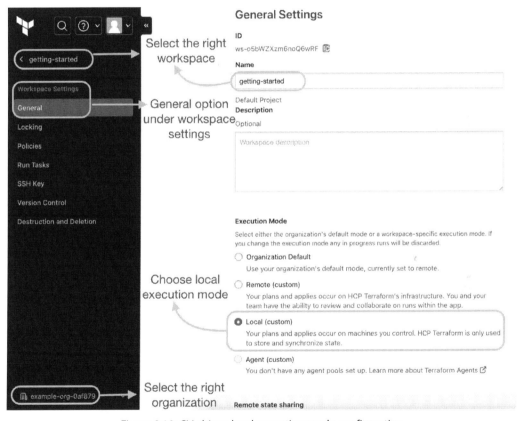

Figure 9.10: CLI-driven local execution mode configuration

6. Save the settings.

7. In the *Remote Execution Mode Using the CLI-Driven Workflow* exercise, you used the `tfc-getting-started` folder on the CLI. This folder has the following configuration files:

    - `backend.tf`: Defines the HCP Terraform organization and workspace where these Terraform runs should happen

    - `provider.tf`: Has a `provider_token` variable and the **fakewebservices** provider required for our example

    - `main.tf`: Has a resource block to create the fake VPC, servers, load balancer, and database

8. In the `main.tf` file, change `cidr_block` to `10.0.0.0/8` in the `fakewebservices_vpc` resource and `count` to `10` in the `fakewebservices_server` resource, as shown in *Figure 9.11*. Do not forget to save this setting.

```
~/tfc-getting-started $ls
LICENSE          README.md       backend.tf       main.tf         provider.tf      scripts
~/tfc-getting-started $cat main.tf
resource "fakewebservices_vpc" "primary_vpc" {
  name       = "Primary VPC"
  cidr_block = "10.0.0.0/8"────────► cidr_block is changed to 10.0.0.0/8
}


resource "fakewebservices_server" "servers" {
  count = 10 ─────────────────────► Number of servers changed to 10

  name = "Server ${count.index + 1}"
  type = "t2.micro"
  vpc  = fakewebservices_vpc.primary_vpc.name
}


resource "fakewebservices_load_balancer" "primary_lb" {
  name    = "Primary Load Balancer"
  servers = fakewebservices_server.servers[*].name
}


resource "fakewebservices_database" "prod_db" {
  name = "Production DB"
  size = 256
}
```

Figure 9.11: CLI-driven local execution mode changes

9. Run `terraform plan` to verify that the modifications appear:

    ```
    terraform plan
    ```

10. You will be prompted to enter a value for `var.provider_token`. This is the same token that was generated in the prerequisite section and stored in the `credentials.tfrc.json` file. You can either copy the content of this file and pass it as input when prompted, or you can pass it as an environmental variable, `TF_VAR_provider_token`.

11. You should see that Terraform is trying to add eight resources and modify two resources, as shown in *Figure 9.12*. The eight servers are added to the load balancer and hence modify that resource too. You also changed `cidr_range` of the VPC, which is another modification.

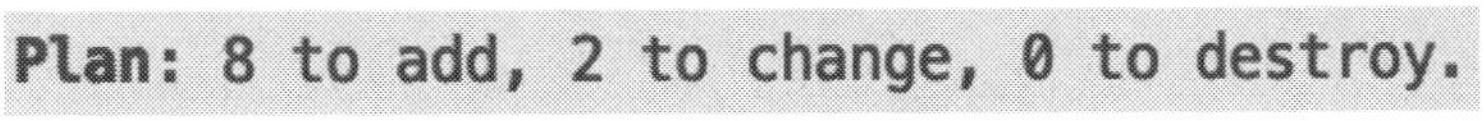

    Plan: 8 to add, 2 to change, 0 to destroy.

    Figure 9.12: `terraform plan` output for local execution mode

12. Run `terraform apply`, which creates/modifies the resources as per the code change:

    ```
    terraform apply
    ```

13. Log in to the HCP Terraform console and navigate to the overview of the workspace on which you are working. You should see that the number of resources has changed from 5 to 13 (10 servers, 1 VPC, 1 load balancer, 1 database), but the timestamp of the run is not updated, as shown in *Figure 9.13*. This is because runs from local execution mode are not shown in the console.

Unlike remote execution mode, local mode does not have the **Runs** option in the workspace that shows all previous `terraform runs`.

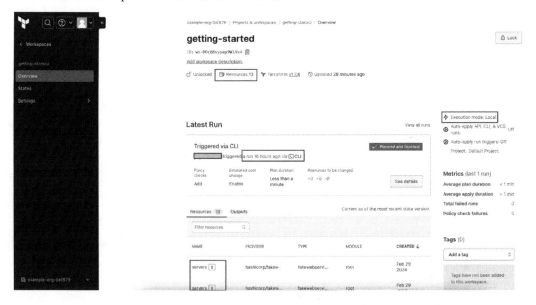

Figure 9.13: CLI-driven local execution mode completion details

14. Notice the execution mode is set to **Local**.

Now that you have learned how to run Terraform in local execution mode using the CLI-driven workflow, you can destroy the resources by running the following command. Enter the API token when prompted. It will delete all 13 resources:

```
terraform destroy –auto-approve
```

Remote Execution Mode Using the VCS/UI Workflow

In this exercise, you will learn how to integrate a VCS with HCP Terraform. You will see how a change committed to the VCS repository will trigger an automatic `terraform plan/apply` in HCP Terraform.

In the VCS/UI workflow, there is only the remote execution mode, and every workspace on HCP Terraform is associated with a repository. If you do not associate your workspace with a specific branch of the repository, it gets associated with a main branch.

HCP Terraform registers webhooks with the VCS provider. Whenever there is a change to the particular branch of the repository that a workspace is associated with, it automatically queues a Terraform run.

A workspace on HCP Terraform is linked only to one branch of the repository, and any changes to the other branches do not trigger Terraform runs.

> **Note**
>
> You must trigger the first run of the workspace manually, after which you can trigger the following runs via the VCS webhook. You will use the **Hashicorp-Certified-Terraform-Associate-003-Exam-guide-Second-Edition** repository in this exercise to learn about the VCS workflow in HCP Terraform.

For the VCS/UI workflow exercise, you will have to complete four tasks:

- Create a public repository in GitHub and populate it with the required Terraform configuration files.
- Integrate this repository with HCP Terraform.
- Test the VCS/UI workflow by committing a change to the repository to test the Terraform runs getting triggered in HCP Terraform.
- Cost estimation for the runs.

The steps required for each of the tasks are explained under the respective headings.

Creating a Public GitHub Repository and Adding Configuration Files

Follow these steps to complete this task:

1. You need to create the VCS repository with the required Terraform configuration files:

    I.   Log in to your GitHub account.
    II. Create a new repository. Since this is for learning, you can create a public repository, as shown in *Figure 9.14*. In this exercise, it is named **terraform-vcs-workflow**.

III.   It is recommended to select `.gitignore` for Terraform, a README, and a license.

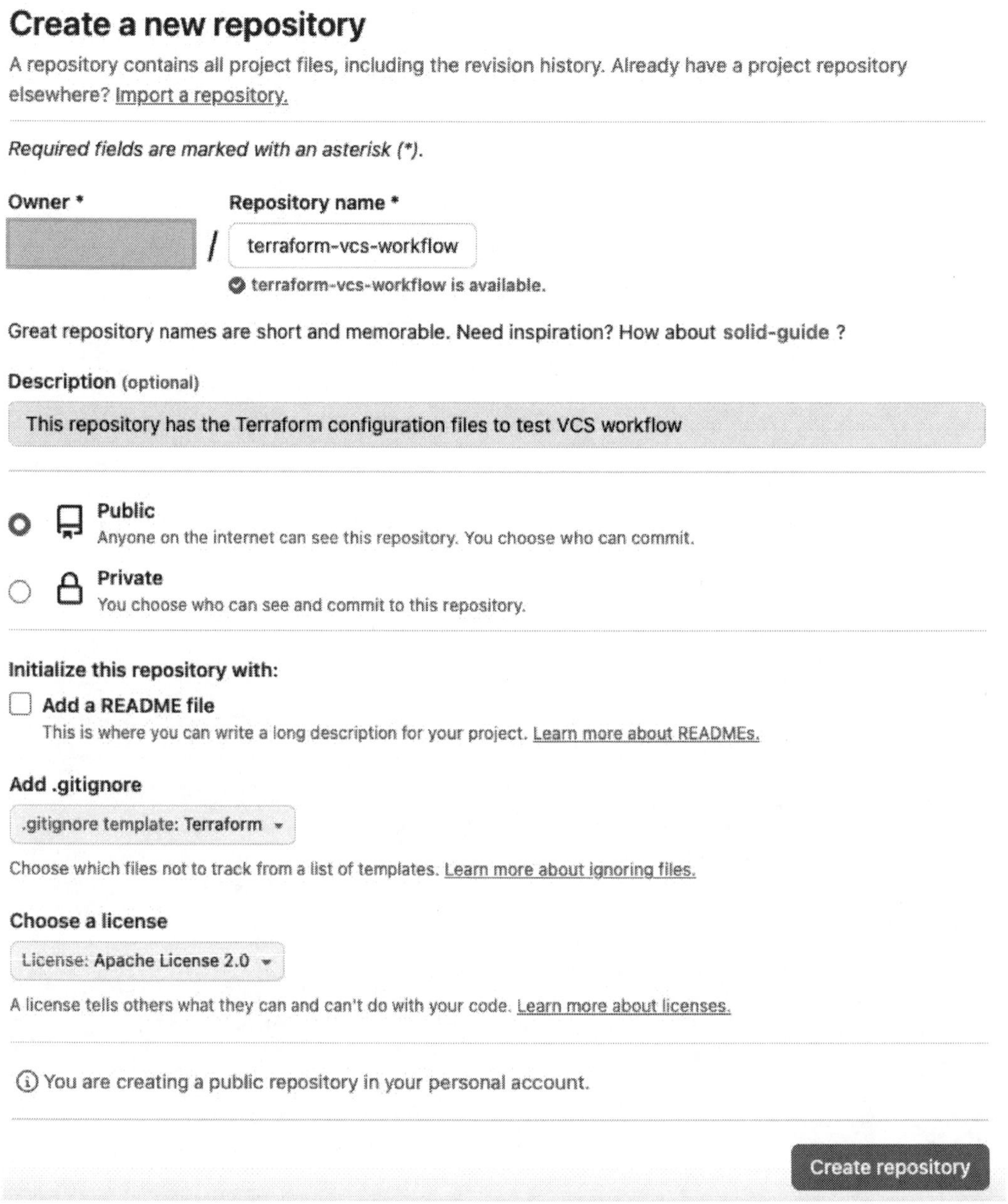

Create a new repository

A repository contains all project files, including the revision history. Already have a project repository elsewhere? Import a repository.

Required fields are marked with an asterisk (*).

Owner *   **Repository name ***

[   ] / [terraform-vcs-workflow]

✓ terraform-vcs-workflow is available.

Great repository names are short and memorable. Need inspiration? How about **solid-guide** ?

Description (optional)

[This repository has the Terraform configuration files to test VCS workflow]

○ **Public**
Anyone on the internet can see this repository. You choose who can commit.

○ **Private**
You choose who can see and commit to this repository.

Initialize this repository with:

☐ **Add a README file**
This is where you can write a long description for your project. Learn more about READMEs.

Add .gitignore

[.gitignore template: Terraform ▾]

Choose which files not to track from a list of templates. Learn more about ignoring files.

Choose a license

[License: Apache License 2.0 ▾]

A license tells others what they can and can't do with your code. Learn more about licenses.

ⓘ You are creating a public repository in your personal account.

[Create repository]

Figure 9.14: Creating a public repository in GitHub

2. Click on the newly created repository and copy the link (as shown in *Figure 9.15*) required to clone this repository to a local machine under the home directory.

```
git clone https://github.com/GIT_USERNAME/terraform-vcs-workflow.
git ~/terraform-vcs-workflow
```

Replace `GIT_USERNAME` with your Git username.

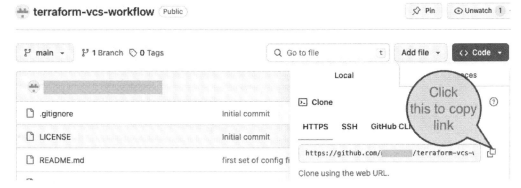

Figure 9.15: Copying the HTTPS link from the GitHub repository

3. In the folder where you have cloned the repo, update the remote endpoint URL (as before, replace `GIT_USERNAME` with your Git username):

```
cd ~/terraform-vcs-workflow
git remote set-url origin https://github.com/GIT_USERNAME/terraform-vcs-
workflow.git
```

4. Copy the configuration files of the **remote-child-module-example** folder used in *Chapter 5, Terraform Modules*, to the **terraform-vcs-workflow** folder.

5. Clone the **Hashicorp-Certified-Terraform-Associate-003-Exam-guide-Second-Edition** repository on your local machine in the home directory:

```
git clone https://github.com/PacktPublishing/Hashicorp-Certified-
Terraform-Associate-003-Exam-guide-Second-Edition.git ~/terraform-
book
```

6. Copy the files to the **terraform-vcs-workflow** folder:

```
cp ~/terraform-book/ch5/terraform-modules/remote-child-module-example/*
~/terraform-vcs-workflow
```

7. In the `providers.tf` file, you will notice the `terraform` block declaring only an AWS provider and no configuration for HCP Terraform. When using the VCS-driven workflow for HCP Terraform, you do not need to define the cloud block in your configuration.

8. Git is tracking the changes in the **terraform-vcs-workflow** folder. Since the new files are copied to this folder, you can add these changes to the Git staging area by running the following command:

```
cd ~/terraform-vcs-workflow && git add .
```

9. Commit the change.

```
cd ~/terraform-vcs-workflow && git commit -m "first set of files
to test VCS workflow"
```

10. Push the changes to the repository created in GitHub:

```
git push
```

11. If you encounter any errors during the code push to the repository, make sure you are correctly authenticated against GitHub using the personal access token. The following URL can help you solve this problem:

```
https://packt.link/xpAav
```

You have completed the creation of the public GitHub repository and have populated the required configuration files within the repository, as shown in *Figure 9.16*. In the next section, you will integrate this repository with HCP Terraform.

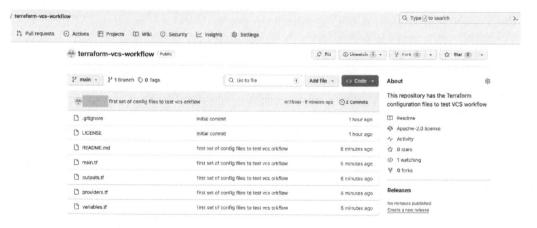

Figure 9.16: Exercise files populated in the GitHub repository

Integrating the VCS Repository with HCP Terraform

Follow these steps to integrate the public repository you created earlier with HCP Terraform:

1. If you have already logged in to HCP Terraform (via the browser), you can continue. You need to log in before proceeding to the next steps.

2. Create a new organization on HCP Terraform by clicking on the **Create new organization** option in the bottom-left corner of the HCP Terraform console, as shown in *Figure 9.17*. In this exercise, the organization is named **packt-learn-terraform**.

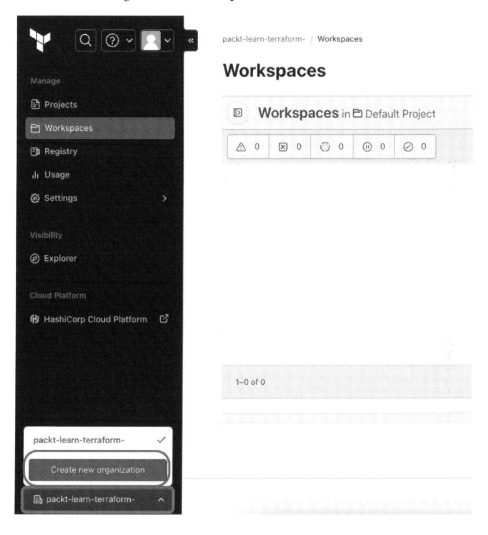

Figure 9.17: Creating a new organization in HCP Terraform

3. Once you have selected the organization and clicked **Create a Workspace**, you will see three options. Select **Version Control Workflow** as shown in *Figure 9.18*.

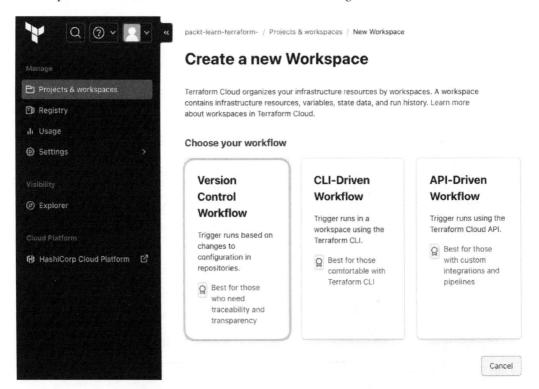

Figure 9.18: Creating a new workspace with `Version Control Workflow`

4. Select `GitHub` for the version control provider and select the `GitHub.com` version from the dropdown on the screen, as shown in *Figure 9.19*. A new window will open, asking you to authorize HCP Terraform to verify and use your GitHub account.

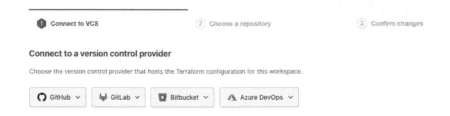

Figure 9.19: Choosing the version control provider

5. If you have multiple GitHub accounts, you will have to select the one you want to use and click the green **Authorize Terraform Cloud** button to authorize the connection, as shown in *Figure 9.20*.

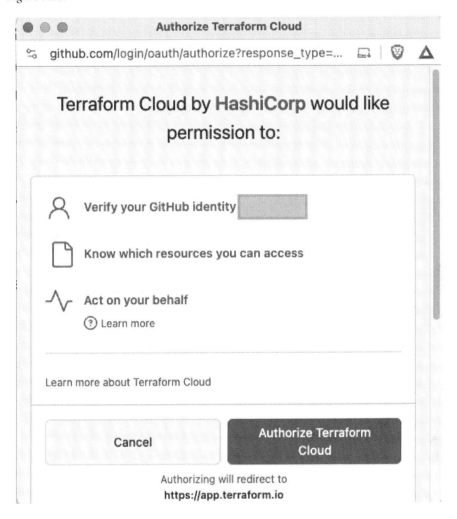

Figure 9.20: Authorization window in GitHub

Note

In *Figure 9.20* and *Figure 9.21*, you can see Terraform Cloud instead of HCP Terraform. HashiCorp is yet to make this name change in these two workflows. Once that update is done, you will see HCP Terraform on those two screens instead of Terraform Cloud.

6.   You will be asked to install Terraform Cloud/HCP Terraform for your GitHub account, as shown in *Figure 9.21*. When prompted, select the organization where you want to install this app. You may select all the repositories on the next screen to make sure the app installation covers all repositories. You can later select a specific repository that needs to be integrated with the workspace.

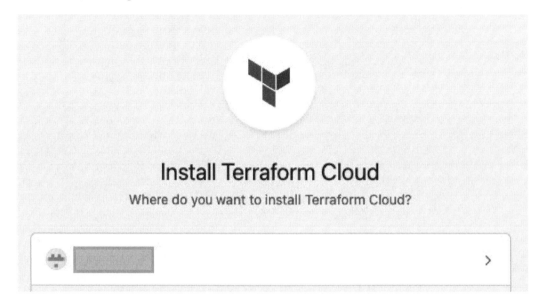

Figure 9.21: Install Terraform Cloud/HCP Terraform in GitHub

7.   Once successfully installed, it displays all the repositories in the account. Choose the repository you want, and the name of the workspace is auto-filled with the same name as the repository.

8. Click on **Create** to create a workspace that is integrated with a VCS repository. Once it has been created, you should see the screen shown in *Figure 9.22*:

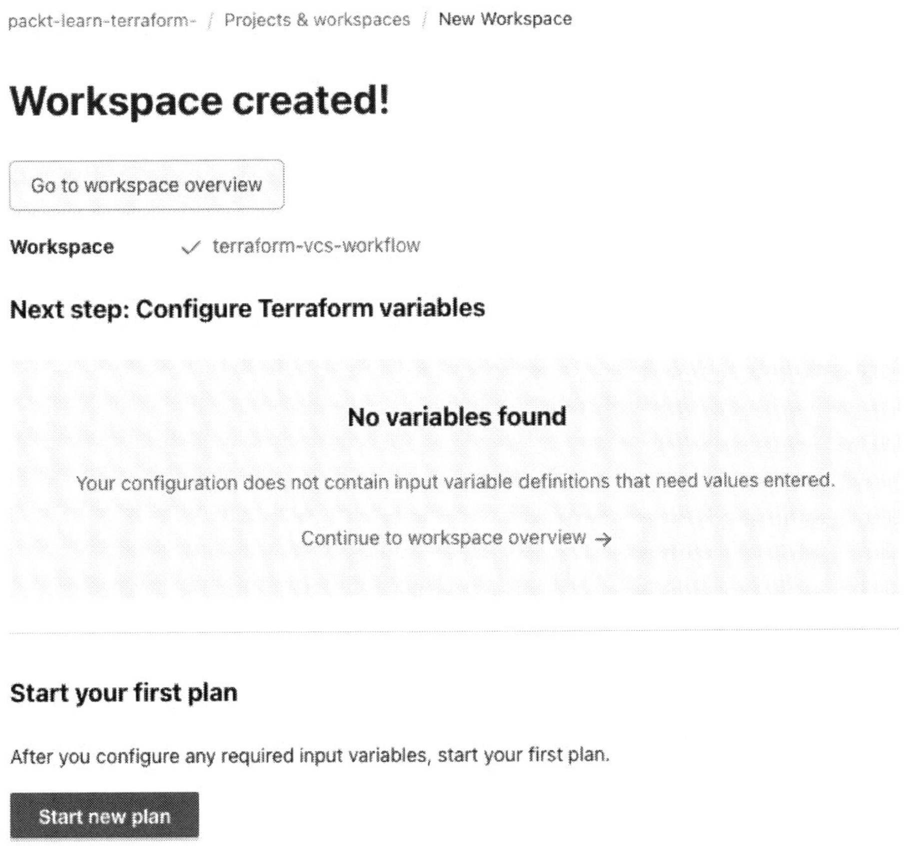

packt-learn-terraform- / Projects & workspaces / **New Workspace**

Workspace created!

Go to workspace overview

Workspace ✓ terraform-vcs-workflow

Next step: Configure Terraform variables

No variables found

Your configuration does not contain input variable definitions that need values entered.

Continue to workspace overview →

Start your first plan

After you configure any required input variables, start your first plan.

Start new plan

Figure 9.22: Successful creation of a workspace

This completes the second task of integrating the VCS repository with HCP Terraform.

Testing the VCS/UI Workflow in HCP Terraform

In this final task of the VCS/UI workflow, you will test the end-to-end flow by committing a change to the repository and verify whether it triggers `terraform plan/apply` in HCP Terraform.

Now you are ready to trigger your first run manually, which can be done by clicking **Start new plan** within the user interface of HCP Terraform.

This first run will fail because the AWS credentials are not configured yet.

The following steps will help you with the final task of making the change to the public repository and triggering `terraform plan` in HCP Terraform. The resources that get provisioned in this task will be in the AWS cloud environment and will cost you money. If you finish this exercise within an hour and delete the resources, the cost should be less than $1.

1. You need to provision an IAM user, assign the required policy, and generate an access key and secret key. For detailed instructions on how to create an IAM user, refer to the following AWS documentation:

    `https://docs.aws.amazon.com/IAM/latest/UserGuide/id_users_create.html`

2. Go to the **Overview** option of the newly created workspace and you will see a **Configure variable** option. Alternatively, you can directly go to the **Variables** option under the workspace.

3. Click on **Add variable** and select **Environment variable** from the variable category.

4. You need to add two variables: **AWS access key (AWS_ACCESS_KEY_ID)** and **AWS secret access key (AWS_SECRET_ACCESS_KEY)**. While adding the secret access key, select the **Sensitive** checkbox as per best practice. Once the variables are added, you should see entries similar to those shown in *Figure 9.23*.

> **Note**
>
> Workspaces support two types of variables: Environment variables and Terraform variables. Environment variables are available in the Terraform runtime environment.

5. Terraform variables are defined in the configuration file, mostly in `variables.tf`. In Terraform CLI, you normally pass the value for these variables via the `.tfvars` file. In HCP Terraform, you pass the value for the variable via the `Terraform` variable.

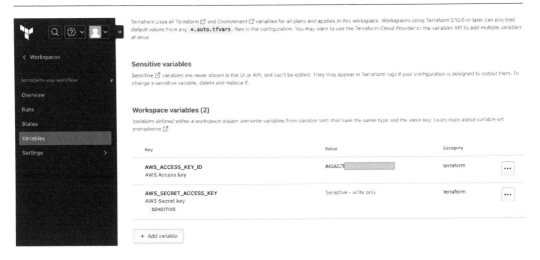

Figure 9.23: Adding AWS credentials as variables

6. Now you have the VCS repository with the required Terraform configuration files, integrated the repository with the HCP Terraform workspace, and configured the AWS credentials to authenticate to AWS for resource provisioning. You can now trigger the **Run** manually to verify whether everything works as planned.

7. You should see `terraform plan` running successfully, as shown in *Figure 9.24*. Toward the end of the plan, there is a prompt asking you to either confirm `terraform apply` or `discard run`.

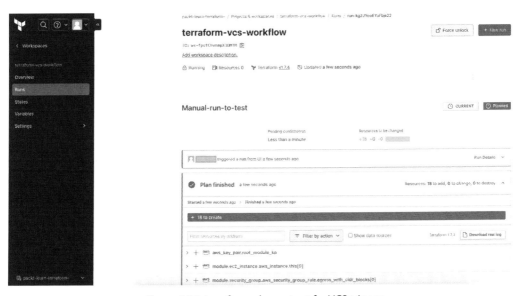

Figure 9.24: terraform plan output for VCS trigger

8. Once you click **Confirm and apply**, add a comment, and click **Confirm plan**, as shown in *Figure 9.25*, the resources will get provisioned.

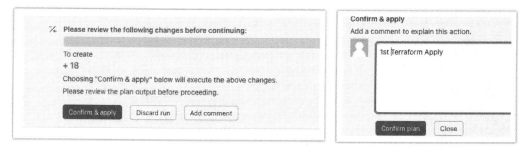

Figure 9.25: Confirm the `Terraform plan` to apply

9. The code has created VPC, subnets, a route table, EC2, and a few other things, as shown in *Figure 9.26*:

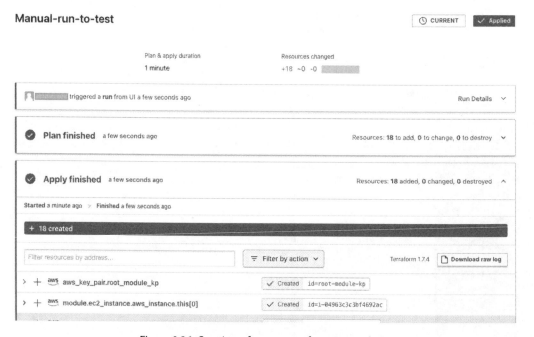

Figure 9.26: Creation of resources after a manual run

10. You can now make changes to the code locally and push it to the GitHub repository. This should automatically trigger `terraform run` in HCP Terraform.

11. Change the keypair name from `root-module-kp` to `vcs-test-kp` in the `main.tf` file, as shown in *Figure 9.27*:

```
resource "aws_key_pair" "root-module-kp" {
    key_name    = "vcs-test-kp"
```

Figure 9.27: Changing the keypair name

12. Now add the changed file to Git:

```
git add .
```

13. Commit the change:

```
git commit -m "changed the name of keypair"
```

14. Push the changes to the repository created in GitHub:

```
git push
```

15. Since the keypair cannot be renamed, it will have to be deleted and recreated. The EC2 instance that uses the keypair will also have to be deleted and recreated. The plan that was triggered automatically should confirm these changes.

16. As soon as the latest code is pushed to the GitHub repository, HCP Terraform picks up the change and runs `terraform plan`. It will present the changes as shown in *Figure 9.28*.

17. Go ahead and hit **Confirm & apply**, add a comment, and hit **Confirm plan**. You will see the resources getting provisioned.

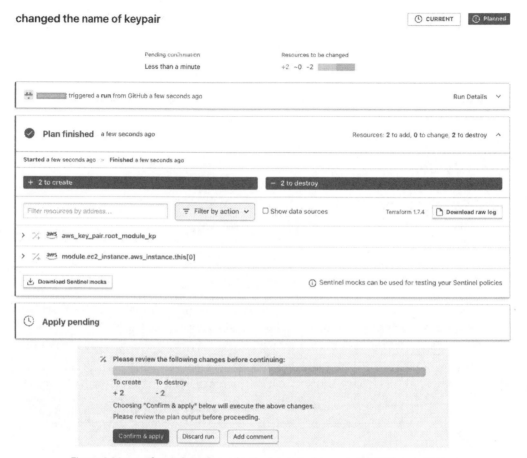

Figure 9.28: terraform plan output for the keypair change in the VCS repository

You can see that the change committed to the VCS repository has triggered the run in HCP Terraform and provisioned the resources once you approved the change.

This completes the VCS repository integration with HCP Terraform task.

> **Note**
>
> HCP Terraform now supports dynamic provider credentials to authenticate to AWS. This is a recommended way of authenticating against AWS for all production requirements.

Cost Estimation Feature

The last task in this exercise is to enable the **Cost Estimation** feature in the organization setting. This will give us a cost estimate for each run to indicate how much will it cost us to provision and run the infrastructure proposed by `terraform run`.

One of the important questions you'll get from your managers is about cost. This feature helps you to get a quick number that can be used for your discussions.

You will have to navigate to **Organization settings** and look for the **Cost Estimation** option. Click on the **Enable Cost Estimation for all workspaces** checkbox, as shown in *Figure 9.29*:

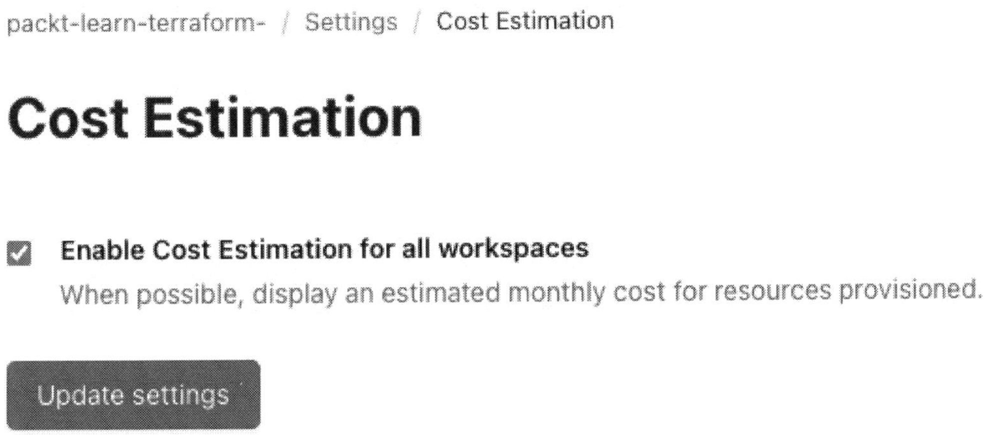

packt-learn-terraform- / Settings / Cost Estimation

Cost Estimation

☑ **Enable Cost Estimation for all workspaces**
  When possible, display an estimated monthly cost for resources provisioned.

Update settings

Figure 9.29: Enabling the Cost Estimation feature at the organization level

To verify that this change is working, we will make a few changes in the configuration file.

Modify the EC2 instance type from `t3.micro` to `t3.small` in the `main.tf` file and push the changes to the repo. Follow the same steps that changed the keypair name in the preceding exercise on the VCS/UI workflow.

This should trigger a run, and this time you should see the estimated cost for this infrastructure provisioning, as shown in *Figure 9.30*.

Please note that the price can vary a bit depending on the pricing changes made by AWS and the region used by you.

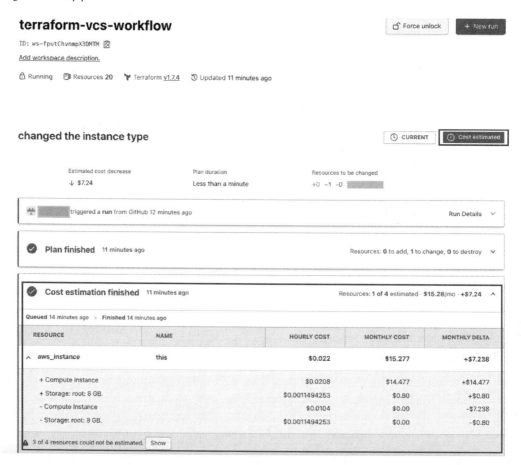

Figure 9.30: terraform plan showing the estimated cost

This completes the task of enabling and testing the Cost estimation feature in the VCS workflow.

Before you move on to the next section, please delete all the resources you have created, along with the workspace and organization in HCP Terraform. Though Terraform resources such as the workspace and organization will not cost you, AWS resources will be charged until they are deleted.

Migrating to HCP Terraform or Terraform Enterprise

If you are using Terraform Community Edition to manage your resources, you can migrate to HCP Terraform or Terraform Enterprise and continue to manage your resources.

The following steps need to be followed to complete the migration:

1. Make a list mapping the Terraform CLI directory with the HCP Terraform workspace.

2. Stop all Terraform operations to prevent any interaction with the state files during the migration.

3. Now you need to let Terraform know that HCP Terraform will be used going forward to manage the infrastructure. You do this by adding the `cloud` block within the `terraform` block of your configuration file. The `cloud` block has mandatory arguments, such as `organization` and `workspaces`, and optional arguments, such as `hostname`, `project`, and `name`. For a single workspace, the following `cloud` block needs to be added (make sure you change the organization and workspace name to the one you have in your HCP Terraform account):

```
terraform {
  cloud {
    organization = "packt-terraform"
    workspaces {
      name = "networking"
    }
  }
}
```

4. This should migrate the state file into HCP Terraform or to Terraform Enterprise, depending on which one you have used.

> **Note**
>
> **Speculative Plans:** These are plan-only runs, that is, these runs can never be applied but will only show the changes that your infrastructure will undergo due to the latest change in the configuration code. In the VCS-integrated workspace, any pull request to the repository will trigger a speculative plan, whereas in the CLI-integrated workspace, the `terraform plan` command will trigger the speculative plan.

Terraform Enterprise Features

If your company has a security mandate to have in-house deployment of the tools used to manage your infrastructure, Terraform Enterprise is the only edition to use.

Terraform Enterprise is the self-hosted distribution of HCP Terraform.

In terms of the features, Terraform Enterprise builds on the feature set of HCP Terraform. We will focus only on the unique additional features that are provided by Terraform Enterprise.

The following features are exclusive to Terraform Enterprise:

- Cross-organization registry sharing.

- Both HCP Terraform and Terraform Enterprise support the creation of multiple organizations and using the private registry within them. However, only Terraform Enterprise supports sharing the modules/providers in the private registry with other organizations in the same Terraform Enterprise instance.

- Runtime metrics (Prometheus) and application-level logging.

- Metrics and logs are very important from an observability perspective, as you will need to understand the state of the application and its performance.

- As Terraform Enterprise is a self-hosted application, you will need to monitor the runtime metrics and also keep an eye on the application logs.

- Runtime metrics need to be explicitly enabled as they are disabled by default. You can use Grafana with Prometheus to visualize these exported metrics.

- The application logs are sent directly to standard output and standard error.

- Air gap network deployment.

- If your company has a restricted network environment so that the tools deployed in your network cannot access the internet, you will have to go with Terraform Enterprise.

- Log forwarding.

- It is a common practice in enterprises to aggregate logs in a single location and pass them through security tools for observability, retain them for compliance, and use them for troubleshooting when needed.

- Terraform Enterprise supports forwarding logs to central locations, which could be external destinations such as **Syslog server** or paid offerings such as Datadog or Splunk. It also supports sending logs to cloud offerings such as AWS S3 and Cloudwatch (only when Terraform Enterprise is running within AWS), GCP Cloud Logging, or Azure Blob storage.

- Support for ServiceNow integration (only the HCP Terraform Plus edition supports this other than Terraform Enterprise).

- Many enterprises use ServiceNow for their workflow automation and prefer using a single tool while working with other applications too. Terraform Enterprise can integrate with ServiceNow, which will help users provision a self-serve infrastructure directly from ServiceNow.

- After the successful integration, end users will be able to use ServiceNow to create workspaces and perform Terraform runs.

- Terraform Enterprise provides an API to back up and restore all its application data.

Terraform Enterprise supports more flexible deployment options, such as Docker Engine (using Compose) and Kubernetes (using Helm).

> **Note**
>
> For a full feature comparison between Terraform Community Edition, HCP Terraform, and Terraform Enterprise, visit the following URL and navigate to the features section:
>
> `https://www.hashicorp.com/products/terraform/pricing`

Summary

In this chapter, you have learned about the various Terraform editions at your disposal after you decide to go with Terraform for infrastructure management. By now, you should have a good understanding of the shortcomings of Terraform Community Edition, when to move to HCP Terraform/Enterprise, and the additional features of these editions. You also learned how to sign up for HCP Terraform and looked at a few exercises that helped you understand how the workflows work and what the local and remote execution modes are.

Policy as code is one of the key features that is used to enforce certain policies around costing, best practices, and compliance. You learned how this can be implemented using Sentinel. Toward the end of the chapter, you looked at the unique features of Terraform Enterprise.

In the next chapter, you will look at some miscellaneous topics that have not been covered so far.

Exam Readiness Drill – Chapter Review Questions

Apart from a solid understanding of key concepts, being able to think quickly under time pressure is a skill that will help you ace your certification exam. That is why working on these skills early on in your learning journey is key.

Chapter review questions are designed to improve your test-taking skills progressively with each chapter you learn and review your understanding of key concepts in the chapter at the same time. You'll find these at the end of each chapter.

> **How to Access these Resources**
>
> To learn how to access these resources, head over to the chapter titled *Chapter 11, Accessing the Online Practice Resources*.

To open the Chapter Review Questions for this chapter, perform the following steps:

1. Click the link – `https://packt.link/HCorp003Ch9`.

    Alternatively, you can scan the following **QR code** (*Figure 9.31*):

Figure 9.31 – QR code that opens Chapter Review Questions for logged-in users

2. Once you log in, you'll see a page similar to the one shown in *Figure 9.32*:

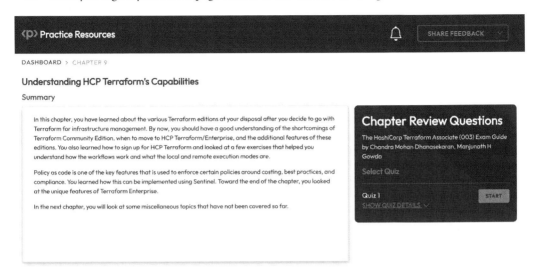

Figure 9.32 – Chapter Review Questions for Chapter 9

3. Once ready, start the following practice drills, re-attempting the quiz multiple times.

Exam Readiness Drill

For the first three attempts, don't worry about the time limit.

ATTEMPT 1

The first time, aim for at least **40%**. Look at the answers you got wrong and read the relevant sections in the chapter again to fix your learning gaps.

ATTEMPT 2

The second time, aim for at least **60%**. Look at the answers you got wrong and read the relevant sections in the chapter again to fix any remaining learning gaps.

ATTEMPT 3

The third time, aim for at least **75%**. Once you score 75% or more, you start working on your timing.

> **Tip**
>
> You may take more than **three** attempts to reach 75%. That's okay. Just review the relevant sections in the chapter till you get there.

Working On Timing

Target: Your aim is to keep the score the same while trying to answer these questions as quickly as possible. Here's an example of how your next attempts should look like:

Attempt	Score	Time Taken
Attempt 5	77%	21 mins 30 seconds
Attempt 6	78%	18 mins 34 seconds
Attempt 7	76%	14 mins 44 seconds

Table 9.1 – Sample timing practice drills on the online platform

> **Note**
>
> The time limits shown in the above table are just examples. Set your own time limits with each attempt based on the time limit of the quiz on the website.

With each new attempt, your score should stay above **75%** while your "time taken" to complete should "decrease". Repeat as many attempts as you want till you feel confident dealing with the time pressure.

10

Miscellaneous Topics

A big congratulations to you for maintaining sheer focus and dedication to your Terraform certification journey – and yes, you have reached the final chapter of this book.

As you will have noticed, the core aspects of the Terraform configuration language were covered initially. This was then followed by learnings on enterprise offerings such as Terraform Cloud and Terraform Enterprise that elevate the overall development experience for software developers. They also enable you to manage production infrastructure seamlessly with minimal overhead.

In this chapter, some topics relevant to the certification exam that could not be covered so far will be discussed. The individual topics are not very extensive, but they add value in special scenarios if the use case demands it.

The topics that will be covered in this chapter are the following:

- Input validations
- Preconditions and postconditions
- The `check` { } block
- Workspaces
- The `dynamic` { } block
- Provisioners
- Handling sensitive data

Technical Requirements

There are sample configuration files with the examples used in the chapter and you can find them at the following link:

```
https://github.com/PacktPublishing/Hashicorp-Certified-Terraform-
Associate-003-Exam-guide-Second-Edition/tree/main/ch10
```

To use the files, the following tools are expected to be available on your workstation:

- An AWS account ID with administrator access credentials

- The AWS CLI (version 2.x.x)

- The Terraform CLI (version 1.5.x or later)

- Visual Studio Code or any text editor

Input Validations

In real-world scenarios, it is very common to get the necessary inputs from the user and provision the infrastructure accordingly. For example, you can assume that you are part of a central DevOps team that is involved in setting up the CICD pipelines for any team requiring your service. In this case, they might need to provide basic inputs such as application name/ID, cloud-specific details such as region, and so on.

If the infrastructure provisioning is automated from your end, such that the workflow will trigger directly when the user provides the input via a ticket, it becomes necessary to run the workflow for valid inputs only. Manual errors in inputs would also need to be filtered as early as possible.

This is where input validations will help, and in Terraform, this can be achieved by adding the `validation` {} block with the `condition` argument specifying the rules in the form of expressions. If the result of the expression is TRUE, the input will be considered valid, and if it's FALSE, Terraform will return an error message.

This is primarily used with variable declarations. Take a look at the following code snippet:

```
variable "app_id" {
  type        = string
  description = "The application id for ECR repo creation."

  validation {
    condition       = length(var.app_id) == 9 && substr(var.app_id, 0,
4) == "app-"
    error_message = "The app_id value must include the prefix \"app-\"
and should be 9 characters long."
  }
}
```

Here, the `app_id` variable is to get the user input for the application ID and that will be used to create the **Elastic Container Registry** (**ECR**) repository for the application to host Docker images. ECR is a managed service from the AWS cloud provider for customers to host their container images in public or private repositories.

If the input does not match the criteria of a length of nine characters or is missing the `app-`, prefix, Terraform will return a coded error message like the one shown in *Figure 10.1*. This is directly related to the resource lifecycle and `terraform applies` will go through only if the specified condition is TRUE. You will further look into other functionalities and how they behave:

```
Error: Invalid value for variable

  on input-validations.tf line 5:
   5: variable "app_id" {

     │
     │ var.app_id is "app-1234"

The app_id value must include the prefix "app-" and should be 9 characters long.

This was checked by the validation rule at input-validations.tf:9,3-13.
```

Figure 10.1 – Error message returned by Terraform

The complete code is available at the GitHub link provided previously – feel free to try it out with your AWS account.

Preconditions and Postconditions

Input validation stops resource creation in the case of invalid inputs if you run the configuration script, which means the validation takes place before the `terraform apply` operation.

But if you want a similar condition(s) to be applied to resources, data sources, or outputs and the evaluation has to be done before and after, based on the scenario, Terraform has `precondition` and `postcondition` to explore.

For resources and data sources, the `precondition` and `postcondition` checks need to be added under the `lifecycle {}` block. The outputs can contain a `precondition` check only without the `lifecycle {}` block. The `precondition` and `postcondition` check will contain the condition and the error message parameters, such as the one you saw with the input validation.

Look at the following code snippet:

```
data "aws_ecr_repository" "repo_data" {
  name = aws_ecr_repository.app_repo.name

  lifecycle {
    precondition {
      condition       = aws_ecr_repository.app_repo.image_tag_mutability
== "IMMUTABLE"
      error_message = "The only value allowed is \"IMMUTABLE\"."
```

```
    }

    postcondition {
        condition       = substr(self.name, 10, 4) == "repo"
        error_message = "Resource suffix \"repo\" missing for the ECR
repo"
    }
  }
}
```

The data {} block here has one precondition and one postcondition specified. precondition will validate whether the image_tag_mutablity argument is set to IMMUTABLE to allow the resource creation. If not, Terraform will return an error message.

postcondition will check whether the repo to be created has the right repo suffix appended at the end. If not, the resource creation will be blocked again, and the error message will be returned. This behavior is the same when applied with resource {} blocks as well.

If you look closely, the self keyword is used to refer to the name attribute within the same data resource block and the validation will come into effect when you issue the terraform plan and terraform apply commands.

In the case of outputs, only precondition is applicable, and that will be validated before the value parameter. Specifying the precondition with the outputs will help save the right output value in the output, and if there are any problems with the latest changes, it will preserve the previous output value with this type of check.

The check {} block

Unlike the input variable validations and the custom preconditions/postconditions, check {} blocks are not tied to the resource lifecycle directly. check {} blocks are used to validate the checks for the overall configuration after the plan/apply operations.

check {} blocks can help perform the functional validation of the provisioned infrastructure after apply – check {} blocks have assert {} block inside them, which, in turn, contain the condition and error_message arguments.

Another major difference is that check {} blocks will allow the terraform plan/apply operation to go through in the case of validation failures. The error message will be written at the end if the defined condition seems to be invalid. This can also be used with data sources.

To understand this block better, we will define an AWS **Simple Storage Service (S3)** bucket and check the `force_destroy` parameter in the `check {}` block:

```
resource "aws_s3_bucket" "app_bucket" {
#   force_destroy = true
}
check "destroy_check" {
    assert {
      condition = aws_s3_bucket.app_bucket.force_destroy == true
      error_message = "The S3 bucket created with the force_destroy
parameter as false"
    }
}
```

During the planning stage, the `force_destroy` parameter value that is going to be set is known, and hence, Terraform will throw the error message shown in *Figure 10.2*.

```
Plan: 1 to add, 0 to change, 0 to destroy.

Warning: Check block assertion failed

  on check-assertions.tf line 7, in check "destroy_check":
    7:        condition = aws_s3_bucket.app_bucket.force_destroy == true

        aws_s3_bucket.app_bucket.force_destroy is false

The S3 bucket created with the force_destroy parameter as false
```

Figure 10.2 – Error message from the check {} block

If you proceed with `apply`, the S3 bucket will still be created, and the error message will also be returned, as shown in *Figure 10.3*.

```
aws_s3_bucket.app_bucket: Creating...
aws_s3_bucket.app_bucket: Creation complete after 6s [id=terraform-                    ?]

  Warning: Check block assertion failed

    on check-assertions.tf line 7, in check "destroy_check":
    7:        condition = aws_s3_bucket.app_bucket.force_destroy == true

      aws_s3_bucket.app_bucket.force_destroy is false

  The S3 bucket created with the force_destroy parameter as false


Apply complete! Resources: 1 added, 0 changed, 0 destroyed.
```

Figure 10.3 – Output from terraform apply

Workspaces

This section is relevant to Terraform CLI workspaces and is different from the Terraform Cloud workspaces covered in the previous chapter.

As you are aware, Terraform configuration files can be configured to use a particular backend to persist the state file data. This has more advantages over the default `local` backend in terms of backup and recovery, shared access within teams, security, and so on.

When you work with the default settings, the configuration stores the state file that belongs to the `default` workspace. If there is a need to manage and work with multiple workspaces for the same configuration, there is a list of compatible backends that support that.

Have a look at a scenario and proceed with a sample exercise to know more:

The accounting team of the **ABC** company is planning to go ahead and use Terraform for their infrastructure provisioning. They will be deploying resources with the same AWS account to support multiple lower environments. AWS S3 is the backend they will be configuring for their scripts.

This approach will help with better management. This will also remove the need to deal with multiple AWS accounts. In this case, the configuration scripts that will be used are the same for all environments, and the resources created must be unique to avoid conflicts.

Instead of creating copies of the configuration for each environment with hardcoded values, you can parameterize the configuration so the resource names are decided dynamically and you can work with a single set.

This is where Terraform workspaces can help; for the above scenario, the S3 backend can be configured to use different workspaces for each environment, and all state files will be created and managed within the same S3 bucket.

The `main.tf` file for the sample exercise is given here:

```
provider "aws" {
  region = "us-east-1"
}

locals {
  queue_prefix = "${terraform.workspace}"
}

resource «aws_sqs_queue» «main_queue» {
  name = "${local.queue_prefix}-accounting-stmt-queue"

  redrive_policy = jsonencode({
    deadLetterTargetArn = aws_sqs_queue.dlq_queue.arn
    maxReceiveCount     = 4
  })
}
resource "aws_sqs_queue" "dlq_queue" {
  name = "${local.queue_prefix}-accounting-stmt-dlq"
}

resource "aws_sqs_queue_redrive_allow_policy" "queue_redrive_policy" {
  queue_url = aws_sqs_queue.dlq_queue.id

  redrive_allow_policy = jsonencode({
    redrivePermission = "byQueue",
    sourceQueueArns   = [aws_sqs_queue.main_queue.arn]
  })
}
```

Here are some things to note:

- The local `queue_prefix` variable will be set based on the current workspace name in the context, and it will decide the final name of the SQS resources to be created.

- The script will create an SQS queue and its respective dead letter queue with a redrive policy. SQS is a fully managed queueing service from AWS to be used in event-driven architectures where different microservices can interact with the queue messages to be processed in an asynchronous fashion. The redrive policy will ensure the unprocessed messages in the dead letter queue will be moved to the standard queue for processing.

More information can be found at the following links:

- `https://docs.aws.amazon.com/sqs`

- `https://docs.aws.amazon.com/AWSSimpleQueueService/latest/SQSDeveloperGuide/sqs-configure-dead-letter-queue-redrive.html`

- The default `local` backend is used as there is no `backend {}` block configured.

- On applying this configuration with the default settings, the SQS resources that will be created are as follows:

  - `default-accounting-stmt-dlq`

  - `default-accounting-stmt-queue`

The `terraform.tfstate` file is stored in the default root directory location as expected. If you want to, use the same script to create the same set of resources for the `dev` environment with the dev prefix.

As a first step, you can go ahead and create the `dev` workspace with the following command:

```
$ terraform workspace new dev
```

Then, the context will be automatically switched to the new `dev` workspace (marked with the asterisk (`*`) symbol), which can be validated with the `terraform workspace list` command, as shown in *Figure 10.4.*

```
$ terraform workspace list
```

```
aces-example> terraform workspace list
  default
* dev
```

Figure 10.4 – terraform workspace list command output

Now, rerun the `plan` and `apply` commands and see the results:

- You will notice that a new `terraform.tfstate.d` folder has been created in the root directory and it has one subfolder, `dev`, which has a new state file created.

- The state file will have the following resources defined and is different from the ones created with the default workspace:

  - `dev-accounting-stmt-dlq`

  - `dev-accounting-stmt-queue`

You can use the same steps to create multiple workspaces with the same configuration without having to manage multiple backends. To destroy the resources created in the respective workspace(s), please use the `terraform workspace select <WORKSPACE_NAME>` command, followed by the `destroy` command.

You can also refer to the `commands.txt` file in the GitHub repository for this chapter, which lists the different commands used with these examples.

The list of supported backends for multiple workspaces is given here:

- **Azure Resource Manager** (**RM**): Blob storage supported by Microsoft

- Consul: Backend to store the state as **Key/Value** (**KV**) in the given path

- COS: Tencent Cloud object storage

- GCS: Google's object storage service

- Kubernetes: Open-source container orchestration platform

- Local: Default backend supported by Terraform

- OSS: Bucket storage option from Alibaba Cloud

- Postgres: Popular relational database

- Remote: Generic remote backend to configure different backends

- S3: AWS object storage platform

The dynamic {} block

The `dynamic {}` block is a special type of block that can be used to generate nested blocks instead of a value. This is different from the `for_each` expression, which dynamically sets the expression value based on the input complex type.

The `dynamic {}` block creates a nested block for special resources, data sources, providers, or provisioner blocks that might accept repeatable nested blocks. A very good example of possible usage is **DynamoDB** table creation using Terraform.

AWS DynamoDB is a non-relational NoSQL database service; it can accept multiple attribute blocks, and these blocks can be automatically constructed using the dynamic {} block if the values can be passed from a complex type variable.

The following configuration snippet uses the dynamic block to define a DynamoDB table with the AccountId and AccountName attributes:

```
resource "aws_dynamodb_table" "account-table" {

    name            = "Accounttable"
    billing_mode    = "PROVISIONED"
    read_capacity   = 2
    write_capacity  = 2
    hash_key        = "AccountId"
    range_key       = "AccountName"

    dynamic "attribute" {
      for_each = var.dynamodb_attributes
      content {
        name = attribute.value["name"]
        type = attribute.value["type"]
      }
    }

    tags = {
      Description = "Account Table"
      CreatedBy   = "dynamic  block"
    }
}
```

You might have a question now – how does this actually work?

- You have a dynamodb_attributes variable with the list(object) type, with each occurrence having the name and type keys.

- The variable will have a couple of values, AccountID and AccountName, that will be set as attributes using the attribute block.

- The dynamic block generates this type by looping over the variable values using the for_each expression and ensures that different attribute blocks are generated before creating the resource.

- The content {} block will actually set the content for the attribute block with the input values passed.

This is helpful in this particular case, but this should not be applied wherever possible, because that could make the configuration complex and difficult to understand. The dynamic blocks can also be used within other dynamic blocks if needed to create multiple-level nested blocks.

One limitation with the `dynamic {}` block is that it can generate nested blocks supported by the resource type but cannot be used for generating meta-argument blocks for **lifecycle** and **provisioner** blocks.

Provisioners

Terraform supports the concept of **provisioners**, which can be used to perform some actions on a local machine executing Terraform or a remote machine provisioned using Terraform that works in sync with other real-world objects.

Local and remote provisioners should be considered as the last option to use in Terraform because it has no control over the actions performed by provisioners and it can depend on multiple things in the local/remote machine. If there are alternatives available from providers to avoid the use of provisioners, they should be considered first as per the Terraform documentation.

Think of a scenario where a team of developers is working on the same set of configuration scripts with local provisioners and there are dependencies on the scripts for a few resources. The local provisioner will mostly work with the software installed on the local machine, and it can have different versions on different machines. Hence, the behavior of the local provisioner will vary and there are chances of dependent resources being impacted.

There are a few situations where provisioners are still used:

- Passing data to virtual machines using `user_data`, metadata, or `custom_data` blocks, based on the cloud provider
- Provisioning files using the `cloudinit_config` data source
- Running configuration management software

The file provisioner

The file provisioner is mainly used to copy files to newly created resources in Terraform or create new files. It supports `ssh` and `winrm` connection modes.

The same resource can contain multiple `file` provisioner blocks if needed, and the parameters supported are as follows:

- `source`: The source file or directory
- `content`: The actual content to be copied to the file in the new resource
- `destination`: The destination file or directory

The `source` and `content` parameters cannot be used at the same time.

A sample file provisioner is given here for reference, and for this example to work, the `configs` folder should be available in the current working directory and SSH access should be enabled on the EC2 machine to be accessible from the local machine running the script:

```
resource "aws_instance" "web" {
  # Copies the configs folder to /etc/configs
  provisioner « file » {
    source      = « ./configs «
    destination = « /etc/configs »
  }
}
```

The local-exec provisioner

The `local-exec` provisioner is used to run commands after the resource is created and it runs on the host machine running Terraform.

The following are the parameters supported for the `local-exec` provisioner:

- `command`: The command to be executed.

- `working_dir`: The working directory for the command to run; if not provided, defaults to the current working directory.

- `interpreter`: The interpreter arguments to pass for the command – examples are [sh, -c] and [/bin/bash, -c].

- `environment`: The name of the environment in key-value pairs for the command.

- `when`: To specify when to execute the command and the valid values are when = destroy. This will run when the resource is destroyed.

- `quiet`: When set to true, the command will not be printed in the output terminal. But still, the output of the command will be displayed.

Here is a sample configuration:

In this example, the `aws configure list` command is executed on the local machine to check the current configuration set for the AWS CLI. For this example to work, the AWS CLI tool should be available on the local machine and a valid configuration profile should exist:

```
resource "aws_instance" "web" {
  # ...
  provisioner "local-exec" {
    command = «aws configure list»
    environment = {
```

```
        env = "prod"
        region = "us-east-1"
      }
    when = destroy
  }
}
```

The remote-exec provisioner

The `remote-exec` provisioner is used to execute the command on the new resource created remotely. This provisioner requires the connection block and it supports both `ssh` and `winrm` connection types.

The following parameters are supported when using this provisioner:

- `inline`: The list of commands to execute on the remote machine using the default shell available on the machine. If the default shell needs to be overridden, the first command in the list should be set to the required shell program.

- `script`: The relative or absolute path of the script available locally to be copied and then executed. This cannot be used if the `inline` or `scripts` option is specified.

- `scripts`: The relative or absolute path of the scripts available locally to be copied and then executed. This cannot be used if the `inline` or `script` option is specified.

When using the `script` or `scripts` option, arguments are not allowed to be passed. In that case, the file provisioner can be used and then the `inline` option can be used to pass the arguments for the command.

As mentioned already, provisioners are not the preferred option for use if providers support an alternative way of executing any commands/scripts when the resource is created.

Here's a sample configuration:

```
resource "aws_instance" "web" {
  connection {
    type     = "ssh"
    user     = "testuser"
    password = base64decode(var.password)
    host     = self.public_ip
  }
  provisioner "remote-exec" {
    inline = [
      "/bin/bash -c echo ${aws_instance.web.id}"
    ]
  }
}
```

Handling Sensitive Data

When you deal with creating and managing cloud resources using Terraform, there could be situations where you will be working with sensitive data such as admin credentials, database user passwords, vault keys, and so on. So, it is very important that you secure the sensitive data, so it is not exposed to the outside world.

The sensitive data is stored in the state file as well, since it must record all the relevant attributes of the provisioned resources to track whether there are any changes made subsequently. So, the state file with the sensitive data is important, and you need a proper strategy to decide where it was stored and accessed.

However, a couple of considerations must be made:

- When the state file is stored with the default `local` backend, the data is stored in plain text format.

- When the state file is stored in a remote backend such as S3, it can be configured to enable encryption at rest so the data will be decrypted and used only when Terraform uses it. Also, bucket policies can be additionally added to enable only specific users to have access to the state file.

The following section looks at the different aspects of handling sensitive data within the Terraform workflow and how to secure them.

AWS Access Keys or Admin Credentials

In AWS, the most common way of provisioning resources is by using admin credentials in the background. There are special cases where the AWS CLI is also expected to be configured already on the host machine running Terraform.

There are multiple ways to set up admin credentials:

- `provider {}` block configuration values

- Environment variables

- Shared credentials/configuration file

- Container credentials

- Instance profile credentials

But the preferred way is to use the environment variables option so that it does not get recorded in the state file as it is and does not use hardcoded credentials.

Variables

Terraform variables are also expected to contain sensitive information sometimes, to be passed for configuration, such as database initial credentials such as usernames and passwords.

In this case, the `sensitive` attribute of the variable has to be set to true, so it is not exposed directly in the console during the `plan` and `apply` operations.

But remember that the variable value will be stored in plain text fashion in the state file. When setting variable values, the environment variables option is preferred with the **TF_VAR_<variable_name>** convention.

You can use the `.tfvars` file to set variable values, but then again, you need to ensure that the configuration scripts with the `.tfvars` file are accessible only to a special group of people.

Another good practice is to fetch the values from an external secret engine such as AWS Secrets Manager, HashiCorp Vault, or similar tools.

This is how you should declare a variable that might contain a sensitive value:

```
variable "database_password" {
  description = "Database password"
  type        = string
  sensitive   = true
}
```

Output Values

Output values also can refer to a variable marked as sensitive in the configuration, like any other variable. In this case, Terraform would throw an **Output refers to sensitive values** error message.

To overcome this issue, the output value also needs to be marked as `sensitive` using the attribute and then the output value will also be hidden from the console output. Again, the values will be recorded in plain text inside the state file.

Next Steps

Now that you have covered miscellaneous topics, you should be good to go ahead and try out the practice exams.

Once you feel confident, schedule the certification exam and get certified with flying colors!

Summary

In this chapter, the focus was more on topics that are not vast but are very important to understand when you want to build and deploy complex applications using Terraform. Provisioners are very helpful if you know how to use them effectively and handle exceptions that can occur. The usage of sensitive data in Terraform needs to be planned well ahead of the project schedule and external secret engines should be utilized whenever possible.

Exam Readiness Drill – Chapter Review Questions

Apart from a solid understanding of key concepts, being able to think quickly under time pressure is a skill that will help you ace your certification exam. That is why working on these skills early on in your learning journey is key.

Chapter review questions are designed to improve your test-taking skills progressively with each chapter you learn and review your understanding of key concepts in the chapter at the same time. You'll find these at the end of each chapter.

> **How to Access these Resources**
>
> To learn how to access these resources, head over to the chapter titled *Chapter 11, Accessing the Online Practice Resources.*

To open the Chapter Review Questions for this chapter, perform the following steps:

1. Click the link – `https://packt.link/HCorp003Ch10`.

    Alternatively, you can scan the following **QR code** (*Figure 10.5*):

Figure 10.5 – QR code that opens Chapter Review Questions for logged-in users

2. Once you log in, you'll see a page similar to the one shown in *Figure 10.6*:

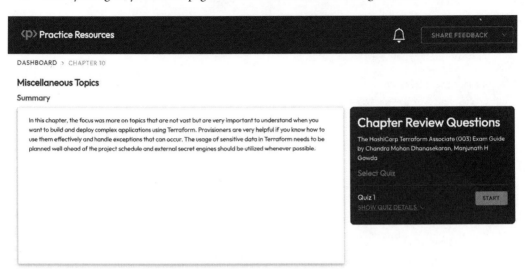

Figure 10.6 – Chapter Review Questions for Chapter 10

3. Once ready, start the following practice drills, re-attempting the quiz multiple times.

Exam Readiness Drill

For the first three attempts, don't worry about the time limit.

ATTEMPT 1

The first time, aim for at least **40%**. Look at the answers you got wrong and read the relevant sections in the chapter again to fix your learning gaps.

ATTEMPT 2

The second time, aim for at least **60%**. Look at the answers you got wrong and read the relevant sections in the chapter again to fix any remaining learning gaps.

ATTEMPT 3

The third time, aim for at least **75%**. Once you score 75% or more, you start working on your timing.

> **Tip**
> You may take more than **three** attempts to reach 75%. That's okay. Just review the relevant sections in the chapter till you get there.

Working On Timing

Target: Your aim is to keep the score the same while trying to answer these questions as quickly as possible. Here's an example of how your next attempts should look like:

Attempt	Score	Time Taken
Attempt 5	77%	21 mins 30 seconds
Attempt 6	78%	18 mins 34 seconds
Attempt 7	76%	14 mins 44 seconds

Table 10.1 – Sample timing practice drills on the online platform

> **Note**
> The time limits shown in the above table are just examples. Set your own time limits with each attempt based on the time limit of the quiz on the website.

With each new attempt, your score should stay above **75%** while your "time taken" to complete should "decrease". Repeat as many attempts as you want till you feel confident dealing with the time pressure.

11
Accessing the Online Practice Resources

Your copy of *HashiCorp Terraform Associate (003) Exam Guide* comes with free online practice resources. Use these to hone your exam readiness even further by attempting practice questions on the companion website. The website is user-friendly and can be accessed from mobile, desktop, and tablet devices. It also includes interactive timers for an exam-like experience.

How to Access These Resources

Here's how you can start accessing these resources depending on your source of purchase.

Purchased from Packt Store (packtpub.com)

If you've bought the book from the Packt store (`packtpub.com`) eBook or Print, head to `https://packt.link/hsh003practice`. There, log in using the same Packt account you created or used to purchase the book.

Packt+ Subscription

If you're a *Packt+ subscriber*, you can head over to the same link (`https://packt.link/hsh003practice`), log in with your `Packt ID`, and start using the resources. You will have access to them as long as your subscription is active.

If you face any issues accessing your free resources, contact us at `customercare@packt.com`.

Purchased from Amazon and Other Sources

If you've purchased from sources other than the ones mentioned above (like *Amazon*), you'll need to unlock the resources first by entering your unique sign-up code provided in this section. **Unlocking takes less than 10 minutes, can be done from any device, and needs to be done only once.** Follow these five easy steps to complete the process:

STEP 1

Open the link `https://packt.link/hsh003unlock` OR scan the following **QR code** (*Figure 11.1*):

Figure 11.1 – QR code for the page that lets you unlock this book's free online content.

Either of those links will lead to the following page as shown in *Figure 11.2*:

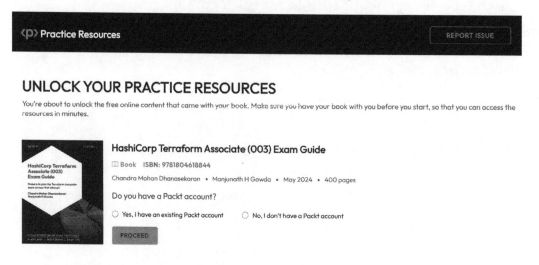

Figure 11.2 – Unlock page for the online practice resources

STEP 2

If you already have a Packt account, select the option `Yes, I have an existing Packt account`. If not, select the option `No, I don't have a Packt account`.

If you don't have a Packt account, you'll be prompted to create a new account on the next page. It's free and only takes a minute to create.

Click `Proceed` after selecting one of those options.

STEP 3

After you've created your account or logged in to an existing one, you'll be directed to the following page as shown in *Figure 11.3*.

Make a note of your unique unlock code:

```
IPW4426
```

Type in or copy this code into the text box labeled 'Enter Unique Code':

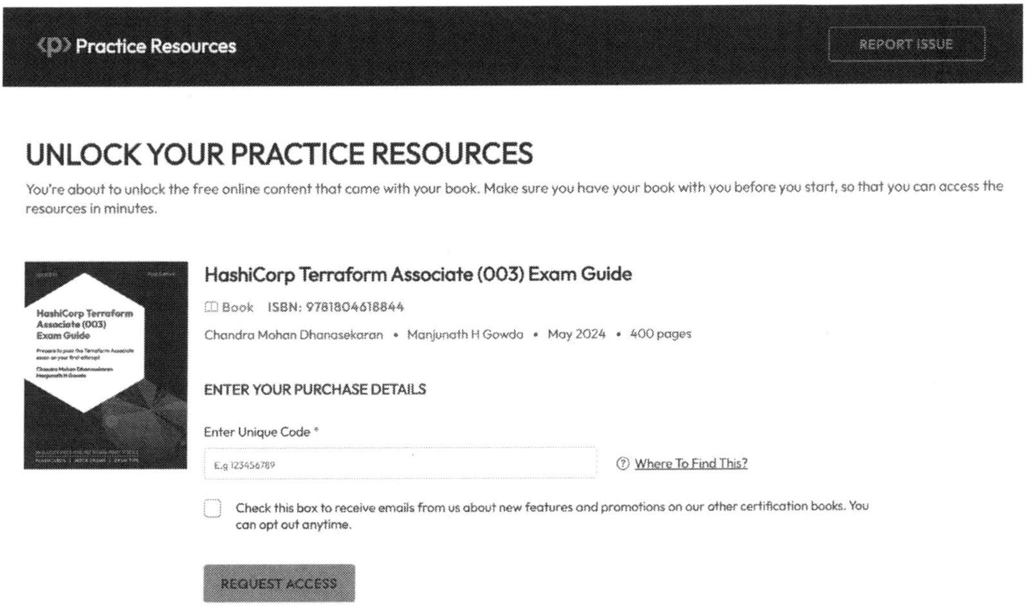

Figure 11.3 – Enter your unique sign-up code to unlock the resources

> **Troubleshooting Tip**
>
> After creating an account, if your connection drops off or you accidentally close the page, you can reopen the page shown in *Figure 11.2* and select `Yes, I have an existing account`. Then, sign in with the account you had created before you closed the page. You'll be redirected to the screen shown in *Figure 11.3*.

STEP 4

> **Note**
>
> You may choose to opt into emails regarding feature updates and offers on our other certification books. We don't spam, and it's easy to opt out at any time.

Click `Request Access`.

STEP 5

If the code you entered is correct, you'll see a button that says, `OPEN PRACTICE RESOURCES`, as shown in *Figure 11.4*:

PACKT PRACTICE RESOURCES

You've just unlocked the free online content that came with your book.

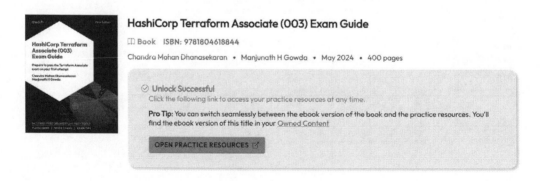

HashiCorp Terraform Associate (003) Exam Guide

Book   ISBN: 9781804618844

Chandra Mohan Dhanasekaran • Manjunath H Gowda • May 2024 • 400 pages

⊘ **Unlock Successful**
Click the following link to access your practice resources at any time.

Pro Tip: You can switch seamlessly between the ebook version of the book and the practice resources. You'll find the ebook version of this title in your Owned Content

`OPEN PRACTICE RESOURCES` ↗

Figure 11.4 – Page that shows up after a successful unlock

Click the OPEN PRACTICE RESOURCES link to start using your free online content. You'll be redirected to the Dashboard shown in *Figure 11.5*:

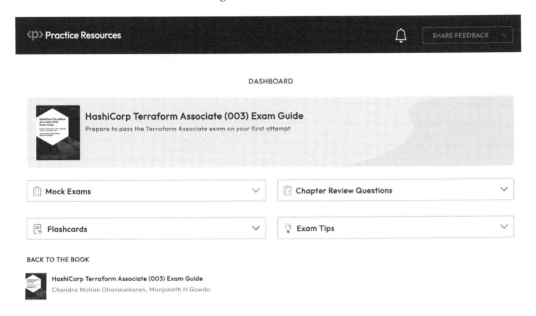

Figure 11.5 – Dashboard page for HashiCorp Terraform Associate (003) practice resources

Bookmark this link

Now that you've unlocked the resources, you can come back to them anytime by visiting https://packt.link/hsh003practice or scanning the following QR code provided in *Figure 11.6*:

Figure 11.6 – QR code to bookmark practice resources website

Troubleshooting Tips

If you're facing issues unlocking, here are three things you can do:

- Double-check your unique code. All unique codes in our books are case-sensitive and your code needs to match exactly as it is shown in *STEP 3*.

- If that doesn't work, use the `Report Issue` button located at the top-right corner of the page.

- If you're not able to open the unlock page at all, write to `customercare@packt.com` and mention the name of the book.

Share Feedback

If you find any issues with the platform, the book, or any of the practice materials, you can click the `Share Feedback` button from any page and reach out to us. If you have any suggestions for improvement, you can share those as well.

Back to the Book

To make switching between the book and practice resources easy, we've added a link that takes you back to the book (*Figure 11.7*). Click it to open your book in Packt's online reader. Your reading position is synced so you can jump right back to where you left off when you last opened the book.

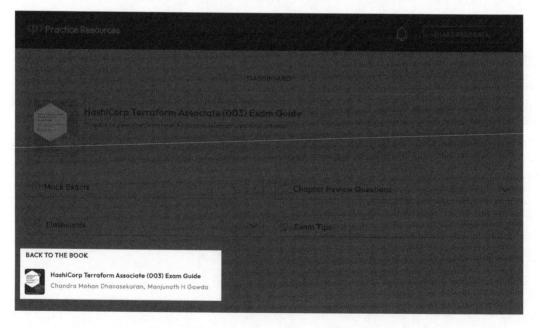

Figure 11.7 – Dashboard page for HashiCorp Terraform Associate (003) practice resources

Index

www.packtpub.com

Subscribe to our online digital library for full access to over 7,000 books and videos, as well as industry leading tools to help you plan your personal development and advance your career. For more information, please visit our website.

Why subscribe?

- Spend less time learning and more time coding with practical eBooks and Videos from over 4,000 industry professionals

- Improve your learning with Skill Plans built especially for you

- Get a free eBook or video every month

- Fully searchable for easy access to vital information

- Copy and paste, print, and bookmark content

At www.packtpub.com, you can also read a collection of free technical articles, sign up for a range of free newsletters, and receive exclusive discounts and offers on Packt books and eBooks.

Other Books You May Enjoy

If you enjoyed this book, you may be interested in these other books by Packt:

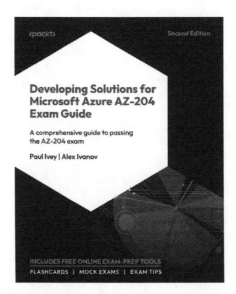

Developing Solutions for Microsoft Azure AZ-204 Exam Guide

Paul Ivey, and Alex Ivanov

ISBN: 978-1-83508-529-5

- Identify cloud models and services in Azure
- Develop secure Azure web apps and host containerized solutions in Azure
- Implement serverless solutions with Azure Functions
- Utilize Cosmos DB for scalable data storage
- Optimize Azure Blob storage for efficiency
- Securely store secrets and configuration settings centrally
- Ensure web application security with Microsoft Entra ID authentication
- Monitor and troubleshoot Azure solutions

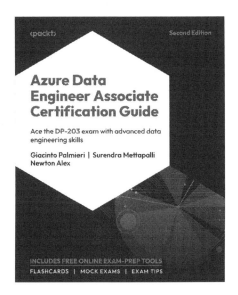

Azure Data Engineer Associate Certification Guide

Giacinto Palmieri, Surendra Mettapalli, and Surendra Mettapalli

ISBN: 978-1-80512-468-9

- Design and implement data lake solutions with batch and stream pipelines
- Secure data with masking, encryption, RBAC, and ACLs
- Perform standard extract, transform, and load (ETL) and analytics operations
- Implement different table geometries in Azure Synapse Analytics
- Write Spark code, design ADF pipelines, and handle batch and stream data
- Use Azure Databricks or Synapse Spark for data processing using Notebooks
- Leverage Synapse Analytics and Purview for comprehensive data exploration
- Confidently manage VMs, VNETS, App Services, and more

Share Your Thoughts

Now you've finished *HashiCorp Terraform Associate (003) Exam Guide*, we'd love to hear your thoughts! Scan the QR code below to go straight to the Amazon review page for this book and share your feedback or leave a review on the site that you purchased it from.

https://packt.link/r/1804618845

Your review is important to us and the tech community and will help us make sure we're delivering excellent quality content.

Download a Free PDF Copy of This Book

Thanks for purchasing this book!

Do you like to read on the go but are unable to carry your print books everywhere?

Is your eBook purchase not compatible with the device of your choice?

Don't worry, now with every Packt book you get a DRM-free PDF version of that book at no cost.

Read anywhere, any place, on any device. Search, copy, and paste code from your favorite technical books directly into your application.

The perks don't stop there, you can get exclusive access to discounts, newsletters, and great free content in your inbox daily.

Follow these simple steps to get the benefits:

1. Scan the QR code or visit the link below:

https://packt.link/free-ebook/9781804618844

2. Submit your proof of purchase.
3. That's it! We'll send your free PDF and other benefits to your email directly.

Made in the USA
Columbia, SC
23 November 2024

47427457R00189